"In his latest book, William A. Taylor delivers a concise and lucid account of the momentous transition from the draft to the all-volunteer force (AVF) and reflects on its significant legacy after fifty years of service. In doing so, he highlights the vital linkages between who serves in the military and how they do so. This book should be required reading for students, scholars, and readers interested in the AVF and its profound relationship to American society."

**Lawrence J. Korb**, *Former Assistant Secretary of Defense*

"Everyone should read William A. Taylor's *The Advent of the All-Volunteer Force*. He provides a wealth of primary sources that readers can explore to understand who serves in America's military. He brilliantly takes the reader from the draft system to the all-volunteer force, demonstrating it as a pivotal moment in American history."

**Jeremy P. Maxwell,** *author of* Brotherhood in Combat: How African Americans Found Equality in Korea and Vietnam

D1666128

# THE ADVENT OF THE ALL-VOLUNTEER FORCE

This book examines the extensive influence of the All-Volunteer Force (AVF) on the past, present, and future of America, demonstrating how the AVF encompasses the most significant issues of military history and defense policy.

Throughout the vast majority of its wars during the twentieth century, the United States relied on a mixture of volunteers who chose to serve and conscripts provided through the Selective Service System, known colloquially as the draft. When the United States emerged as a world superpower in the aftermath of World War II, U.S. policymakers also depended on the draft during peacetime. Drawing on primary source documents, this book guides readers through the transition from the draft to the AVF and analyzes its history, results, challenges, and implications. Each chapter provides an overview of the issues of the time, recounts the ensuing debates and developments around them, and examines how they manifested themselves relative to the advent of the AVF and American society during times of peace and war.

Combining narrative with documents, *The Advent of the All-Volunteer Force* is a valuable resource for students, scholars, policymakers, and general readers interested in modern American history, military history, and the dynamic linkages between policy, politics, and American society.

**William A. Taylor** is the Lee Drain Endowed University Professor of Global Security Studies at Angelo State University.

## Critical Moments in American History
*Edited by William Thomas Allison, Georgia Southern University*

**The Marshall Plan**
A New Deal for Europe
*Michael Holm*

**The Espionage and Sedition Acts**
World War I and the Image of Civil Liberties
*Mitchell C. Newton-Matza*

**McCarthyism**
The Realities, Delusions and Politics Behind the 1950s Red Scare
*Jonathan Michaels*

**Three Mile Island**
The Meltdown Crisis and Nuclear Power in American Popular Culture
*Grace Halden*

**The 1916 Preparedness Day Bombing**
Anarchy and Terrorism in Progressive-Era America
*Jeffrey A. Johnson*

**America Enters the Cold War**
The Road to Global Commitment, 1945–1950
*Kevin Grimm*

**Title IX**
The Transformation of Sex Discrimination in Education
*Elizabeth Kaufer Busch & William E. Thro*

**The "Silent Majority" Speech**
Richard Nixon, the Vietnam War, and the Origins of the New Right
*Scott Laderman*

**When Women Won the Vote**
The Final Decade, 1910–1920
*Sandra Opdycke*

**The Gulf of Tonkin**
The United States and the Escalation in the Vietnam War
*Tal Tovy*

**The Advent of the All-Volunteer Force**
Protecting Free Society
*William A. Taylor*

# THE ADVENT OF THE ALL-VOLUNTEER FORCE

Protecting Free Society

*William A. Taylor*

Routledge
Taylor & Francis Group

NEW YORK AND LONDON

Designed cover image: Vietnam Draft. Young men who have been drafted wait in line to be processed into the U.S. Army at Fort Jackson, Columbia, South Carolina, May 1967. © IanDagnall Computing / Alamy Stock Photo

First published 2023
by Routledge
605 Third Avenue, New York, NY 10158

and by Routledge
4 Park Square, Milton Park, Abingdon, Oxon, OX14 4RN

*Routledge is an imprint of the Taylor & Francis Group, an informa business*

© 2023 Taylor & Francis

The right of William A. Taylor to be identified as author of this work has been asserted in accordance with sections 77 and 78 of the Copyright, Designs and Patents Act 1988.

ISBN: 978-0-367-47683-0 (hbk)
ISBN: 978-0-367-47682-3 (pbk)
ISBN: 978-1-003-03583-1 (ebk)

DOI: 10.4324/9781003035831

Typeset in Bembo
by MPS Limited, Dehradun

For the more than two million Americans serving in the All-Volunteer Force and the many millions more who have done so at some point during its 50 years.

To my wife, Renee, and children, Madison and Benjamin

By William A. Taylor

*The Advent of the All-Volunteer Force*
*George C. Marshall and the Early Cold War*
*Contemporary Security Issues in Africa*
*Military Service and American Democracy*
*Every Citizen a Soldier*

# CONTENTS

List of Figures                                                                    x
List of Abbreviations                                                            xii
Acknowledgments                                                                 xiii
Timeline                                                                           xv

Series Introduction                                                                1

1   Conscription in America: The Draft during the 1940s and 1950s                  2

2   In Pursuit of Equity: The Draft during the 1960s                              19

3   How to End the Draft: The Campaign for the AVF during
    the 1960s                                                                     36

4   The First Indispensable Step: The Gates Commission                           52

5   Our Commitment to Freedom: The AVF and Its Legacy                            70

Documents                                                                         95
Bibliography                                                                     189
About the Author                                                                 197
Index                                                                            198

# FIGURES

1.1 President Richard M. Nixon 4

1.2 Director of the Selective Service System Maj. Gen. Lewis B. Hershey (middle), Georgia Neese Clark, and Secretary of the Interior Oscar Chapman at the Washington Hotel for a meeting 7

1.3 "We must be ready to back up what we say" 11

2.1 Secretary of Defense Robert S. McNamara during a cabinet meeting at the White House 24

2.2 Honorable Burke Marshall during a meeting in the White House Cabinet Room 26

2.3 President Lyndon B. Johnson reading a document in the White House interior as Gen. William C. Westmoreland looks on 31

3.1 President and Mrs. Lyndon B. Johnson, Senate Majority Leader Mike Mansfield, and Speaker of the House John McCormack salute House Minority Leader Gerald R. Ford 38

3.2 President Lyndon B. Johnson meets with Richard Nixon during the campaign in the Cabinet Room at the White House 43

4.1 Outgoing President Lyndon B. Johnson welcomes incoming President Richard M. Nixon to the White House on inauguration day 53

4.2 President Nixon greeting and talking to U.S. Army soldiers of the First Infantry Division in Dian, South Vietnam 56

4.3 Thomas S. Gates Jr. and Gerald R. Ford seated by the fireplace in the Oval Office 65

4.4 Gerald R. Ford and Melvin R. Laird talking at the White House 67

5.1 President Nixon and Pat Nixon pose for an official state portrait by the stairway with Gen. Lewis B. Hershey and Mrs. Hershey before attending a state dinner honoring General Hershey 72

5.2   President Nixon in the Oval Office during a meeting with Gen.
      William C. Westmoreland, former U.S. Military Assistance
      Command, Vietnam (MACV) commander and Secretary of
      Defense Melvin Laird                                               73
5.3   Melvin R. Laird seated near the fireplace in the Oval Office       81

# ABBREVIATIONS

AVF     All-Volunteer Force
CNAS   Center for a New American Security
CSIS    Center for Strategic and International Studies
DOD    Department of Defense
EO      Executive Order
FG      Federal Government
FY      Fiscal Year
GRFL   Gerald R. Ford Library
HSTL   Harry S. Truman Library
LBJL    Lyndon B. Johnson Library
NARA   National Archives and Records Administration
PL      Public Law
POW   Prisoner of War
RG     Record Group
RMNL  Richard M. Nixon Library
SMOF  Staff Member and Office Files
SSS     Selective Service System
UMT   Universal Military Training
VFW   Veterans of Foreign Wars
WHCF  White House Central Files

# ACKNOWLEDGMENTS

Many people helped in numerous ways along the journey of writing this book. I wish to acknowledge my sincere gratitude for their invaluable assistance.

At the Harry S. Truman Library, archivists Randy Sowell and David Clark provided expertise, guiding me through a plethora of materials. Sam Rushay and Jen Vitela encouraged the promotion of my work to a wide audience, even when a global pandemic made doing so a logistical challenge. The Truman Library Institute provided me a grant that funded extensive research, while Lisa Sullivan administered the details with steady encouragement. At the Dwight D. Eisenhower Library, Kevin M. Bailey identified promising lines of inquiry. The Eisenhower Foundation furnished me a travel grant that afforded most productive research, while Meredith Sleichter and Lisa Kijowski assisted with its implementation. At the Lyndon B. Johnson Library, John Wilson identified useful sources, especially records on the Vietnam War and the Selective Service System during it. A Moody Research Grant from the Lyndon B. Johnson Foundation backed this work. I am most grateful to Samantha Stone, members of the selection committee, and LBJ Foundation for supporting this project. At the Gerald R. Ford Library, Stacy Davis coordinated details, while John O'Connell and Jeffrey Senger assisted me at the library. A research grant from the Gerald R. Ford Presidential Foundation defrayed the costs of extensive research at the Ford Library. At the Richard M. Nixon library, Dorissa Martinez and Jon Fletcher offered much appreciated help. The Nixon library proved useful because of its vast White House Central Files, Subject Files and Nixon Administration White House Special Files, which reinforced Martin Anderson's central role in the advent of the AVF.

The Association for Documentary Editing (ADE) awarded this project the 2020/ 2021 Sharon Ritenour Stevens prize, affording valuable financial support for archival research and document collecting. This prize was memorable because of my esteem for Sharon's instrumental work as associate editor of the George C. Marshall papers.

Carol Deboer-Langworthy administered the award and organized an engaging roundtable of current and past winners for the 2021 ADE annual meeting.

I feel most fortunate to have spent my entire academic career at Angelo State University (ASU) in San Angelo, Texas. I arrived upon graduating with my PhD degree in history from George Washington University and have progressed through all academic ranks, serving now as the Lee Drain Endowed University Professor of Global Security Studies. The leadership team of Ronnie D. Hawkins Jr., president; Donald R. Topliff, provost and vice president for academic affairs; Clifton Jones, vice provost; Michael W. Salisbury, dean of the College of Graduate Studies and Research; John E. Klingemann, dean of the College of Arts and Humanities; and Joseph C. Rallo, chair of the Department of Security Studies and Criminal Justice, have led ASU with exceptional vision. They have ensured that ASU is a great place to work and embodies a thriving family of administrators, faculty, staff, students, and community members.

The entire team at Routledge has been remarkable, including Kimberley Smith and Emily Irvine. William T. Allison, series editor for Critical Moments in American History, has always been a stalwart supporter of my work. From the first time that I met him in 2010—when I was a graduate student and he was a department chair—Bill has modeled the absolute best of the historical profession through his teaching, research, and service, as well as his enthusiastic engagement and admirable collegiality. Kimberley, Emily, Bill, and I worked together to navigate this project through the difficulties of an unexpected global pandemic. I am most proud to be an author with Routledge and appreciate all the backing from this prestigious publisher and this fine group of colleagues and now dear friends. Lawrence J. Korb and Jeremy P. Maxwell took precious time out of their busy schedules to read the manuscript and to provide positive endorsements.

As with all my endeavors, my family has been the most faithful. My parents, Richard and Diane Taylor, have always provided encouragement to follow my dreams. My other parents, Dennis and Linda Lesniewski, have been thoughtful as well. As a family, we sadly lost Dennis during the completion of this project. We all dearly miss him, and I know that this book made him proud. My wife, Renee, and our two amazing children, Madison and Benjamin, deserve the most credit. This book is dedicated to them.

Of course, even with such a supportive community of archivists, colleagues, publishers, and family, any errors that remain are mine alone.

# TIMELINE

| | |
|---|---|
| September 16, 1940 | President Roosevelt signed Selective Training and Service Act of 1940 |
| July 31, 1941 | Roosevelt appointed Lewis B. Hershey director of Selective Service System |
| March 31, 1947 | Selective Training and Service Act expired |
| June 24, 1948 | Selective Service resumed |
| June 19, 1951 | President Truman signed Universal Military Training and Service Act |
| 1955 | Congress renewed the draft for four years |
| 1959 | Congress renewed the draft for four years |
| 1963 | Congress renewed the draft for four years |
| June 1966 | DOD draft study concluded |
| July 2, 1966 | President Johnson established Marshall Commission |
| February 1967 | Marshall Commission issued *In Pursuit of Equity* |
| June 30, 1967 | Congress renewed the draft for four years |
| July 1, 1967 | Congress changed Universal Military Training and Service Act to Military Selective Service Act |
| July 4, 1967 | Martin Anderson provided memorandum to Richard M. Nixon outlining rationale for the AVF |
| October 10, 1967 | Anderson expanded his outline on the AVF with analysis of how to achieve it |
| November 8, 1967 | Congress repealed restrictions on the percentage of women in American military service |
| October 17, 1968 | Presidential candidate Nixon's radio address announced his intention to end the draft and transition to the AVF |
| January 20, 1969 | President Nixon's first inauguration |
| March 27, 1969 | Nixon established Gates Commission |

| | |
|---|---|
| May 13, 1969 | Nixon announced his plans on draft reform and sent legislation to Congress |
| May 15, 1969 | Gates Commission held its first meeting |
| June 27, 1969 | Laird delivered a progress report on the AVF during the first five months of the Nixon administration |
| October 10, 1969 | Nixon administration announced retirement of Hershey |
| November 26, 1969 | Nixon signed Draft Reform Bill, implementing a lottery selection system |
| February 16, 1970 | Curtis W. Tarr became director of Selective Service System |
| February 20, 1970 | Gates Commission issued its final report |
| April 23, 1970 | Nixon issued Executive Order 11527, which phased out occupational and paternity deferments |
| January 28, 1971 | Nixon sent special message to Congress about draft reform |
| June 30, 1971 | Draft law expired |
| September 28, 1971 | Nixon signed extension of Military Selective Service Act for two years only |
| August 28, 1972 | Nixon and Laird both issued progress reports on the AVF |
| June 30, 1973 | Draft ended |
| July 1, 1973 | Advent of the AVF |

# SERIES INTRODUCTION

Welcome to the Routledge *Critical Moments in American History* series. The purpose of this new series is to give students a window into the historian's craft through concise, readable books by leading scholars, who bring together the best scholarship and engaging primary sources to explore a critical moment in the American past. In discovering the principal points of the story in these books, gaining a sense of historiography, following a fresh trail of primary documents, and exploring suggested readings, students can then set out on their own journey, to debate the ideas presented, interpret primary sources, and reach their own conclusions—just like the historian.

A critical moment in history can be a range of things—a pivotal year, the pinnacle of a movement or trend, or an important event such as the passage of a piece of legislation, an election, a court decision, a battle. It can be social, cultural, political, or economic. It can be heroic or tragic. Whatever they are, such moments are by definition "game changers," momentous changes in the pattern of the American fabric, paradigm shifts in the American experience. Many of the critical moments explored in this series are familiar; some less so.

There is no ultimate list of critical moments in American history—any group of students, historians, or other scholars may come up with a different catalog of topics. These differences of view, however, are what make history itself and the study of history so important and so fascinating. Therein can be found the utility of historical inquiry—to explore, to challenge, to understand, and to realize the legacy of the past through its influence of the present. It is the hope of this series to help students realize this intrinsic value of our past and of studying our past.

**William Thomas Allison**
*Georgia Southern University*

DOI: 10.4324/9781003035831-1

# 1

# CONSCRIPTION IN AMERICA

## The Draft during the 1940s and 1950s

## Introduction

On February 20, 1970, the President's Commission on an All-Volunteer Armed Force, known as the Gates Commission after its chair, Thomas S. Gates Jr., transmitted its final report to President Nixon. In it, the eminent group of civilian and military leaders advocated ending the draft and creating the All-Volunteer Force (AVF).[1] In something that the group characterized as "Protecting the Free Society," they praised the AVF regarding its applicability to American democracy:

> Since the founding of the republic, a primary task of the government of the United States has been to provide for the common defense of a society established to secure the blessings of liberty and justice. Without endangering the nation's security, the means of defense should support the aims of the society. The armed forces today play an honorable and important part in promoting the nation's security, as they have since our freedoms were won on the battlefield at Yorktown. A fundamental consideration that has guided this Commission is the need to maintain and improve the effectiveness, dignity, and status of the armed forces so they may continue to play their proper role.[2]

That "proper role" is a pivotal subject of much debate, both past and present.

This book provides a brief synopsis of the move away from the draft that culminated with the advent of the AVF in 1973 and presents a valuable collection of key documents related to that critical moment in American history. Most of this book explores characters, debates, arguments, actions, and countermoves related to military service during the 1960s and 1970s, although I endeavor to provide useful context from before and after. Much of my previous work deals with military service, including both the draft and AVF. My sincere hope is that it,

DOI: 10.4324/9781003035831-2

combined with the research and documents in this book, proves useful for readers in a wide range of courses examining such important topics as U.S. history, military service, war and society, military history, compulsion versus volunteerism, and the delicate balance between national security and individual liberty in American democracy. In addition, general readers and military servicemembers interested in a brief overview of how and why the United States moved away from the draft to the AVF will find this work beneficial. Throughout, I also guide readers toward other works that provide worthwhile insights on related topics and differing interpretations.

My thesis is straightforward. The advent of the AVF was a critical moment in American history. This massive change during an ongoing war included all the elements of a major drama. The ensuing story reveals a draft that had proven necessary for quite some time and an older generation of civilian and military leaders that had grown quite comfortable with its continued use. Yet, demographic changes altered the way in which the draft operated and resulted in heightened attention to the myriad inequities that the draft entailed. Richard M. Nixon, ever the opportunist, seized on resistance to the draft for his own political ends. American society swirled with fundamental questions regarding the best pursuits for its youth. Over time, implications related to race and gender within military service promoted more equal opportunity for previously marginalized communities (Figure 1.1).

These vital themes endure. Debates regarding the AVF have proven persistent, encompassing both unresolved matters emanating from its advent and new questions resulting from its subsequent evolution. My purpose is to show that—in addition to the obvious military policy matters at hand—questions of who serves in the U.S. military and how they do so reveal much about American society writ large. Those affairs reside at the intersection of policy, politics, and society, never wholly military in their nature and yet not quite civilian either.

This book employs an innovative methodology that utilizes primary sources from numerous archives across the country to present a succinct narrative about the advent of the AVF. Along the way, I incorporate relevant secondary sources, including long-studied classics and the most recent additions. My hope is that this approach provides readers with a brief introduction to both this historical topic and its prevailing literature. In addition, I have compiled numerous key documents that appear as a collection after the narrative. The document collection will prove quite useful for students and scholars embarking upon their own research. It makes many primary sources accessible for researchers seeking to explore further this fundamental topic.

The narrative consists of five chapters that tell the story of the advent of the AVF. Chapter 1, "Conscription in America," introduces the overall work and provides an overview of the draft during World War II, the campaign for universal military training (UMT) after it, the resurgence of the draft in 1948, and its subsequent emphasis during the Korean War.

**FIGURE 1.1**  President Richard M. Nixon. January 6, 1972

*Source*: Courtesy Richard M. Nixon Library.

Chapter 2, "In Pursuit of Equity," reveals how the twin developments of amplified U.S. military engagement in the Vietnam War and the baby boom generation coming of age combined to place the inequity of the draft front and center in American society. It also details Project 100,000; the DOD draft study; the Marshall Commission; and the Johnson administration's continued support of the Selective Service System despite the draft's growing unpopularity.

Chapter 3, "How to End the Draft," details the nascent campaign for the AVF that appeared during the 1964 presidential campaign and gained momentum thereafter. Advocates promoted numerous rationales for the AVF, including military, economic, and political ones. The year 1968 marked a turning point as Nixon made the matter central to his presidential campaign and subsequent administration.

Chapter 4, "The First Indispensable Step," shows the pivotal role of the Gates Commission. Once in office, President Nixon tasked this group of prominent leaders with crafting the rationale for the AVF and producing a way to achieve it. The advisory body tackled such complicated issues as politics, economics, race, and compulsion. The Gates Commission unanimously endorsed the AVF and provided its blueprint.

Chapter 5, "Our Commitment to Freedom," charts the advent of the AVF, including the necessary draft reforms that preceded it. Much angst accompanied the momentous transition, as policymakers questioned the appropriate timing. Once implemented, the AVF produced early outcomes, chief among them the Total Force Concept. I conclude with some reflections on the legacy of the AVF after 50 years of service.

Following this brief narrative, I provide a document collection consisting of sixteen major sources that tell the story in their own way. Because I present the documents in chronological order, readers can discern the subtle shift away from the draft toward the AVF. Readers benefit from seeing events unfold in both narrative and document forms, reinforcing one another while encouraging readers to leverage both tools for their own forays into historical research.

There is a lively, varied, and robust literature on the AVF. Most work on it falls into five general types. First, there are studies that examine the AVF, the transition to it, or one specific component of it.[3] Second, there are works that commemorate its various anniversaries.[4] Third, there are projects that explore alternatives, including the draft, UMT, national service, and, more recently, private security contractors.[5] Fourth, there are surveys that examine aspects related to military service, including recruiting and retention, who serves and how they do so, civil-military relations, and such vital matters as combat, race, gender, and sexuality.[6] Fifth, there are works that critique the AVF. Questions regarding its fairness, efficiency, and sustainability have accompanied its advent. Many remain to this day.[7]

This book contributes a work that tells the essential story of the advent of the AVF in multiple unique ways. It provides a compelling narrative based on primary sources, a useful guide to the existing literature, and a valuable document collection that serves as a starting point for further research. *The Advent of the All-Volunteer Force* is an ideal subject primer and research starter for students, scholars, and readers interested in studying the AVF, military service, American society, and examining the crucial linkages between them all.

## The Draft During the 1940s

The draft was nothing new in U.S. history. It had been used in multiple forms throughout America's major wars, including the American Civil War, World War I, and World War II.[8] Of course, the way that the draft operated in each of these conflicts was quite different. In the twentieth century, the draft during the two world wars differed because the first occurred during wartime, while the second was the first peacetime draft in U.S. history. The Selective Service System commented on the 1940 draft:

> Though it was passed in the shadow of war, it had to conform to peacetime restrictions. It lacked the urgency of the World War I Act which was passed after the declaration of war. It was a training and service act with emphasis on training. Otherwise, it followed the general principles of the World War I Act and provided for the same democratic processes.[9]

The Selective Service System often characterized the draft as "democratic," although it captured the major difference between the two draft laws during the twentieth century. Congress passed the 1917 law in a wartime environment, and officials quickly implemented it. The 1940 draft law was preventive in nature, delivered in peace, and took more time.

Beginning in 1940, the draft maintained a pervasive presence in the lives of American youth that would endure for more than three decades. In large part, wartime demands necessitated it. Throughout that extensive period, one individual personified the draft, Lewis B. Hershey.[10] "It must be recognized that over the years since 1940 at least," Hershey observed, "the great bulk of manpower has gone into the Armed Forces under some degree of duress." When military requirements skyrocketed, as they did during major wars, there simply were not enough volunteers. The draft influenced more than just those inducted. It permeated American society from the first moment of registration. "This influence begins with the anticipation by the 17-year-old of his imminent obligation to register with the Selective Service System," Hershey divulged. "It develops in intensity with every step of the System's processing, the final and most motivating being found physically, mentally, and morally acceptable for military service."[11]

## Sidebar 1.1: Lewis B. Hershey

Lewis Blaine Hershey (September 12, 1893–May 20, 1977) was the longtime director of the Selective Service System, serving from August 1941 to February 1970. As a result of his nearly three decades in that powerful position, Hershey became a towering figure and personified the draft to many Americans. Hershey often characterized military service as an obligation of citizenship and argued that the draft was a necessary, and indeed positive, feature of U.S. society. President Nixon eventually replaced Hershey as director in order to remove one of the staunchest and most vocal supporters of the draft. In doing so, Nixon paved the way for the advent of the AVF (Figure 1.2).

**FIGURE 1.2**   Director of the Selective Service System Maj. Gen. Lewis B. Hershey (middle), Georgia Neese Clark, and Secretary of the Interior Oscar Chapman at the Washington Hotel for a meeting. September 6, 1950

*Source:* Courtesy Harry S. Truman Library.

Such pressure bore results in the form of draft-motivated volunteers. The process of the draft—registration, classification, examination, and induction—ratcheted up stress on young Americans traversing its stages. For many, the closer they came to induction, the more they considered volunteering. In doing so, they exerted some control over their respective branch of service, military occupational specialty, and duty station. The draft applied coercion to enlist throughout the entire process. "At that point another substantial number enlist each month. With every rise in monthly call there is a concomitant rise in enlistments," Hershey acknowledged. "The pressure to enlist is clear and unmistakable."[12]

As a result, there was a direct link between the draft and volunteers. Historian Peter S. Kindsvatter observed that the U.S. Army Research Branch during World War II

> discovered that except for adventure seekers, draftees sought safe jobs, and only a small fraction of those who had managed, by whatever means, to land a safe job (defined as "noninfantry") had any desire to leave it to join the infantry.[13]

Hershey reinforced that from the outset draft-motivated volunteers existed. "Registrants took time by the forelock and used the period prior to being drafted to make their own choice of the arms and services," he explained. "In short, it was not a free recruiting or enlistment situation. The gentle pressure of the Selective Service System was ever present."[14] Estimates widely varied but ranged from 25 percent to 50 percent of total volunteers in active forces and even higher in the reserves and National Guard. By these accounts, draft-motivated volunteers and draftees comprised roughly half of military personnel.[15] Over the course of World War II, the draft impacted millions of Americans. Historian George Q. Flynn recorded, "During the war the nation had peacefully registered 49 million men, selected 19 million, and inducted 10 million."[16]

## Universal Military Training

In addition to the draft, there were other plans that loomed large during the 1940s. The most prominent was UMT. Beginning in 1943, such military leaders as Gen. George C. Marshall, U.S. army chief of staff, and Brig. Gen. John M. Palmer, Marshall's designated spokesperson on UMT, advocated for it.[17] In their conception, every 18-year-old male in American society would complete six months of basic training—followed by six more months of large-unit training—and then return to their civilian lives. Boosters contended that doing so would create a large and trained General Reserve, which the United States could rapidly mobilize in the case of a national emergency.

Until UMT materialized, the Truman administration needed either to maintain the Selective Service System or to rely exclusively on volunteers. At President Truman's request, Howard C. Petersen, assistant secretary of war, outlined in June 1946 the War Department's top three legislative priorities for the immediate post-World War II era, "listed in order of importance."[18] The military's ranked priority list included extending the Selective Training and Service Act of 1940 (H.R. 6064), "unifying the departments and agencies of the Government relating to the common defense" (S. 2044), and establishing control of atomic energy (S. 1717). Therefore, the top three legislative priorities of the military at that time were selective service, unification, and control of atomic weapons.[19] It is important to note that selective service was a short-term goal for Truman during the 1940s, to be extended only until military leaders, primarily those in the Army, implemented UMT. This theme proved consistent until UMT died with the Pyrrhic victory of the Universal Military Training and Service Act of 1951. While Truman had sought to retain the draft in 1946 because the United States had just emerged from World War II, he pivoted in 1947 due to his staunch support for, and misplaced confidence in, Congress enacting UMT in the postwar era.

Others urged caution, however. Paul H. Griffith, national commander of the American Legion, pleaded with Sen. J. Howard McGrath (D-RI) on February 16, 1947, to ensure that UMT materialized. "Three and one half million men who fought our country's two world wars know from first hand experience the value of national security and the folly of unpreparedness," Griffith exclaimed. "They are appalled to learn that their government contemplates sabotage of the proposed UMT program, recommended by high government officials and demanded by the public, through a one billion dollar cut in Army appropriations."[20] The American Legion, along with the Veterans of Foreign Wars (VFW), touted the benefits of UMT, although their respective visions of the program often varied from one another, the Army, and Truman administration.[21]

Griffith reinforced the official support of the American Legion, and its more than three million members, for UMT. Its backing was staunch, sustained, and unwavering. Griffith reasoned that the alternating cycle of mobilizing for war and then demobilizing afterward was both expensive and counterproductive. Such flux invited aggression, precipitated additional mobilizations, and required exorbitant expenditures in future wars. A smaller, but more consistent, investment in UMT would prevent this feast and famine approach. Other influential observers, most notably Marshall, held similar views on the cyclical nature of preparedness.[22]

On March 3, 1947, Truman proposed to Congress "that there be no extension of the Selective Training and Service Act at this time." The reason was straightforward. The campaign for UMT was well underway, and Truman hoped that it would replace the draft as America's long-term military mobilization mechanism.

> Because I am confident that the Congress and the Nation stand ready both now and in the future to take such action as may be necessary to assure the security of the Nation, and because there are now reasonably good prospects of maintaining at adequate strength the Army and Navy without resort to Selective Service,

Truman explained, "I believe we can liquidate the Selective Service System, except for its records."[23] Truman anticipated that his move would generate additional momentum toward UMT. "He did so with the warning that if voluntary enlistments could not procure the number of men required by the armed services, reenactment would be requested," the Selective Service System later recorded.[24] His maneuver accomplished only one part of these intertwined goals. The draft expired on March 31, 1947. Congress, however, refused to implement UMT.

By July 1947, several UMT bills traversed the halls of Congress. Harry L. Towe (R-NY) sponsored H.R. 4278, and the Armed Services Committee reported it to the House on July 26, 1947. Chan Gurney (R-SD) sponsored two bills, S. 651 and S. 652. Both remained "pending in Senate Committee."[25] These UMT bills spent most of their time in committee and did not make much progress for two reasons. First, there were so many versions of the concept of UMT that the myriad plans diluted support for any particular one. Second, UMT represented a political lightning rod. Historians Debi and Irwin Unger, along with Stanley Hirshson, recognized, "To some, on the political left, the UMT proposal seemed another effort to confront the Soviet Union and a further expansion of the emerging Cold War."[26] Political resistance on the right proved more substantial. As a result of the

1946 midterm elections, Republicans had seized control of both chambers of Congress for the first time since 1931. Arriving in Washington en masse in early 1947, they were reluctant to pass priorities of the Truman administration and grew willing to block the White House on most domestic issues, even if the two parties found some bipartisan agreement on foreign policy. While polling indicated that far more Americans supported the general idea of UMT than opposed it, most advocates could not agree on specific details. Those individuals and groups who opposed it stood vocal and vociferous.[27]

The House mustered limited progress. The Armed Services Committee held hearings and reported H.R. 4278, but the House Rules Committee declined to release it. The Senate Armed Services Committee, on the other hand, produced two UMT bills, S. 651 and S. 652, but scheduled no hearings.[28] The interesting thing was that the House Armed Services Committee held hearings and reported a bill. The House Rules Committee, however, refused to let it proceed. Historian James M. Gerhardt observed, "Thus the second campaign for UMT ended, as had the first, with this central feature of the Administration's hopes for a postwar military establishment resting quietly on the congressional shelf."[29] In the Senate, there were multiple UMT bills but no hearings.

With the draft expired, the United States embarked on a trial run of the AVF. The experiment was short, and the results were not promising. "For the next 12 months the military services waged one of the most extensive recruiting campaigns in U.S. peacetime history," *U.S. News and World Report* later recalled. "The Army alone set aside 20 million dollars for recruiting. Posters and pamphlets flooded the country." Recruiting materials accentuated skills, benefits, and travel that accrued from military service without highlighting such stresses as difficult training and potential combat. Glamorizing military service failed to attract the necessary recruits. From July to December 1947, the Army alone recruited "38,000 fewer than were sought." The shortfalls were significant because the U.S. military had fallen from its all-time high during World War II, a gargantuan 12.3 million strong, to only 1.4 million personnel by 1948, "and this was 15 percent below authorized strength." On March 17, 1948, President Truman "ended the volunteer experiment," urging Congress to pass his three postwar priorities related to national security. The first was implementation of a UMT program as the long-term military mobilization solution. The second was a temporary resumption of the draft as a short-term measure until UMT became manifest. The third was enactment of the European Recovery Act, also known as the Marshall Plan[30] (Figure 1.3).

Because the House Rules Committee held the Towe legislation hostage, there was an attempt to make that bill a "special order of business" to force it out of the Rules Committee to the overall House. On the other side of Congress, the Senate made partial inroads and held committee hearings on UMT in March 1948.[31] With two bills in the Senate, committee work produced a "proposed omnibus bill including reenactment of selective service."[32] The House UMT bill remained in the Rules Committee. The Senate moved forward with an omnibus bill that

**FIGURE 1.3** "We must be ready to back up what we say." Cartoon by Clifford K. Berryman. March 18, 1948

*Source*: Courtesy Center for Legislative Archives.

combined UMT with the draft. Congress then removed the UMT provisions and simply reenacted the draft.

Geopolitical pressure also built until the situation proved highly volatile and potentially explosive in a war scare with the Soviet Union in 1948.[33] Therefore, the lapse in the draft was fleeting. Truman reinstated it in 1948 because he found himself with no other viable military mobilization strategy. There was no functioning UMT program in place other than the Experimental Demonstration Unit, a battalion-sized pilot program at Fort Knox, Kentucky, dubbed the "Fort Knox Experiment."[34] Therefore, Truman brought back the draft in 1948 but envisioned it as only a temporary bridge to the permanent enactment of UMT.

On June 24, 1948, President Truman signed the Selective Service Act of 1948. For the second time in less than a decade, young Americans were subject to the draft during peacetime. The act resurrected the Selective Service System "with 54 State Headquarters, 3,900 local boards and 4,500 full-time clerks." It accomplished two things. First, it reintroduced the draft into American society. Second, it motivated volunteers to join. "Although the 1948 Act authorized the drafting of a maximum of 250,000 men in Fiscal Year 1949," Hershey recorded, "the effect of the induction of 35,000 men in November, December and January so stimulated enlistments that no further calls were necessary until July of 1950, after the start of the Korean conflict."[35]

The act included a ninety-day moratorium on inductions, making late September the earliest possible inductions. The *New York Times* reported a "rush of inductees to sign up in the National Guard before the act became law" and declared that such a development was "good neither for the Guard nor the Selective Service."[36] It also highlighted the perennial connection between the draft and draft-motivated volunteers, in this case into the National Guard. While deflating the campaign for UMT and reinstating the draft, the act made no major changes to the Selective Service System. Political scientist James M. Gerhardt remarked:

> In sum, the Selective Service Act of 1948 left unanswered some important questions about the equity and impact of its operation, about the kind of military force structure it was eventually to provide, and indeed about the very nature and duration of the security threat it was to meet.[37]

The downsizing of the military diminished use of the draft. From November 1948 to mid-January 1949, the military services received only 35,000 inductees. By February 1949, there was no need for any draftees due to falling force levels. This situation remained consistent until the Korean War.[38] The Truman administration, seeking budget cuts amid fierce partisan politics, pared down the military. As a result, the draft was in effect but inactive. The outbreak of the Korean War changed everything.

## The Draft During the 1950s

On June 25, 1950, the U.S. military had fallen to 1,459,000 personnel.[39] That same day, North Korea's communist military attacked across the 38th parallel into South Korea, thereby launching the Korean War. The United States rapidly sent forces, although they were woefully outnumbered and ill prepared. U.S. forces soon fell back to the Pusan Perimeter, and the United Nations provided international assistance under U.S. leadership.[40]

The abrupt outbreak of the Korean War revitalized the Selective Service System, which had laid largely dormant since the end of World War II. With the onset of severe fighting on the Korean peninsula and a U.S. military that was not ready for hostilities, the onus of providing personnel fell to the draft. Once the Korean War began, draft calls spiked. "The call for September which was originally set at 10,000 grew to 50,000 in a few days. At the end of September more than 56,000 registrants had been inducted," the Selective Service System recorded. "Nearly 600,000 men were inducted in Fiscal Year 1951. The top for a single month was 87,000."[41] The draft, therefore, provided a mechanism for wartime expansion that exclusive reliance on volunteers failed to fulfill.

The suddenly amplified personnel requirements of the Korean War still paled in comparison to the global conflagration of World War II. These vast differences in scale created newfound complications in managing the draft during the early 1950s. "There are inherent administrative difficulties in partial mobilization operations of Selective Service which are not encountered on a large-scale operation such as World War II," admitted Hershey, "during which time almost as many men were delivered in one month as were inducted during the first year of the Korean operation." Contrasting the total war experience of World War II with the limited approach of the Korean War, Hershey identified one of the resulting problems of directing the draft during the Cold War, even when fighting occurred. "In a partial mobilization," Hershey admitted, "the drafting of veterans is not favored by the public."[42]

Many Americans noticed the high proportion of World War II veterans, by some estimates as many as 600,000, serving in the Korean War and argued that even if necessary, such reliance on them twice in short order was patently unfair.[43] The draft visited other tragedies on veterans and their families. Baltimore resident Marie Tuder, the mother of Sgt. William R. List, received on May 28, 1951, notice that her son was killed in action in Korea. A little more than one week later on June 9, a draft summons arrived, "ordering him to report immediately for draft registration." Colonel Henry C. Stanwood, Maryland state director for the Selective Service System, confessed that he was "terribly sorry" for the agonizing error.[44]

Hershey perceived that "low calls require greater selectivity" and that "a large part of the populace is strictly on a business-as-usual basis." The reasons for these challenges were simple. During World War II, the immense scale of the draft had required gigantic draft calls every month. As a necessary condition to meet these enormous personnel demands, deferments had remained low and had proved the exception. The limited war in Korea, in contrast, required augmenting the use of the draft but at a much smaller scale. Therefore, the selective aspect of the system became more pronounced. "Back of each of these difficulties are two basic factors—public lethargy and a greater than necessary supply of registrants," Hershey explained.[45]

As a result, the Selective Service System experienced unique dilemmas implementing the draft during the Korean War. Many of them arose from the limited nature of the conflict. World War II had required a total mobilization that was unprecedented in scope. In some ways, these circumstances made it easier for the system to handle the draft and proved less controversial because of the perception that the draft was a shared burden, even if there were always exceptions.[46] In stark contrast, the Korean War was a limited mobilization wherein the U.S. military required draftees in much greater numbers than during peacetime but not in the totality that they had been called during World War II. While still faint during the 1950s, a troubling dichotomy emerged that portended upsetting implications if exacerbated. On the one hand, an increased number of draftees proved sufficient to heighten criticism of the draft. On the other, that number proved inadequate to galvanize public sentiment behind either the Korean War or widespread notions of shared sacrifice.

The Korean War produced a massive expansion of the U.S. military, much of it facilitated by the draft. George C. Marshall, secretary of defense, informed President Truman that as of March 21, 1951, the number of personnel in the armed forces was "exactly double" prewar levels. Marshall boasted that attaining such vaulted strength, more than 2.9 million servicemembers, took "less than nine months" compared to "more than 21 months" during World War II.[47] Truman needed this build-up to address battlefield requirements on the Korean peninsula. The administration sought it too, however, to enact the strategy of the Cold War as it entered a new phase characterized by geopolitical tensions and proxy wars. Whereas World War II had demonstrated the necessity of the draft for large-scale mobilization and its lingering presence during peacetime, the subsequent Korean War normalized its use throughout much of the 1950s.

On June 19, 1951, President Truman signed the Universal Military Training and Service Law. The law extended the draft for another four years and "set up a system of universal military training for all young men for the first time in the nation's history," remarked Harold B. Hinton, correspondent for the *New York Times*. In a major understatement, the newspaper reported, "The universal training feature will go into effect at some unspecified time in the future."[48] It never did. In stark contrast to the act's name, it demurred on UMT but reinstituted the draft. "The Truman administration had failed to convince opponents that UMT was an American, democratic, or necessary measure," observed historian Amy J. Rutenberg. "The idea of universal military training was, in effect, politically dead, as was the civic republican ideal of masculine citizenship it represented."[49]

As the Korean War ground to a bloody stalemate and produced in 1953 an uneasy yet enduring armistice, the use of the draft subsided. As it did, so too did widespread controversy regarding it. Even though the Selective Service System had become "a permanent agency" in 1951, the authority to draft young Americans was not automatic. Instead, Congress had to renew it every four years. Congress obliged in 1955 amid little debate.[50] Four years later, the same result occurred. "Its extension in 1959 was overwhelming, with only one vote against it," the Selective Service System chronicled.[51] Throughout most of the 1950s, therefore, significant criticism of the draft remained muted. There were vigorous debates about other forms of military service, UMT, for instance, and about deferments, although limitations in their use dampened vociferous condemnation.

Overall, however, there was not significant consternation about the continued renewal of the draft during peacetime. Such a situation combined with past experience to demonstrate several important lessons about the draft during the 1940s and 1950s. First, it had proven least controversial when either the need was great, as during World War II and to a much lesser degree the Korean War, or when the overall use of the draft was low and therefore benign for most Americans, as it was during the 1940s after World War II and during the 1950s after the armistice of the Korean War.

## Resistance against an AVF

The three major critiques of a potential AVF during the 1940s and 1950s were that there were not enough volunteers to be found, it was not flexible enough, and it was not desirable for civil-military relations. In the aftermath of World War II, most military leaders and analysts agreed that there were not enough volunteers to maintain a military of the size required for the newfound role of the United States as a world superpower. During the 1950s, this fear became especially palpable due to

U.S. unpreparedness for the Korean War and necessary reliance on draftees to fight that conflict. Others upheld that an AVF was not flexible enough to meet the demands of the Cold War. U.S. military planners assumed that communist nations, led by the Soviet Union, sought to expand their power at times and places that would prove difficult to predict. Therefore, having the draft available as a malleable means either to increase or to decrease quickly the size of the U.S. military proved crucial. A third argument arose that would prove enduring: a potential AVF would not be desirable for a number of reasons related to civil-military relations. Therefore, a clear shift occurred from a two-pronged feasibility contention—based first on raw numbers and second on the Cold War context—to a social undesirability claim.

## Notes

1 Historical figures used a variety of labels to describe what observers now refer to as the AVF, including All-Volunteer Armed Force(s), All-Volunteer Army, and All-Volunteer Military Force, among others. The accepted term today is the All-Volunteer Force (AVF), which is the word that I use throughout this volume for standardization and because it is the most recognized idiom of the many that were used interchangeably throughout this lengthy debate.

2 President's Commission on an All-Volunteer Armed Force, *The Report of the President's Commission on an All-Volunteer Armed Force* (Washington, DC: U.S. Government Printing Office, 1970), 5 (hereafter cited as Gates Commission). The title of this book reflects the words "Protecting Free Society" in the quotation presented earlier. A similar practice is used in the chapter titles.

3 Jennifer Mittelstadt, *The Rise of the Military Welfare State* (Cambridge, MA: Harvard University Press, 2015); Beth Bailey, *America's Army: Making the All-Volunteer Force* (Cambridge, MA: Belknap Press of Harvard University Press, 2009); Bernard Rostker, *I Want You! The Evolution of the All-Volunteer Force* (Santa Monica, CA: RAND, 2006); and Robert K. Griffith Jr., *The U.S. Army's Transition to the All-Volunteer Force, 1968–1974* (Washington, DC: Center of Military History, 1997).

4 Karl W. Eikenberry, "Reassessing the All-Volunteer Force," *Washington Quarterly* 36, no. 1 (Winter 2013): 7–24; Barbara A. Bicksler, Curtis L. Gilroy, and John T. Warner, eds., *The All-Volunteer Force: Thirty Years of Service* (Washington, DC: Brassey's, 2004); David R. Segal, Thomas J. Burns, William W. Falk, Michael P. Silver, and Bam Dev Sharda, "The All-Volunteer Force in the 1970s," *Social Science Quarterly* 79, no. 2 (June 1998): 390–411; and Morris Janowitz and Charles C. Moskos Jr., "Five Years of the All-Volunteer Force: 1973–1978," *Armed Forces and Society* 5, no. 2 (Winter 1979): 171–218.

5 Amy J. Rutenberg, *Rough Draft: Cold War Military Manpower Policy and the Origins of Vietnam-Era Draft Resistance* (Ithaca, NY: Cornell University Press, 2019); William A. Taylor, *Every Citizen a Soldier: The Campaign for Universal Military Training after World War II* (College Station: Texas A&M University Press, 2014); Deborah D. Avant, *The Market for Force: The Consequences of Privatizing Security* (Cambridge: Cambridge University Press, 2005); George Q. Flynn, *The Draft, 1940–1973* (Lawrence: University Press of Kansas, 1993); and Charles C. Moskos, *A Call to Civic Service: National Service for Country and Community* (New York: Free Press, 1988).

6 Douglas W. Bristol Jr. and Heather Marie Stur, eds., *Integrating the US Military: Race, Gender, and Sexual Orientation since World War II* (Baltimore: Johns Hopkins University Press, 2017); William A. Taylor, *Military Service and American Democracy: From World War II to the Iraq and Afghanistan Wars* (Lawrence: University Press of Kansas, 2016); Peter S. Kindsvatter, *American Soldiers: Ground Combat in the World Wars, Korea, and Vietnam* (Lawrence: University Press of Kansas, 2003); Peter D. Feaver and Richard H.

Kohn, eds., *Soldiers and Civilians: The Civil-Military Gap and American National Security* (Cambridge, MA: MIT Press, 2001); David R. Segal, *Recruiting for Uncle Sam: Citizenship and Military Manpower Policy* (Lawrence: University Press of Kansas, 1989); and Eliot A. Cohen, *Citizens and Soldiers: The Dilemmas of Military Service* (Ithaca, NY: Cornell University Press, 1985).

7 Dennis Laich, *Skin in the Game: Poor Kids and Patriots* (Bloomington, IN: iUniverse, 2013); Andrew J. Bacevich, *Breach of Trust: How Americans Failed Their Soldiers and Their Country* (New York: Henry Holt, 2013); and Kathy Roth-Douquet and Frank Schaeffer, *AWOL: The Unexcused Absence of America's Upper Classes from Military Service—and How It Hurts Our Country* (New York: HarperCollins, 2006).

8 For the American Civil War, see Timothy J. Perri, "The Evolution of Military Conscription in the United States," *Independent Review* 17, no. 3 (Winter 2013): 429–439, esp. 430–432. For World War I, see John W. Chambers, *To Raise an Army: The Draft Comes to Modern America* (New York: Free Press, 1987). For World War II, see J. Garry Clifford and Samuel R. Spencer, *The First Peacetime Draft* (Lawrence: University Press of Kansas, 1986).

9 Selective Service System, "Its Concept, History and Operation," September 1967, p. 3, box 72, folder Selective Service System, "Its Concept, History and Operation," September 1967, RG 147, Entry 36, Selective Service System, Histories of the SSS, National Archives and Records Administration, College Park, MD (hereafter cited as NARA).

10 On Hershey, see George Q. Flynn, *Lewis B. Hershey: Mr. Selective Service* (Chapel Hill: University of North Carolina Press, 1985).

11 Lewis Hershey, "The Selective Service System during the Administration of President Lyndon B. Johnson, November 1963–January 1969, Volume I Administrative History," 1969, p. 60, box 1 Selective Service System, Volume I, Volume II, Parts I & II, folder Vol. 1-Narrative History Chapters III–Chapter IX, Administrative History, Lyndon B. Johnson Library, Austin, TX (hereafter cited as LBJL).

12 Ibid.

13 Kindsvatter, *American Soldiers*, 10. On the same page, the author comments, "In a similar vein, a survey of Vietnam veterans showed that as many as two-thirds of those who had volunteered were 'draft-motivated.'"

14 Selective Service System, *Selective Service in Peacetime: First Report of the Director of Selective Service, 1940–1941* (Washington, DC: U.S. Government Printing Office, 1942), 17.

15 The Gates Commission quantified draft-motivated and true volunteers. For active forces as of June 30, 1965, the group calculated that of 1,357,000 first-term personnel, only 768,000 (57 percent) were true volunteers. For active forces as of June 30, 1967, they estimated that of 2,100,000 first-term personnel, only 819,000 (39 percent) were true volunteers. Gates Commission, *Report on an All-Volunteer Armed Force*, 48–49.

16 Flynn, *The Draft*, 85.

17 The campaign for UMT after World War II had precedents, most notably the Plattsburg Movement before, during, and after World War I. On Plattsburg, see J. Garry Clifford, *The Citizen Soldiers: The Plattsburg Training Camp Movement, 1913–1920* (Lexington: University Press of Kentucky, 1972). While Marshall was the most prominent proponent because of his vaunted international status, Palmer conceived the specifics. On Marshall, see Mark A. Stoler, *George C. Marshall: Soldier-Statesman of the American Century* (Boston: Twayne, 1989). On Palmer, see I. B. Holley, *General John M. Palmer, Citizen Soldiers, and the Army of a Democracy* (Westport, CT: Greenwood, 1982).

18 Howard Petersen, "Memorandum to the President," June 21, 1946, pp. 1, 3, box 1309, folder OF 419-B Pending Legislation 1945–February 1947, Congress, Harry S. Truman Papers, Official File, Harry S. Truman Library, Independence, MO (hereafter cited as HSTL).

19 On unification, see Demetrios Caraley, *Politics of Military Unification: A Study of Conflict and the Policy Process* (New York: Columbia University Press, 1966). On control of atomic energy, see Richard G. Hewlett and Francis Duncan, *A History of the United*

*States Atomic Energy Commission*, vol. 2, *Atomic Shield, 1947–1952* (University Park: Pennsylvania University Press, 1969) and Richard G. Hewlett and Oscar E. Anderson Jr., *A History of the United States Atomic Energy Commission*, vol. 1, *The New World, 1936–1946* (University Park: Pennsylvania State University Press, 1962).

20 Paul Griffith to Howard McGrath, February 16, 1947, p. 1, box 23, folder Military Training, Compulsory, 1947, J. Howard McGrath Papers, HSTL.

21 On prior advocacy and for differences, see "2 Veterans Groups Back Youth Draft," *New York Times*, June 6, 1945.

22 On Marshall's views, see Joe Majerus, "From War to Global Peace Strategist: George C. Marshall and the Fundamentals of International Peace and Security," *International Journal of Military History and Historiography* (2021): 1–32, doi: https://doi.org/10.1163/246833 02-bja10027 (accessed June 7, 2022).

23 Harry Truman, "Message to the Congress of the United States," March 10, 1947, p. 1, box 1309, folder OF 419-B Pending Legislation March 1947, Congress, Harry S. Truman Papers, Official File, HSTL.

24 Selective Service System, "Its Concept, History and Operation," September 1967, p. 33, box 72, folder Selective Service System, "Its Concept, History and Operation," September 1967, RG 147, Entry 36, Selective Service System, Histories of the SSS, NARA.

25 "Summary of Status of Legislation Relating to Recommendations of the President, 80th Congress, Second Session," January 27, 1948, p. 1, box 1309, folder OF 419-B Pending Legislation 1948, Congress, Harry S. Truman Papers, Official File, HSTL.

26 Debi and Irwin Unger with Stanley Hirshson, *George Marshall: A Biography* (New York: HarperCollins, 2014), 393.

27 On opposition, see Taylor, "A Pig in a Poke," in *Every Citizen a Soldier*, 67–87.

28 Bureau of the Budget, Fiscal Division, "Presidential Recommendations in 1947 Messages," January 27, 1948, p. 3, box 1309, folder OF 419-B Pending Legislation 1948, Congress, Harry S. Truman Papers, Official File, HSTL.

29 James M. Gerhardt, *The Draft and Public Policy: Issues in Military Manpower Procurement, 1945–1970* (Columbus: Ohio State University Press, 1971), 73.

30 "When the Draft Stopped—Just Before the Korean War," *U.S. News and World Report*, March 9, 1970.

31 "Summary of Status of Legislation Relating to Recommendations of the President, 80th Congress, Second Session," March 12, 1948, p. 1, box 1309, folder OF 419-B Pending Legislation 1948, Congress, Harry S. Truman Papers, Official File, HSTL.

32 "Summary of Status of Legislation Relating to Recommendations of the President, 80th Congress, Second Session," April 9, 1948, p. 1, box 1309, folder OF 419-B Pending Legislation 1948, Congress, Harry S. Truman Papers, Official File, HSTL.

33 On the war scare, see Frank Kofsky, *Harry S. Truman and the War Scare of 1948: A Successful Campaign to Deceive the Nation* (New York: St. Martin's, 1995).

34 William A. Taylor, "The Cavalcade of Universal Military Training: Training and Education within the Experimental Demonstration Unit," *Marine Corps University Journal* 9, no. 1 (Spring 2018): 97–119.

35 Selective Service System, "Its Concept, History and Operation," September 1967, p. 33, box 72, folder Selective Service System, "Its Concept, History and Operation," September 1967, RG 147, Entry 36, Selective Service System, Histories of the SSS, NARA.

36 "The Draft Act Signed," *New York Times*, June 25, 1948.

37 Gerhardt, *Draft and Public Policy*, 122.

38 "When the Draft Stopped—Just Before the Korean War," *U.S. News and World Report*, March 9, 1970.

39 Ibid.

40 On the Korean War, see Allan R. Millett, *The War for Korea, 1950–1951: They Came from the North* (Lawrence: University Press of Kansas, 2010) and Allan R. Millett, *The*

*War for Korea, 1945–1950: A House Burning* (Lawrence: University Press of Kansas, 2005). On U.S. readiness, see Thomas E. Hanson, *Combat Ready? The Eighth U.S. Army on the Eve of the Korean War* (College Station: Texas A&M University Press, 2010).

41 Selective Service System, "Its Concept, History and Operation," September 1967, p. 33, box 72, folder Selective Service System, "Its Concept, History and Operation," September 1967, RG 147, Entry 36, Selective Service System, Histories of the SSS, NARA.

42 Ibid.

43 "Double Jeopardy in Defense," *Washington Post*, December 20, 1953; "AMVETS Push Fight against GI Draft," *Los Angeles Times*, November 17, 1950.

44 "Draft Order Sent to Dead Veteran Held Regrettable," *Washington Post*, June 19, 1951.

45 Selective Service System, "Its Concept, History and Operation," September 1967, p. 33, box 72, folder Selective Service System, "Its Concept, History and Operation," September 1967, RG 147, Entry 36, Selective Service System, Histories of the SSS, NARA.

46 There were more than 10 million draftees and some 52,000 conscientious objectors during World War II. On the latter, see Nicholas A. Krehbiel, *General Lewis B. Hershey and Conscientious Objection during World War II* (Columbia: University of Missouri Press, 2011).

47 George Marshall to Harry Truman, March 20, 1951, p. 1, box 132, folder Secretary of: Military, Harry S. Truman Papers, President's Secretary's Files, HSTL.

48 Harold Hinton, "Draft-U.M.T. Bill Signed by Truman," *New York Times*, June 20, 1951.

49 Rutenberg, *Rough Draft*, 65.

50 C. P. Trussell, "House, 394-4, Backs Draft Extension," *New York Times*, February 9, 1955; "Senate Votes to Extend Regular and Doctor Draft," *Los Angeles Times*, June 17, 1955. The Senate passed the draft by voice vote.

51 Selective Service System, "Its Concept, History and Operation," September 1967, p. 12, box 72, folder Selective Service System, "Its Concept, History and Operation," September 1967, RG 147, Entry 36, Selective Service System, Histories of the SSS, NARA.

# 2

# IN PURSUIT OF EQUITY

## The Draft during the 1960s

During the 1960s, U.S. military involvement in the Vietnam War expanded. President Johnson's commitment of ground troops in 1965 symbolized a direct engagement.[1] As a result, U.S. force levels in Vietnam skyrocketed. To meet these higher requirements, the Johnson administration intensified use of the draft, and draft calls rose. Because of the baby boom, however, these changes effected a smaller percentage of the overall pool of young Americans. Essentially, there were far more people of military age than needed, even with military needs rising.

### Increased Use of the Draft during the 1960s

The Pentagon recorded that its total personnel worldwide was stable until 1965. "Average military strength was fairly constant between 30 June 1963 and 30 June 1965," DOD reported, "ranging from 2,702,000 in fiscal year 1963 to 2,668,000 in fiscal year 1965." This total, roughly 2.7 million personnel, rose in 1965 and only three years later had grown by almost 30 percent. The cause was heightened U.S. involvement in Vietnam. "With the expansion of Southeast Asia operations, military strength increased to over 3,546,000 by 30 June 1968," the Pentagon documented.[2]

The Johnson administration made the critical decision to do so without a large-scale mobilization of reserves. The Pentagon admitted, "A buildup of this magnitude without mobilization or recall of substantial numbers of reserve personnel is unprecedented in the military history of the United States." Without the addition of reservists, it proved quite difficult to expand the military to these heightened levels without also raising draft calls. The Department of Defense maintained that such a departure from past experience granted the Johnson administration options given the vast uncertainties ahead. "The United States was enabled to keep its reserve forces intact in the event of other contingencies which might require their

DOI: 10.4324/9781003035831-3

use during the time of Vietnam operations," the Pentagon claimed.[3] Regardless, the Johnson administration intentionally accomplished this large expansion without mobilizing the reserves and instead relied on the draft more and more. There were also important political motives for the Johnson administration. The draft was certainly unpopular but was already in use. Mobilizing the reserves would have been another disliked move on top of existing criticisms of the draft. Scholar Norman Friedman observed, "The U.S. Army later considered Johnson's decision to avoid the pain of mobilization the key to disaster in Vietnam."[4]

## Demographic Changes during the 1960s

Massive demographic changes in American society also occurred during the 1960s. They made the potential draft pool much larger than even what was needed for these enlarged demands. Selectivity, and by extension deferments, proliferated. Young Americans had been exposed to the draft during World War II and the Korean War, which was not particularly popular but was generally viewed as necessary demonstrated by the fact that Congress repeatedly renewed the draft with little controversary and less fanfare.[5] The fundamental transition to a much smaller percentage of young Americans being inducted as a result of expanded deferments proved much more contentious. Such a subtle yet momentous shift generated attendant critiques. These developments also shined additional attention toward the draft's problems, their solutions, and potential alternatives. At this critical moment in American history, these dynamics made the AVF seem to many observers like a viable and desirable alternative.

Knowledgeable observers noticed these occurrences and commented on their implications. Hanson W. Baldwin, military correspondent for the *New York Times*, related the demographics boom to the U.S. military.[6] "The maintenance of an armed force of 3,000,000 men will require—if past experience is a guide—an annual average input of more than 700,000 men," Baldwin explained. "However, the population explosion has greatly increased the potential pool of military manpower; the number of men reaching 18 in 1965 was 50 percent higher (1,720,000) than it was in 1955 (1,150,000)." Baldwin forecast that such variation was not temporary. Instead, it would continue and even accelerate. "By 1974, this figure will have reached 2,120,000, an 84 percent increase in less than 20 years," Baldwin presaged. "The nation's total military age manpower pool is now about 33,000,000 men (aged 18 to 44) as compared to only 28,000,000 at the end of World War II."[7] There were far too many young men than needed, even in the context of Vietnam. There was no way that they were all going into the military, so the prevailing question became how the Selective Service System would decide whom to induct. Such a conundrum led to expanded deferments and increased disparities.

The Johnson administration was not oblivious to these major demographic trends. Bradley H. Patterson Jr., executive director of the National Advisory Commission on Selective Service, informed Joseph Califano, special assistant to the president, that the U.S. population had significantly grown, beginning in 1960, and charted historical force levels of the military. Patterson showed the active duty strength of the military, as well as enlistments and inductions, and revealed expanding and contracting force levels over time, as well as the vital role of the draft in meeting those recurring fluctuations.[8]

When the majority of young men had to serve in the past, roughly 70 percent in the 1950s, there was less controversy because such a situation was a generally shared burden, even if few liked it. When war broke out, as occurred with the Korean War, the shared burden mitigated dissent and dampened controversy. With the baby boom, this percentage contracted even in the face of the increasing size of the armed forces. Such a dynamic evaporated any shared burden because far fewer served, less than 50 percent by the late 1960s. In addition, this percentage was dropping. As a result, the major debate regarding military service reoriented from applying a shared burden to determining how to choose this shrinking minority from the burgeoning youth population. It thereby sparked dissent and amplified opposition.

Of course, the original focus on equity, even if genuine in theory, was anything but equal in reality. Significant shortcomings regarding troubling socioeconomic imbalances and vast racial disparities were rife. The decentralized nature of the Selective Service System granted autonomy to local draft boards. In turn, these local draft boards woefully lacked representation and were far too willing to make decisions based on privileged notions of class and race. In the face of the demographic onslaught of the baby boom, the Selective Service System lost control over any semblance of equity. It became ever more difficult to ensure equity when the system offered more and more deferments because it needed a smaller and smaller percentage of a rapidly enlarging youth population. The ramping up Vietnam War combined with demographics to form a combustible mix, with all these disparities aggravated by combat assignments and mounting casualties. The whole system began to crack.[9]

## Project 100,000

The Johnson administration also sought to connect military service to its broader vision of the Great Society. The most prominent, and controversial, example was Project 100,000.[10] As a result, the Johnson administration made a direct connection between military service and widespread poverty. In its analysis, poverty prevented young men from qualifying for military service by failing to reach required standards. In Johnson's calculus, combating one would help address the other and vice versa.[11] The Johnson administration also connected current military service with future civilian achievement. It held that failure to qualify for military service could limit forthcoming opportunities for American youth, providing one of the underlying rationales for Project 100,000.

By the mid-1960s, "growing concern" in the highest echelons of government "about the fact that one-third of our nation's youth were being declared unfit for military service under standards established by the Department of Defense" became central to debates over military service. The problem resulted from differing institutional perspectives between the various military services and the Selective Service System. The Pentagon divulged, relying on

> the high mental standards for enlistment and induction in effect at the time, the Services were rejecting a substantial segment of the manpower pool known as Category IV's—men who score between the 10th and 30th percentile on the Armed Forces Qualification Test.

The military services rejected these youth even though the Selective Service System did not. "Under the Selective Service Law, however, registrants scoring AFQT 10 or higher must be accepted by the Services irrespective of aptitude test scores or educational level during times of war or national emergency."[12] As a result of the dissonance, there was mounting cognizance of the high rejection rates, which had increased from approximately 25 percent to 33 percent at the same time that demand for military personnel was sharply rising, from 2.5 million personnel in 1965 to 3.5 million service members by 1968.

In September 1965, the Pentagon had reduced accession requirements "to determine whether some portion of these rejectees for service could qualify." It repeated the test in March 1966. "These initial revisions demonstrated that many thousands of men who had previously not been accepted could be trained and used effectively," concluded DOD leaders.[13] Once the spur of high rejection rates became urgent, policymakers assessed whether some of those turned away could serve under new standards. They determined from the results to shift standards. These initial trials paved the way for a larger endeavor, Project 100,000.

On August 23, 1966, Robert S. McNamara, secretary of defense, addressed the VFW convention in New York and "announced a program to accept men who would have been rejected for military service—40,000 the first year and 100,000 each year thereafter." The Pentagon christened the endeavor Project 100,000.[14] With this inauguration, McNamara launched an effort destined for widespread publicity and ample criticism. It occurred in two phases, with 40,000 initial entrants followed by 100,000 annually. There was a high correlation between rising demand for servicemembers and the initiation of Project 100,000. Both appeared shortly after U.S. combat troops arrived in Vietnam.

## Sidebar 2.1: Robert S. McNamara

Robert Strange McNamara (June 9, 1916–July 6, 2009) served as secretary of defense from 1961 to 1968 during the John F. Kennedy and Lyndon B. Johnson administrations. A previous president of the Ford Motor Company, McNamara was one of a well-known group of former business executives, colloquially known as the "Whiz Kids," who joined the government to serve under President Kennedy.

McNamara brought many business practices to the Pentagon, most notably systems analysis. During his tenure as secretary of defense, McNamara became most closely associated with such controversial issues as the draft, the Vietnam War, and Project 100,000. As secretary of defense, McNamara strongly supported the draft and recommended its continuance.

The Pentagon documented the "profile" of New Standards men, the label military leaders gave to these previously rejected personnel. On average, they were just over 20 years old. Roughly 40 percent were racial minorities. Approximately 38 percent were unemployed, and 57 percent did not possess a high school diploma. Even though most had completed tenth grade, their median scores placed them on a sixth-grade reading level. An estimated 14 percent scored below the fourth-grade level on reading.[15] The unusual program aroused notice because participants in Project 100,000 were generally poor, many were African American, and some 37.7 percent received orders to "Combat Specialties."[16] The *Wall Street Journal* reported that McNamara expected the program to produce "fully satisfactory soldiers" and that he envisioned a "gigantic spinoff" by returning them to American society better off than when they entered military service.[17] McNamara failed to acknowledge that many would never come back from Vietnam.

## DOD Draft Study

Another major effort related to the draft during the Johnson administration was the Department of Defense (DOD) draft study. In response to emerging censures of the draft amid growing U.S. involvement in the Vietnam War, Johnson in 1964 had instructed McNamara to examine the matter. Johnson anticipated, of course, a positive appraisal. The results of the DOD draft study substantiated Johnson's reliance on the draft to support the Vietnam War. The review was one of the most thorough examinations in many years. After two long years of intensive research, Secretary McNamara publicly released it in early July 1966[18] (Figure 2.1).

Two weeks prior, Joseph C. Califano, White House domestic affairs advisor, privately informed President Johnson of its contents. "The study shows conclusively that a draft is needed (unless we are willing to spend billions upon billions of dollars to attract men into the services)," Califano divulged, "but it will raise basic questions concerning the current deferment system." Califano admitted to the president that "these are not new questions" but worried that its public release, combined with ongoing hearings in the House led by L. Mendel Rivers (D-SC), would "stir up more public discussion" regarding the draft. Califano warned, "This is bound to put you on the spot, at least to the extent of the question, 'What is the President going to do about it?'"[19]

**FIGURE 2.1**   Secretary of Defense Robert S. McNamara during a cabinet meeting at the White House. February 9, 1968

*Source:* Courtesy Lyndon B. Johnson Library.

The Pentagon's report emphatically, albeit not surprisingly, maintained that the draft was indispensable. McNamara identified the strength of the study as its thoroughness, entailing two years of rigorous research. He felt confident that such a comprehensive assessment would assuage public concerns. The final report, however, also contained detailed analysis of many problems within the Selective Service System, primarily inequities caused by deferments. Therefore, the DOD draft study unintentionally illuminated the inconsistent nature of the deferment system related to socioeconomic class because poor Americans disproportionally suffered and in terms of race because African Americans experienced disparate treatment and unfair results. Historian George Q. Flynn discerned that "the study caused more political problems for the president by pointing out the class and race biases of the deferment system."[20]

Johnson wasted little time in attempting to seize the initiative. In doing so, he honed in on the study's assessment of the AVF. "A major objective of the study was to assess the possibility of meeting our military manpower requirements on an entirely voluntary basis in the coming decade," Johnson reiterated. Paying short shrift to the many problems with the draft, the president reinforced that the final report proved that the draft worked and that the AVF was a wishful pipe dream. "The study revealed that there is no question about the success of the Draft in meeting military manpower requirements in the past," Johnson underscored. "It also revealed that, without the Draft, we would be unable to meet our requirements for increased men, officers and reservists in the decade of the 1970's." Not content to argue that the

AVF was an unrealistic goal, Johnson depicted the dangerous situation that it would usher in. "In fact, we would be able to sustain a force only two-thirds the size of today's military force without the Draft, and our reserve organizations would be drastically curtailed," Johnson predicted. "There would be severe shortages in technically qualified personnel, both officer and enlisted."[21]

While underpinning reasons to retain the draft, the DOD study also buttressed critiques of the AVF. The Pentagon's primary criticism was exorbitant costs. "The study examined the possibility of obtaining an all-volunteer force by increasing compensation of first-term military personnel," President Johnson disclosed. "It found that compensation would have to be two to three times as great as present levels, and that this would increase defense costs by as much as $17 billion annually to sustain pre-Viet Nam force levels."[22] Therefore, the DOD concluded in 1966 that the AVF was unrealistic, unsustainable, and extravagant. In the end, the report argued that even if the military services could obtain the required number of volunteers, which DOD claimed was a doubtful proposition, then the Pentagon could not afford to fund the massive pay increases required to do so.

## Marshall Commission

Around the same time in 1966 that the Pentagon finalized its study of the draft, President Johnson launched his own effort aimed at analyzing the Selective Service System and determining the feasibility of the AVF. On July 2, 1966, Johnson issued Executive Order 11289, thereby creating the National Advisory Commission on Selective Service.[23] Burke Marshall, former assistant attorney general in charge of the Civil Rights Division during the Kennedy administration, led the effort that quickly bore his name.[24] Marshall approached his task with earnestness, seeking to ameliorate the growing inequities of the draft. Historian George Flynn observed, "For political reasons, Marshall sought to change the draft, despite some testimony favoring the status quo."[25] Achieving significant reform of the Selective Service System, especially while it was a central pillar supporting an ongoing war, proved a daunting task (Figure 2.2).

Joining Marshall was an accomplished group of 19 other respected leaders from American society, including Kingman Brewster Jr., president of Yale University; Thomas S. Gates Jr., chair of the board for Morgan Guaranty Trust Company; Oveta Culp Hoppy, editor and chair of the board for the *Houston Post*; Anna Rosenberg Hoffman, former assistant secretary of defense for manpower and personnel during the Truman administration; Paul J. Jennings, president of the International Union of Electrical, Radio, and Machine Workers, AFL–CIO; James H. McCrocklin, president of Southwest Texas State College; Jeanne L. Noble, Center for Human Relations Studies at New York University; and Gen. David Monroe Shoup, U.S. Marine Corps (retired), among others.[26] The eminent group began their work at 10 a.m. the Saturday morning of July 30, 1966, in the White House.[27] Over eight months, the Marshall Commission met and explored both the draft and the AVF.

**FIGURE 2.2**   Honorable Burke Marshall during a meeting in the White House Cabinet Room. February 28, 1967

*Source*: Courtesy Lyndon B. Johnson Library.

Journalists followed the progress of the Marshall Commission, and its deliberations fostered debate about the draft and potential alternatives. Hanson W. Baldwin, renowned military affairs correspondent for the *New York Times*, previewed many of the central findings of the commission's final report in late November 1966, presumably obtained through leaked material.

> The present draft law has proved to be an extremely flexible instrument for the recruitment of military manpower; it has met needs, without undue strain, varying from more than 400,000 men a month in World War II, to 65 men in June of 1961.[28]

In doing so, he captured the draft's most touted feature, its elasticity. Baldwin was not a staunch advocate of compulsion, however. He had criticized earlier proposals for UMT and instead encouraged military service by highly trained volunteers. Therefore, any concessions by Baldwin regarding strengths of the draft carried additional clout.

Baldwin revealed that the "definitive conclusion is that the draft—though perhaps in modified form—will be with us for a while." The reason was simple. The nation was at war, and the draft was a principal component of waging it. "It would be unthinkable to shift the entire manpower procurement process into new and totally untried channels—least of all, in the midst of a war," Baldwin admitted. He highlighted the necessity of additional "inducements to military professionalism" in order for the AVF to become viable and envisioned a future, although not a present, where the shift could occur. "In time, when the nation is experiencing a more relative degree of peace than is true today," Baldwin contemplated, "it might even be desirable to embark—for a limited test period—on a 'trial run' of an all-volunteer force."[29] In his informed assessment, Baldwin highlighted a central obstacle. There was a war being waged. He foreshadowed the logic that the AVF might have to wait for peace. Baldwin's sentiments, based on military calculations, unconsciously illuminated the political aspects of the shift. The advent of the AVF made more sense politically than militarily during a critical moment in American history. Baldwin, a lifelong and prominent military expert, underscored that it was incomprehensible to shift the nation's whole military personnel procurement system during a war.

As the Marshall Commission prepared to release its final report, another element surfaced, a generational divide. "As you probably know, Burke Marshall's Commission was sharply criticized at the National Student Association convention and widely thereafter among students because it had no members under 30," Harris Wofford, president of the State University of New York at Old Westbury, informed Califano. In addition to a noticeable lack of younger members, especially students, the Marshall Commission suffered from the perception that it represented a different, and distinctly older, perspective on military service. "From the little I heard of the Commission's deliberations, I have the impression that this criticism turned out to be more justified and important than I had suspected," Wofford continued. "The Commission members generally did seem to be thinking in a world other than the one understood by the under-30 generation."[30] This older generation came of age during World War II and saw military service as an obligation anytime that the nation was at war. Youth, including many students, protested that elder leaders were making rules that impacted those who lacked a proper voice.[31]

Burke Marshall transmitted his commission's final report to President Johnson in February 1967. Marshall emphasized that he did so "on the authority and with the approval" of the entire membership and reinforced that the commission explored "very difficult and intensely important" topics in a most comprehensive manner. In eight months of intensive study, the group and its staff had generated hundreds of pages of detailed analysis and more than 3,500 pages of transcripts.[32]

The Marshall Commission report was indeed quite thorough. It entailed nine separate chapters, comprehensively analyzing the draft on a number of grounds ranging from its necessity to possible alternatives to how it worked.[33] In the end, the Marshall Commission found the draft necessary but recommended a complete overhaul to centralize its operation. Doing so, the group hoped, would standardize the draft and ameliorate its most glaring inequities. Members also proposed an awareness campaign to counteract "widespread public ignorance" about the system, although a reasonable observer could counter that the American public understood the draft—and its many failings—all too well.[34] More important, the Marshall Commission advised, "The present 'oldest first' order of call should be reversed so that the youngest men, beginning at age 19, are taken first" and advocated for an "impartially and randomly determined" induction process.[35] Finally, the group urged ending all student and occupational deferments with few exceptions; examining more choices on induction timing; broadening opportunities for women in military service; lowering induction standards through new programs, "insofar as it proves practicable"; and ensuring that the reserves and National Guard did not "provide immunity from the draft."[36]

The Johnson administration sensed that the group's recommendations presented both opportunities and complications. On the one hand, the commission endorsed keeping the draft. On the other, it proposed a complete restructuring.[37] While a centralized approach would lessen inconsistencies that invited disparagement, such a major overhaul as the Vietnam War intensified was not something that Johnson found enticing.

Occurring roughly simultaneous with the Marshall Commission, Congress conducted its own study of the draft. The same "criticism" of the draft that had led President Johnson to appoint the Marshall Commission "eventually induced the Armed Services Committee of the House to initiate its own, independent inquiry," recorded Hershey. Chaired by famed World War II hero Gen. Mark W. Clark, the group began its work in November 1966, four months after the Marshall Commission, but published its report on February 28, 1967, just before Burke Marshall's group released its conclusions and recommendations. Hershey perceived strengths and weaknesses in the Clark Panel's approach. "It did not have among its members any who were experienced with the System's program and administration. This was advantageous because it made for impartiality of analysis," Hershey discerned. "It was disadvantageous because it was difficult to review philosophy and operation without a knowledge of basic elements and principles." The Clark Panel's report, in stark contrast to the Marshall Commission, characterized the existing draft system "as a reflection of decentralized-democracy-at-work and recommended continuance without major change." In the end, the Clark Panel's report was "largely a repudiation" of the Marshall Commission. Four months later, Congress passed and Johnson signed an extension of the draft, maintaining the existing system intact.[38]

Both the Marshall Commission and Clark Panel reinforced the necessity of the draft. They came to quite different conclusions, however, on what form it should take. The Marshall Commission sought to shift the entire Selective Service System from decentralized to centralized. The Clark Panel was content to have the draft remain as it was. Such a stark contrast represented a constant tension within the Selective Service System. If it was decentralized, then there was more local control. If it was centralized, then there was more standardization. One cost of decentralization was that local boards were wildly inconsistent on particular decisions. When Congress renewed the draft with the Selective Service Act of 1967, it followed the Clark Panel's report, keeping the draft, maintaining its decentralization, and failing to address inequity, which the Marshall Commission had highlighted.

## Johnson Administration's Support of the Draft

While President Johnson maintained that the draft was necessary for national security and committed to its continued use for the foreseeable future, his administration also

sought a three-pronged strategy to offset reliance on it. First, the Johnson administration pursued modest reforms of the draft to address its most controversial inequities.
Second, the Johnson administration promoted increased volunteerism by improving
quality of life for servicemembers. Third, the Johnson administration began reducing
the need for draftees through various means, including Project 100,000, civilianization
efforts, and recruiting more women. The Johnson administration made modest efforts
on quality of life within military service. Examples included annual military pay raises
from 1963 to 1966, "averaging a total increase of 33 percent in basic pay"; medical
care for active duty dependents, retirees, and retiree dependents; Cold War GI Bill of
Rights; Vietnam Conflict Servicemen and Veterans Act of 1967; additional studies on
military compensation and retirement benefits; and medical scholarships for physicians, dentists, and health professionals.[39]

"At the same time that we have been increasing the incentives for volunteer
service," Johnson proclaimed, "we have also taken steps to reduce our requirements for men who must be drafted." The Johnson administration attempted to
reduce personnel requirements so as to lessen reliance on the draft. Johnson
stressed how Project 100,000 "revised mental and physical standards to admit
young men who were being rejected—more than half of whom had sought to
volunteer," thereby adding heretofore rejected personnel. It also used civilians to
fill jobs previously held by servicemembers. "During fiscal 1967, 74,000 former
military jobs will be filled by civilians," Johnson explained. "During the next fiscal
year, an additional 40,000 such jobs will be so filled. If these measures were no
taken, our draft calls would have to be much higher." "Finally," Johnson explained, "the Secretary of Defense is taking steps to expand opportunities for
women in the Services, thus further reducing the number of men who must be
called involuntarily for duty."[40]

Even so, President Johnson remained adamant that the draft had to stay. "But in
spite of all we can and will do in this regard," Johnson explained, "we cannot
realistically expect to meet our present commitments or our future requirements
with a military force relying exclusively on volunteers." Johnson presented several
reasons why not. The first was the need for draft-motivated volunteers. "We
know that vulnerability to the draft is a strong motivating factor in the decision of
many young men to enlist," Johnson divulged. "Studies have shown that in the
relatively normal years before the build-up in Vietnam, two out of every five
enlistees were so motivated. Since then, the proportion has been considerably
higher." The second was that there were simply not enough volunteers vis-a-vis
U.S. commitments. "Research has also disclosed that volunteers along could be
expected to man a force of little more than 2 million," Johnson revealed. He
compared that anticipated number of volunteers with the actual size of the U.S.
military in 1967—3.3 million strong and rising. The mismatch was not just a
temporary aberration. Johnson revealed that the average size of the U.S. military
from 1953 to 1968 had been 2.7 million, "substantially greater" than the anticipated number of volunteers at that time. Pointing to the many comprehensive
studies of the draft and AVF to date, Johnson conceded that estimates of the costs

of the AVF widely varied, "but clearly they would be very high." Most important for Johnson was "the position of weakness to which an exclusively volunteer force—with no provision for selective service—would expose us." Johnson argued that the draft provided an elasticity with which to respond to crises. It could be ratcheted either up or down on a monthly basis depending on prevailing circumstances. In short, it was convenient and adjustable. "The sudden need for more men than a volunteer force could supply would find the nation without the machinery to respond," Johnson warned. "That lack of flexibility, that absence of power to expand in quick response to sudden challenge, would be totally incompatible with an effective national defense."[41]

In his final analysis, Johnson averred that the AVF "would force us to gamble with the Nation's security ... . The draft is one of the essential and crucial instruments which assures us of that flexibility." As a result, Johnson recommended that Congress extend it for another four years prior to its expiration on June 30, 1967.[42] There was no ambiguity in Johnson administration policy. It was unyielding about conscription and insisted that there was no way the United States could maintain a large military solely, with volunteers (Figure 2.3).

President Johnson signed the Military Selective Service Act of 1967, extending induction authority for another four years until June 30, 1971. Much remained the same. What had changed, however, was that the renewal in 1967 was the first time since World War II where it had been highly controversial. As a result, support for the draft eroded, and proponents of the AVF gained momentum. Observers even characterized draft renewal as "a distinct setback" for Johnson's draft reforms because "the measures amounted to a victory for Representative L. Mendel Rivers, the South Carolina Democrat who is chairman of the House Armed Services Committee, and other Southern conservatives who oppose any basic change in the draft process." Even Burke Marshall lamented, "In my judgment, the new bill makes the system worse than it was before."[43] The Military Selective Service Act of 1967 was the last gasp of the Johnson administration regarding the draft and renewed the draft until 1971 with no substantive reform. The only alteration was that the president now had the authority to end graduate deferments, except for medical and dental students, after a one-year moratorium. Undergraduate deferments remained intact. This extension also prevented the president from taking the youngest first in random selection, handicapping the president's ability to reform the most unpleasant aspects of the draft.

## Unpopularity of the Draft

Neither the Marshall Commission nor the Johnson administration's unflinching support of the draft stifled festering antagonism toward its continuation. Instead, the renewal of the draft in 1967 for another four years, an event that had repeatedly occurred for 20 years with little uproar, intensified its unpopularity. "After the first flush of coming of age, an 18-year-old boy may begin to sweat," wrote Anthony Wolff in *Look* magazine. "In his wallet, keeping company with his

**FIGURE 2.3**   President Lyndon B. Johnson reading a document in the White House interior as Gen. William C. Westmoreland looks on. November 16, 1967

*Source*: Courtesy Lyndon B. Johnson Library.

driver's license as part of the thin dossier that proves he's a man, is a card from Uncle Sam that says the Government has a lien on his life." The blurry lines between youth, adulthood, masculinity, and citizenship all swirled around the draft. Wolff recognized:

> In most states, he may not buy a drink, vote, marry without parental consent or sign a legal contract, but he knows that his Government can arrogate to its own purpose two years of his irreplaceable youth and subject it to unfamiliar indignities, perhaps to death.[44]

The draft had become a central facet of American society. Indeed, it was an American institution. It was a supposed ritual of manhood, one that impacted every 18-year-old male. It illuminated the connection between military service as an institution and American youth as a demographic, revealing that the two were intimately, although not always consensually, connected. Determining the best pursuits for American youth—military service, college education, gainful employment—remained a perennial question.

Myriad problems plagued the draft. Marginalized groups had almost no representation on local draft boards, fortifying charges that the draft discriminated. One government analysis of the 16,632 local draft board members throughout the nation revealed that only 213 (1.3 percent) were African American and only 240 (1.5 percent) were Hispanic.[45] Such an unacceptable shortcoming provided a nexus for two important issues related to military service: race and compulsion. If the nation retained compulsory military service, then race became magnified when conditions were discriminatory. Marginalized communities understandably lacked confidence that they were treated fairly if they were not represented on the local draft boards that made the very decisions regarding who was drafted. President Johnson intermittently and inadequately sought to improve this shortcoming, but even slight advancements left the system far below any meaningful measure of representation.

The draft also resulted in military complications. Numerous difficulties on battlefields in Vietnam—desertion, drugs, racism, demoralization, insubordination, fragging—all surfaced with alarming frequency and troubling implications. Such developments created a vicious cycle. Highly publicized hindrances within the ranks made recruiting more difficult, thereby ensuring greater reliance on the draft. More and more draftees perpetuated, and in some cases aggravated, the same setbacks. "One reason for morale problems was the large number of draftees sent to Vietnam," Congressional Quarterly recorded. "At the end of 1968, draftees accounted for 38 percent of all American troops stationed in Vietnam. In the Army, the figure was much higher." Desertion rates in the Army rose in 1967 and continued to rise throughout the decade. Draftees, some 12 percent of whom had graduated from college, proved more willing to challenge orders and more likely to lack motivation given that they had not chosen to serve. Desertions rose steadily from 1966 (15 per 1,000) and peaked in 1971 (73 per 1,000). By comparison, desertion rates during the Korean War ranged from 14 per 1,000 in 1951 to a high of 22 per 1,000 in 1953.[46]

Most important, the unpopularity of the draft conjoined opposite ends of the political spectrum. "The right and the left wing are poles apart on what policy the United States should follow in Vietnam," Neil Sheehan reported in the *New York Times*, "but the war has united them on one issue—their joint desire to abolish the draft and to create an entirely volunteer armed force."[47] Indeed, the Vietnam War and increased use of the draft to wage it had created a strange coalition of antiwar, antidraft supporters on the left with prowar, antidraft supporters on the right. Such an odd combination breathed powerful life into the impetus against the draft and support for the AVF through a unique political context at a critical moment in American history.

Sheehan captured the divergent motives but common goals of political factions usually in strong opposition. "The left, profoundly disturbed by American involvement in Vietnam, wants to abolish the draft in the hope that the elimination of this source of military manpower will inhibit similar involvement in the future," he perceived. In stark contrast, "The right, which favors an aggressive foreign policy and escalation in Vietnam, opposes the draft because it is against conscription on principle and because it wants a military establishment that is as highly professional as possible."[48] Such a confluence of shared resentment against the draft and staunch support for the AVF proved crucial for the advent of the latter. It represented a growing coalition of people with diametrically opposed motives sharing a common goal through an unintentional, informal, and temporary political alliance. It also demonstrated the importance of politics to policy, which, in turn, impacted American society.

## Notes

1 On escalation after 1965, see Brian VanDeMark, *Road to Disaster: A New History of America's Descent into Vietnam* (New York: Custom House, 2018), 230–231, 249, 254, 262, 275–276, 432–433.

2 Department of Defense, "Volume IV: Manpower, 1963–1969," p. 7, box 2 Department of Defense, 1963–1969, Volume IV, Manpower, folder 1 Administrative History of the Department of Defense, Volume IV-Manpower, Administrative History, LBJL.

3 Ibid.

4 Norman Friedman, *The Fifty-Year War: Conflict and Strategy in the Cold War* (Annapolis, MD: Naval Institute, 2000), 323.

5 Congress renewed the draft during the early Cold War by overwhelming majorities in the House and simple voice votes in the Senate, indicating that its extensions up to 1967 were not particularly controversial.

6 On Baldwin, see Robert B. Davies, *Baldwin of the Times: Hanson W. Baldwin, A Military Journalist's Life, 1903–1991* (Annapolis, MD: Naval Institute, 2011).

7 Hanson Baldwin, "The Draft Is Here to Stay, but It Should Be Changed," *New York Times*, November 20, 1966.

8 Bradley Patterson, "Note to Mr. Joseph Califano, Special Assistant to the President, Re: Printing Schedule for the Commission's Report," February 21, 1967, esp. chart 2 and chart 9, box 391, folder FG 698 2/6/67–2/21/67, Papers of Lyndon B. Johnson, President, 1963–1969, EX FG 698, LBJL.

9 White House Press Secretary, "To the Congress of the United States: Message on Selective Service," March 6, 1967, p. 2, box D74, folder Draft, Gerald R. Ford Congressional Papers, Gerald R. Ford Library, Ann Arbor, MI (hereafter cited as GRFL).

10 See Geoffrey W. Jensen, "A Parable of Persisting Failure: Project 100,000," in *Beyond the Quagmire: New Interpretations of the Vietnam War*, ed. Geoffrey W. Jensen and Matthew M. Stith (Denton: University of North Texas Press, 2019), 145–179; Thomas Sticht, "Project 100,000 in the Vietnam War and Afterward," in *Scraping the Barrel: The Military Use of Substandard Manpower, 1860–1960*, ed. Sanders Marble (Bronx, NY: Fordham University Press, 2012), 254–270; and David A. Dawson, *The Impact of Project 100,000 on the Marine Corps* (Washington, DC: History and Museums Division, Headquarters U.S. Marine Corps, 1995).

11 On Johnson's War on Poverty, esp. the complex interplay between presidential rhetoric and public policy, see David Zarefsky, *President Johnson's War on Poverty: Rhetoric and History* (Tuscaloosa: University of Alabama Press, 1986).

12  Department of Defense, "Volume IV: Manpower, 1963–1969," p. 222, box 2 Department of Defense, 1963–1969, Volume IV, Manpower, folder 2 Administrative History of the Department of Defense, Volume IV-Manpower, Administrative History, LBJL.

13  Ibid.

14  Ibid., 222–223.

15  Ibid., 230.

16  Ibid., 234.

17  "McNamara Announces Plan for Military to Take in Men Who Now Fail in Tests," *Wall Street Journal*, August 24, 1966.

18  John Norris, "Study Recommends Earlier Draft Callup," *Washington Post, Times Herald*, July 1, 1966.

19  Joseph Califano, "Memorandum for the President," June 20, 1966, p. 1, box 390, folder FG 698 National Advisory Commission on Selective Service 11/23/63–9/9/66, Papers of Lyndon B. Johnson, President, 1963–1969, GEN FG 695, LBJL.

20  Flynn, *The Draft*, 190.

21  Lyndon Johnson, "Dictation by Assistant Secretary of Defense for Manpower Morris," June 25, 1966, p. 1, box 390, folder FG 698 National Advisory Commission on Selective Service 11/23/63–9/9/66, Papers of Lyndon B. Johnson, President, 1963–1969, GEN FG 695, LBJL.

22  Ibid., 2.

23  Lyndon Johnson, "Executive Order 11289," July 2, 1966, p. 1, box 390, folder FG 698 National Advisory Commission on Selective Service 11/23/63–9/9/66, Papers of Lyndon B. Johnson, President, 1963–1969, GEN FG 695, LBJL.

24  On Marshall, see Owen Fiss, "Burke Marshall: A Reluctant Hero," in *Pillars of Justice: Lawyers and the Liberal Tradition* (Cambridge, MA: Harvard University Press, 2017), 65–77.

25  Flynn, *The Draft*, 195.

26  For a full membership listing, see National Advisory Commission on Selective Service, *In Pursuit of Equity: Who Serves When Not All Serve?* (Washington, DC: U.S. Government Printing Office, 1967), v (hereafter cited as Marshall Commission).

27  Burke Marshall, "Book Telegram—Address List Attached," July 18, 1966, p. 1, box 390, folder FG 698 National Advisory Commission on Selective Service 11/23/63–9/9/66, Papers of Lyndon B. Johnson, President, 1963–1969, GEN FG 695, LBJL.

28  Hanson Baldwin, "The Draft Is Here to Stay, but It Should Be Changed," *New York Times*, November 20, 1966. Baldwin analyzed the Marshall Commission report in excruciating detail but published this article prior to public release of the report in February 1967.

29  Ibid.

30  Harris Wofford to Joseph Califano, January 26, 1967, p. 1, box 391, folder FG 698 11/17/66–2/5/67, Papers of Lyndon B. Johnson, President, 1963–1969, EX FG 698, LBJL.

31  Such a contention was visible in the nexus between the Vietnam War and the 26th Amendment to the U.S. Constitution, which granted eighteen-year-olds the right to vote. See Jennifer Frost, *"Let Us Vote!": Youth Voting Rights and the 26th Amendment* (New York: NYU Press, 2022).

32  Burke Marshall to Lyndon Johnson, February 1967, p. 1, box 391, folder FG 698 2/6/67–2/21/67, Papers of Lyndon B. Johnson, President, 1963–1969, EX FG 698, LBJL.

33  Marshall Commission, *In Pursuit of Equity*, vii.

34  Ibid., 4–6. Quote on 6.

35  Ibid., 6.

36  Ibid., 7.

37  Joseph Califano, "Memorandum for the President," January 19, 1968, p. 1, box 367, folder FG 600/Task Force/Selective Service System, Papers of Lyndon B. Johnson, President, 1963–1969, EX FG 600/Task Forces/Science and Technology, LBJL.

38 Lewis Hershey, "The Selective Service System during the Administration of President Lyndon B. Johnson, November 1963–January 1969, Volume I Administrative History," 1969, p. 91, box 1 Selective Service System, Volume I, Volume II, Parts I & II, folder Vol. 1-Narrative History Chapters III–Chapter IX, Administrative History, LBJL.

39 White House Press Secretary, "To the Congress of the United States: Message on Selective Service," March 6, 1967, pp. 4–5, box D74, folder Draft, Gerald R. Ford Congressional Papers, GRFL.

40 Ibid., 5.

41 Ibid., 5–6.

42 Ibid.

43 Neil Sheehan, "Johnson Extends Draft Four Years under Old Rules," *New York Times*, July 1, 1967.

44 Anthony Wolff, "Draft Board No. 13," *Look* 32, no. 7 (April 1968): 28.

45 Bradley Patterson, "Memorandum for Joseph Califano," November 17, 1966, p. 2, box 391, folder FG 698 11/17/66–2/5/67, Papers of Lyndon B. Johnson, President, 1963–1969, EX FG 698, LBJL.

46 *Congress and the Nation: A Review of Government and Politics*, vol. 3, *1969–1972* (Washington, DC: Congressional Quarterly, 1973), 192–193.

47 Neil Sheehan, "Draft Is Uniting Right with Left," *New York Times*, May 22, 1967.

48 Ibid.

# 3

# HOW TO END THE DRAFT

## The Campaign for the AVF during the 1960s

As the draft grew more unpopular throughout the 1960s, several important things occurred. First, its many flaws—uncertainty, inconsistency, and inequity—became accentuated throughout American society. Second, the search for an alternative intensified, something that had not gained much traction until the U.S. fully committed in 1965 to the Vietnam War. Beforehand, many observers had accepted that exclusively relying on volunteers could not maintain the force levels required for the Cold War. Beginning around 1965, however, calls for the AVF grew. Such a development created a unique milieu that proved fertile ground through a combination of factors, including ideological, economic, and political ones.

### A Nascent Campaign for the AVF

Displeasure with the draft and openness to alternatives had entered national politics during the 1964 presidential election. The Republican National Convention adopted its party platform on July 14, 1964, at San Francisco, California. In it, Republicans vowed a "re-evaluation of the armed forces' manpower procurement programs with the goal of replacing involuntary inductions as soon as possible by an efficient voluntary systems, offering real career incentives."[1] The following month, on August 25, the Democratic National Convention approved its own. While not advocating to replace the draft, Democrats admitted that it needed wholesale reform and promised to "pursue our examination of the selective service program to make certain that it is continued only as long as it is necessary and that we meet our manpower needs without social or economic injustice."[2] The inequity of the draft had become a political issue for both parties. Their respective platforms addressed the problem, although Republicans took a more critical role as the party outside the White House.

DOI: 10.4324/9781003035831-4

A nascent movement for the AVF emerged that both critiqued the Johnson administration for failing to reform the draft and, more important, advocated to eliminate it altogether. Not surprisingly, most detractors of the administration were Republicans, especially in the House of Representatives. Two early advocates of the AVF were Thomas B. Curtis (R-MO) and Donald Rumsfeld (R-IL). During 1967, they called on President Johnson, first in March and again that June, to release the entire records of the Marshall Commission. In response to Congress extending the draft with little change during summer 1967 and despite many recommendations for modification from the Marshall Commission, Curtis and Rumsfeld charged that "the American public cannot evaluate the work of the Commission without examining the working papers and background papers upon which the Commission presumably based its conclusions." Furthermore, they alleged that Congress had "ignored the recommendations of the National Advisory Commission and continued the present Selective Service System virtually without change." Curtis and Rumsfeld maintained that the AVF was deserving "of considerably more attention … than was given to it in the deliberations of the Commission."[3]

By November 1967, other prominent voices joined the movement. Members of Congress, including Robert T. Stafford (R-VT), Frank Horton (R-NY), Richard S. Schweiker (R-PA), Garner E. Shriver (R-KS), and Charles W. Whalen Jr. (R-OH), published *How to End the Draft: The Case for an All-Volunteer Army*. While these five representatives authored the book, 15 others endorsed it. *How to End the Draft* provided more than 30 recommendations to move from the draft to the AVF. Hoping to make "the debate on the draft as constructive and responsible as possible," the group lamented that the topic was "generally treated only in emotional terms." Anticipating that such a thorough project by multiple members of Congress highlighted vast possibilities, the group proclaimed, "*How to End the Draft* is, to the best of our knowledge, the first effort to define systematically a specific program of action which can lead to an all-volunteer service and the elimination of draft calls."[4]

Advocates of the AVF continued to press the Johnson administration on two related fronts: they assailed the inequities of the draft and contended that the AVF was not only possible but desirable. In what they characterized as "a blistering attack" on both President Johnson and Lieutenant General Hershey, the authors charged that both men had, on seven specific points, "irresponsibly failed to deal constructively with an issue as important as the draft—especially in war time when the draft imposes on young men the risk of death." The end result, the group insisted, was "disappointment and outrage" regarding Johnson's and Hershey's inability to reform the draft and unwillingness to advance the AVF.[5]

Their major complaints included the administration's dismissal of the Marshall Commission recommendations, its initiation of a second task force headed by Hershey that subsumed the Marshall Commission's work, its failure to move toward youngest-first selection, Hershey's refusal to implement reforms that his own task force recommended, the administration's refusal to make public either the Hershey Task Force or Marshall Commission papers, and its resistance to create national standards for the Selective Service System.

## Arguments for the AVF during the 1960s

During the 1960s, arguments for the AVF surfaced from many quarters. Some proponents made military claims, while others advanced libertarian ones. Perhaps most common—and most contested—were economic reasons. Less openly stated than other arguments, political machinations drove much of the movement toward the AVF.

Military explanations took many shapes, but many centered on the notion that mass armies were anachronistic given rapid advances of technology. Representative Gerald R. Ford (R-MI), House minority leader, maintained that moving toward the AVF would create a more effective military. "Suppose you were to wake up one morning and see these headlines: 'The Draft is Dead'—'Draft Finished'—'Congress Repeals Draft Law,'" he rhetorically asked. "You'd probably feel like celebrating. Most mothers, fathers, sisters, brothers, and sweethearts in the country would be cheering"[6] (Figure 3.1).

Ford explained that Rear Adm. Lester E. Hubbell had led "a distinguished panel" that examined the possibility of the AVF. After extensive study, the group

**FIGURE 3.1** President and Mrs. Lyndon B. Johnson, Senate Majority Leader Mike Mansfield, and Speaker of the House John McCormack salute House Minority Leader Gerald R. Ford. Circa 1967

*Source:* Courtesy Gerald R. Ford Library.

had issued its findings—known as the Hubbell Report—"that outlined a formula designed to achieve just that—the end of the draft." Ford complained, however, that even though the report was "of critical importance to all of us," the Johnson administration had withheld it from the public.[7]

The Hubbell Report was one of the first efforts to advocate compensation reform as the way to create the AVF. Also known as the First Quadrennial Review of Military Compensation, the Hubbell Report admitted, "The hard facts are that we are not now attracting, retaining, and motivating to career military service the kind and numbers of people our uniformed services need."[8] Bernard Rostker, renowned expert on the AVF, perceived, "What is important is that nothing directly came of these recommendations because of the Hubbell Study's focus on the career force and its design of a salary system that was not extended to first-term personnel."[9]

Ford's arguments rested on an altered conception of military service, shifting from an obligation of citizenship toward a career comparable to civilian life. Basing his military arguments on the Hubbell Report and agreeing with its conclusions, Ford relayed that "today's soldier must be something of an all-around specialist. He must understand highly technical weaponry. He must know more than a little about today's social problems. And above all, he must be something of an international diplomat."[10]

In return, Ford argued that military service members should be rewarded on par with any civilian holding comparable responsibilities. "Now, in civilian life, anyone with these qualifications would be eligible for a very good salary; indeed, would deserve and get it," Ford explained. "The Hubbell report suggests that the military man should be as highly paid as his civilian counterpart." Increasing pay for servicemembers was not Ford's ultimate goal, however. It was merely a means to an end. The ultimate objective was the end of the draft and ensuing advent of the AVF. "A military career would become as attractive as a wellpaid [sic] civilian career," Ford explained. "To many, it would be more attractive. In time, our army would develop into a career service, thus putting an end to the need for Selective Service."[11] By significantly raising compensation, as previously outlined by Hubbell and his commission, Ford and other boosters of the AVF proposed that they could transform the conception of military service from a calling to a career. Doing so would attract the necessary volunteers, end reliance on the draft, and foster the conditions necessary to make the AVF not only possible but sustainable. Of course, doing so necessitated increased pay, expanded benefits, improved conditions, and recharacterizing military service, all of which were massive undertakings.

Other voices offered additional military arguments. One such advocate was Lt. Gen. Ira C. Eaker, a highly respected U.S. Air Force retired general. Sensing that efforts for draft reform and consideration of the AVF were "meeting with approval," Eaker launched a scathing critique of the draft. "Abolition of the draft is long overdue," he complained. "It is remarkable that such an inequitable and inefficient system has been tolerated so long." Eaker's reasons for abhorrence of the draft were plain. He judged that American society would never apply the same principles to civilian work and risk compelling people who were either untrained or uninterested in their vocation to labor in high-risk environments. "No one would favor conscripting men to be airline pilots and mechanics, giving them a few weeks of training and then turning the safety of air passenger traffic over to their unskilled hands," Eaker pointed out. He compared that compelling paradigm to the reality that the U.S. military had been doing something similar for almost three decades. "Yet we have followed such a system in selecting our fighting men," Eaker regretted. "Who would put his money into a business where the employees hated their jobs, planned to leave at the earliest opportunity and in no case would serve more than two or three years? Yet a draft army is expected to win victories."[12] It proved interesting that Eaker was from the Air Force. The Navy, Air Force, and Marine Corps proved far more receptive to the AVF because, for the most part, those services accrued sufficient volunteers. The Army, in contrast, required the draft the most to reach its desired force levels.

Military arguments for the AVF were not the only ones percolating in American society. Libertarian ones surfaced that focused on the dichotomy between individual freedom and selective service. Members of Congress, especially Republicans in the Senate, pursued this rationale. One such individual was Mark O. Hatfield (R-OR), a naval officer who had served in the Pacific theater during World War II. Later on, Hatfield had served as governor of Oregon for eight years and then won election to the U.S. Senate as a Republican. Once in office, Hatfield contended that Congress had sacrificed a sacred pillar of American democracy, individual liberty, at the altar of expedient convenience and mundane routine. In essence, Congress and the military had grown so accustomed to the draft that they now found it both comfortable and preordained. "We must have the foresight to accept logic over habit, reason over the retarding security of tradition. We must dispel the myth that the draft, besides being undesirable, is also inevitable," Hatfield warned. Otherwise, the outcome would be as obvious as its was insidious: Congress would simply continue the draft as it had for three decades. "Again and again Congress will be asked to extend the draft," Hatfield presaged. "Our committees will provide one 'study' after another." Instead, Hatfield proposed something new, the AVF, and now. He was less concerned with the myriad challenges of achieving the AVF than he was of the risk that inaction would place Congress, and the American people, in a perpetual state of sacrificing individual liberty when there was another distinct possibility. "But the time for studies is over. In my opinion, Congress should enact legislation immediately to provide for an orderly transition to a volunteer military," Hatfield proposed. "It is never too late to start moving away from the draft—and toward the restoration of liberty, equity and military efficiency that a truly volunteer military would bring."[13]

It was not only members of Congress who seized on libertarian arguments to make the case for the AVF. Working out of Apartment 6M, 85 Fourth Avenue, New York, a group of concerned citizens formed the Association for a Volunteer Army. They used the "Don't Tread on Me" flag as their symbol and Daniel Webster as their muse. The clique promoted his quote:

> Where is it written in the Constitution, in what article or section is it
> contained, that you may take children from their parents, and parents from
> their children, and compel them to fight the battles of any war, in which the
> folly or the wickedness of Government may engage it?[14]

The group seized on one of the main libertarian arguments for the AVF: the draft
was anathema to individual liberty in American democracy. For its members, the
only solution was to end the draft at once and swiftly move toward the AVF.

Economic arguments came to define much of the rationale. Well-known
economists, including Milton Friedman, Sol Tax, James C. Miller III, and Edward
F. Renshaw, made a trailblazing case for the AVF that rested on the novel concept
of conscripted time as a hidden tax.[15] When the Selective Service System drafted
young men, these economists reasoned that it simultaneously did two things, both
of which were negative. First, the draft removed young men from the civilian
economy against their will. Second, the military then paid them artificially low
wages because the services did not have to compete for them as civilian businesses
did. As a result, the campaign for the AVF gained growing support from economists, first in discourse and later in implementation.

Renshaw, a distinguished scholar in the Economics Department at the State
University of New York at Albany, observed, "In the last decade it has become
increasingly respectable for economists to apply their tools of analysis to such
problems as selective service." Renshaw explained that an unusual congruence had
occurred wherein economists from widely divergent viewpoints had formed a
general consensus. Renshaw juxtaposed leading economists Milton Friedman and
John Kenneth Galbraith, "men who are not normally on the same side of most
issues," revealing that the duo had arrived at "essentially the same conclusion"
regarding the need to eliminate draft and move toward the AVF.[16]

Most indicative of growing animus for the draft among economists and mobilization of economic analysis for the AVF was the University of Chicago's
Conference on the Draft held in December 1966, referred to by attendees as the
Chicago Conference. At this large gathering of influential economists, "proponents of every conceivable manpower procurement policy were invited." An
accord began to form. "As a result of arguments presented, over 60 of the 100
conferees signed a petition supporting the concept of a volunteer army," remembered Renshaw.[17] This meeting propelled many attendees to become more
involved. The organizers submitted the resulting papers to the Marshall
Commission and published them in a volume, edited by Sol Tax, entitled *The
Draft: A Handbook of Facts and Alternatives*. This forceful book consolidated economic rationales against the draft and heralded the possibility of economics con-
tributing to the campaign for the AVF.

While both the Marshall Commission and Congress had resisted the early
entreaties of these economists and instead renewed the draft in 1967, the group
sensed that their work was drawing converts. "It is clear than an increasing number

of congressmen have been convinced that an end to selective service is feasible," Renshaw recollected, singling out Rep. Thomas B. Curtis (R-MO) as one member who "believes that gradual abolition of the draft and institution of a volunteer military is not only in the interest of our young men but also would raise the quality of our defense and save the government money in the end."[18] Economists countered one of the major critiques of the AVF, its high costs. Total federal expenditures at the time were roughly $170 billion per year, with defense spending approximately $70 billion annually. Milton Friedman pointed out that these figures made the AVF costs reasonable.[19]

Political arguments proved less publicized but more significant. Two inter-related political factors played a major role: burgeoning resistance against the draft and increasing unpopularity of the Vietnam War. Throughout the campaign for the AVF, myriad machinations occurred out of public view that characterized the AVF as a potential opportunity, first to seize and then to solidify political power. Richard Nixon commandeered this issue during the 1968 presidential campaign and immediately solidified it upon entering the Oval Office. Early in his ad-ministration, his advisors reassured him that "an orderly end of the draft would be a dramatic proposal that might help to convince the President's critics of a sincere plan to quickly reduce U.S. involvement in an unpopular war."[20] Such a political calculus wedded Nixon to the AVF and proved critical to its advent. Nixon's campaign pledge to end the draft garnered significant political advantage by blunting the two biggest obstacles facing his administration early on: the draft and the Vietnam War. Nixon perceived that the AVF could solve both problems at once. First, ending the draft could remove the major cause of youth unrest around the country. Second, the AVF would likely decrease the size of the military and thereby limit forces available for deployment to Vietnam.

## Sidebar 3.1: Richard M. Nixon

Richard Milhous Nixon (January 9, 1913–April 22, 1994) was the 37th president of the United States, serving from 1969 to 1974. Running in a close election race with Humbert Humphrey, the incumbent vice president in the Johnson adminis-tration, Nixon made the advent of the AVF a central theme of his presidential campaign and subsequent administration. In doing so, Nixon saw great political opportunity in jettisoning two intertwined challenges facing his new administration—the draft and the Vietnam War. Once elected, Nixon fulfilled his campaign promise and pursued the AVF with steadfast determination. Many observers characterized the AVF as one of the great legacies of the Nixon administration, although in hindsight Nixon would question the move.

**FIGURE 3.2**  President Lyndon B. Johnson meets with Richard Nixon during the campaign in the Cabinet Room at the White House. July 26, 1968

*Source*: Courtesy Lyndon B. Johnson Library.

All these arguments for the AVF—military, libertarian, economic, and, most powerful, political—demonstrated swelling support from diverse groups. These forces were largely unaligned, agreeing in principle on the need for the AVF even when they differed on the exact reasons why. As a result, during the 1960s advocates of the AVF presented myriad reasons for it: increasing military effectiveness; preserving ideals regarding personal freedom; improved economics in the form of both removing the obvious inequity of artificially low pay for first-term enlisted servicemembers and potential budget savings, even if pay increased, from reduced force levels; and politics driven by significant, and growing, discontent over the draft directed at the military, the commander in chief, and Congress (Figure 3.2).

## Richard Nixon's Presidential Campaign

Even though the conditions necessary for the advent of the AVF had congealed around heightened resistance to the draft, increased unpopularity of the Vietnam War, and a newfound openness to reconsider volunteerism as the basis for American military service, the movement had yet to find its true champion. That disciple appeared during summer 1967 in the unlikely form of Richard Milhous Nixon.[21] Campaigning for the presidential nomination of the Republican Party, Nixon was nothing if not an opportunist. In many ways, he sensed a critical moment in American history and leveraged it for political gain. Nixon committed to the AVF and made it a central part of his presidential campaign and subsequent administration.

Economist Martin Anderson, director of policy research for Nixon's presidential campaign, provided Nixon in 1967 a sweeping distillation of the rationale for the AVF. As a result of the election, Anderson later became a close advisor to the president and Nixon's primary point person on this issue. Anderson provided one of the first comprehensive sketches of why the AVF was necessary and how it could be achieved. Much of that reasoning revolved around the concept of a "hidden tax," wherein the draft taxed both a person's time through compulsion and their income through artificially low wages. "It has been estimated that enlisted men could earn at least $3,600 a year in civilian jobs," Anderson informed Nixon. "Thus, they pay a *hidden tax* of $1,200 a year—twice that paid by the average taxpayer."[22] Drafted enlistees earned an annual income of $2,400 during their first tour of duty. Because the civilian equivalent was $3,600 a year, enlistees paid a "hidden tax" of $1,200. Such reasoning framed the campaign for the AVF and melded around the sentiment that "conscription is a tax."[23]

In addition, conscription produced negative consequences. One of the most damaging was high turnover. Draftees entered the service for a short period of time, and the vast majority left at the first opportunity. "Fully 93 percent of draftees leave the military as soon as possible," Anderson divulged. The limited stint for draftees meant that a significant portion of their entire time was spent training, with very little occasion remaining for actual duty. Shortly after most draftees completed their training and became proficient at their respective jobs, they left military service, causing the inefficient cycle to begin anew. "Their expensive training is largely wasted," Anderson revealed. "A much higher percentage of volunteers will make the military a career, and utilize their valuable skills in the defense of the country."[24] This situation meant that the military services reliant upon the draft became quite inexperienced over time. Approximately 43 percent of the entire Army at that time had less than one year of experience.[25]

Anderson's outline for candidate Nixon was comprehensive. It highlighted a vast range of relevant factors, including economic ones characterized by the "hidden tax," national security ones based on turnover, and moral ones that found "involuntary servitude to the State" especially abhorrent. To these manifold reasons for the AVF, Anderson added two more—politics and society. "Clearly explained and understood, it is likely that most Americans would support an all-volunteer armed force," Anderson revealed. He implied the political possibilities that this situation represented for Nixon: "Upwards of 20,000,000 young men and their families and friends would have the uncertainty associated with the draft removed. They would be able to plan their futures—civilian or military—and make their own choices." The clear suggestion was that relief from the draft might motivate some, or even most, of this large group to vote. There were social benefits as well. "A well-paid career in the armed forces would be viewed as an attractive opportunity," Anderson clarified. "It would provide well-paying, important work that many young people would be proud to have."[26] As early as 1967, therefore, the Nixon campaign had developed a broad spectrum of arguments in favor of the AVF, including moral, national security, economic, political, and social ones. Politics and economics assumed greater significance as the campaign for the AVF intensified.

The conclusion was evident. Anderson recommended to Nixon to seize the issue of the AVF because it had numerous factors supporting it. Anderson urged:

> Because it is moral and fair, because it increases our national security, and because it is economically feasible, we should give high priority to the goal of establishing an all-volunteer armed force with fair, decent wages that will offer the young men of our country the opportunity to participate in its defense with dignity, with honor and as free men.[27]

This rationale became the basis for the movement that followed, even as the relative emphasis on particular factors waxed and waned.

Of course, the Nixon campaign admitted that there were also many elements arrayed against the advent of the AVF, including peril to national security, too few volunteers, challenges of implementation during the ongoing Vietnam War, exorbitant costs, heightened possibility of a coup, removal of military service as an obligation, racial imbalance in the military, and acute difficulty of raising sufficient volunteers during war, regardless of pay increases, among others.[28] The Nixon campaign highlighted these hurdles early on in anticipation of having to counter them as things progressed.

Annelise Graebner Anderson, Nixon campaign aide, later recounted how Nixon, Martin Anderson, and Robert B. Semple Jr. from the *New York Times* flew together on Eastern Airlines on November 17, 1967. During the flight, Semple asked for Nixon's position on the draft. Nixon argued that the United States should end the draft and move toward the AVF based on Martin Anderson's memorandum. The next day, the *New York Times* published an article on Nixon's comments. Nixon and Hubert Humphrey were very close in the polls at that time. Martin Anderson suggested that Nixon make ending the draft and creating the AVF one of his major polices during the campaign.[29]

## A Major Turning Point in 1968

The 90th Congress, convening from 1967 to 1969, played a complementary role in evaluating the draft and the AVF. Because Congress was not monolithic, however, this dynamic had two divergent results. First, an increasing minority of members took stances against the draft and advocated studies of the AVF, if not outright support of the latter. Hershey observed, "The numbers of proposals introduced, the number of statements issued, and the specificity of the proposals all registered increases." Second, many of the powerful congressional committee chairs still maintained loyalty to President Johnson and by extension supported the draft, even if only out of fealty for their party's leader. As a result, significant legislative action either against the draft or for the AVF languished in Congress. "This minority in the Congress recognized that the Committees with legislative jurisdiction would not take up any of the bills introduced," Hershey revealed. The result was that the impetus for change shifted from Congress to the more public, and therefore more fluid, presidential campaign, "where there was every indication that perhaps more so than in any presidential election year in the past 20, the draft would be a topic of campaign rhetoric and perhaps of more formal treatment in party platforms in 1968."[30]

Prior to 1968, the attention on the draft had involved legislative inquiries on how to improve it and whether it was necessary. "While the Selective Service System was made a permanent agency in 1951," Hershey admitted, "its authority to induct men who were not deferred has a fixed expiration date." The renewal in 1963, as those before it, had proved uncontroversial. The House of Representatives voted 387-3 to extend the draft until 1967, while the Senate simply conducted a voice vote. "In June 1967, it was extended until 1971," Hershey detailed.[31] The year 1968 marked a major shift. The draft had become a major political issue, with criticism against it taking center stage and coalescing with the Nixon campaign's initial moves.

The 1968 presidential election marked a watershed moment for the AVF. Both parties sought to capitalize on this emerging issue and took much stronger stances than four years prior. The Republican Party promised, "When military manpower needs can be appreciably reduced, we will place the Selective Service System on standby and substitute a voluntary force obtained through adequate pay and career incentives," while the Democratic Party more reservedly, but no less notably, "included a phrase about the all-volunteer concept," recorded Congressional Quarterly.[32]

Nixon was not the one to create the AVF idea but rather the one who capitalized on it at the critical moment. The political, social, economic, and military environments of the 1960s combined to create significant discontent with both the draft and the Vietnam War and thereby spurred debates about the possibility, feasibility, and desirability of the AVF. This was especially true with the end of the Johnson administration, which itself proved beholden to the draft. Without it, Johnson feared that it would prove near impossible to maintain the force levels necessary to pursue his military and foreign policy objectives related to the Vietnam War.

Nixon seized the issue, and observers took notice. Nick Thimmesch, correspondent for *Newsday*, characterized Nixon as "a temporary hero on many campuses" for quickly following up on his popular campaign pledge to end the draft with a concrete strategy to do so. Sensing that most American young men "possess a wide range of visceral feelings about selective service, most of them negative," Thimmesch reasoned that Nixon's "detailed plan" for moving away from the draft and toward the AVF "must make them feel a little better." Acknowledging that the 1965 escalation of U.S. involvement in the Vietnam War made the draft "a sorrier and messier subject," the reporter conceded that the biggest drawback, both for the young men drafted and for the politicians attempting to use the draft, was its fundamental, and increasingly obvious, inequity. "It seems that the smart boys, mostly white and collegiate, managed to get deferred and that the poor to middling boys, mostly non-collegiate, got drafted and later shot at," Thimmesch decried. "Besides, the draft served as a marvelous target for all manner of protestors, including the baby doctor, Benjamin Spock, and the real heavyweight champion of the world, Muhammad Ali."[33]

Of course, the unpopularity of the draft did not make the AVF inevitable, or even viable. The United States Youth Council polled young Americans and revealed an interesting, and problematic, dichotomy. Roughly 61 percent of youth supported the concept of the AVF. At the same time, however, approximately 58 percent of the same youth indicated that they would not volunteer for it. Even more knotty was the assessment that "in a showdown, the latter figure would probably be a lot higher."[34] Nixon's proposals prompted consistent approval of ending the draft but only lukewarm indications that enough youth would volunteer. Such a scenario was politically advantageous for Nixon but foreshadowed enduring trials for the AVF.

## Nixon's Crusade against Hershey

Standing in Nixon's way were stalwart supporters of the draft, none so much as Hershey. By 1968, Hershey personified the draft, making him a patriotic hero to some but an anachronistic villain to far more. As a result of Hershey's lengthy association with the Selective Service System over the course of more than three decades, he attained iconic status. President Nixon set out to end the draft and to remove Hershey from influence.

Behind the scenes, President Nixon had cast his verdict: Hershey must go. "The President has made the decision to replace General Hershey as Director of Selective Service, and feels that we should lay the ground work first by using our veterans groups to give us recommendations on a replacement," H. R. Haldeman revealed.[35] Removing the powerful director of the Selective Service System and most emblematic supporter of the draft would ease the transition to the AVF.

Peter M. Flanigan became the point person within the Nixon administration to move Hershey aside and argued that doing so would accrue political advantage for the president. "While General Hershey remains in [sic] an intelligent and engaging human being," Flanigan acknowledged, "the disadvantages of his image among those subject to the draft are obvious." Even though Hershey had become a larger-than-life figure due to his lengthy involvement with the draft and had crafted significant bonds with powerful figures in Congress, Flanigan urged that his time had come. "In spite of his strong ties on the Hill, I think that the Administration would benefit from his retirement," Flanigan recommended.[36]

Other powerful figures joined the plot against Hershey. On May 7, 1969, Stephen Hess on the White House staff informed John Ehrlichman, White House counsel, that support for the administration's move against Hershey was growing and "would be pleasing to youth." Hess highlighted the recent support from Kingman Brewster, president of Yale University, for the removal of Hershey. "Kingman Brewster yesterday stressed the symbolic importance of replacing General Hershey as Director of the Selective Service System."[37]

Less than three weeks later, Hershey struck back. He went on the record in opposition to the AVF, averring, "It won't work and it isn't the American way."[38] Hershey made these comments in secret congressional testimony. His private remarks, however, were subsequently made public. Hershey refused to back down once they aired. His opposition to the AVF during spring 1969 demonstrated a widening—and by this point irreconcilable—schism between Hershey and the Nixon administration, which had in private pushed for his resignation for several months. Even though the Nixon administration had already decided to remove Hershey, his unflinching antagonism toward the AVF cemented the case against him.

Everyday Americans also spoke out. Allan Marin wrote to President Nixon, angrily asking, "Why don't you retire Lieutenant General Lewis B. Hershey?" Understandably without direct knowledge of the unfolding plot against Hershey from the White House, Marin could not comprehend why Nixon seemingly failed to see the obvious: for Nixon to achieve his articulated goal to unify the country, Hershey must go. "Why are you unable to understand the extent to which this man is resented and even hated?" Marin demanded. "Perhaps more than any other single individual, he personifies everything the American people detest about the Pentagon, and the military mind it houses."[39] Other letters poured in making similar points, demonstrating the polarizing figure that Hershey had become by the late 1960s and the political liability that he represented to the Nixon administration.

On October 10, 1969, President Nixon made public his plan to remove Hershey. Jonathan C. Rose, special assistant to Nixon, later recalled that eliminating Hershey was "akin to firing J. Edgar Hoover or something of that sort." To achieve that end, Rose recommended, "What you have to do is appoint him to a high-powered advisory post and give him a fourth star," something that had earlier been suggested to President Johnson by his advisors to no avail.[40] Nixon approved a promotion, from three-star to four-star general, and gave Hershey the vacuous position of advisor to the president on manpower mobilization, effective on February 16, 1970. In doing so, Nixon wielded the coup de grâce against Hershey, removing him from the Selective Service System and placing him into a consultative role away from the limelight. Hershey was 76 years old at that time. In his new role, Nixon ensured that Hershey "will assist in the transition to a 'youngest-first' draft system and help develop a standby draft system for the period when the nation adopts an all-volunteer armed force," coopting one of the most fervent, and vocal, supporters of the draft into the campaign for the AVF, albeit much to Hershey's chagrin.[41]

The political maneuver did not go as smoothly as planned. President Nixon's preferred replacement for Hershey, Charles J. DiBona, encountered stiff resistance from Congress. The Nixon administration had hoped that DiBona's nomination and subsequent leadership would garner support from American youth due to the former Rhodes Scholar DiBona's vastly younger age than Hershey's—37 years old compared to 76. "Our boy, Di Bona, could face serious opposition if nominated," warned Patrick J. Buchanan, White House assistant and speechwriter. Buchanan pinpointed the opposition to DiBona to the Senate Armed Services Committee, and relayed that Bryce Harlow, assistant to the president for legislative and congressional affairs, "does not think he could be confirmed. Harlow thus thinks it would be a grave error to commit to him right now, or even to say we are going to have one next week." Buchanan ended with a simple recommendation for Nixon: "do not commit to Di Bona."[42] There was strong resistance against DiBona on Capitol Hill, led by Margaret Chase Smith, powerful chair of the Senate Republican Conference. The Nixon administration eventually succeeded in appointing Dee Ingold as acting director on February 16, 1970, before Curtis W. Tarr became director less than two months later on April 6.[43] For the first time in nearly three decades, Lewis B. Hershey was not the director of the Selective Service System.

## Notes

1 Republican National Convention, "Republican Platform, 1964," July 14, 1964, pp. 15–16, box 11, folder WHCF: SMOF Martin Anderson All Volunteer Armed Force [4 of 4], White House Central Files, Staff Member and Office Files, Martin Anderson Files, Richard M. Nixon Library, Yorba Linda, CA (hereafter cited as RMNL).

2 Democratic National Convention, "Democratic Platform, 1964," cited in *Congressional Record*, September 29, 1964, p. 1, box 11, folder WHCF: SMOF Martin Anderson All Volunteer Armed Force [4 of 4], White House Central Files, Staff Member and Office Files, Martin Anderson Files, RMNL.

3 Thomas Curtis and Donald Rumsfeld, "Press Release," July 2, 1967, p. 30, box D74, folder Draft, Gerald R. Ford Congressional Papers, GRFL. For their actual letter to President Johnson, see Donald Rumsfeld and Thomas Curtis to Lyndon Johnson, June 29, 1967, in the same location.

4 Robert Stafford et al., "Summary Statement upon Publication of 'How to End the Draft,'" November 13, 1967, pp. 1, 4, box D74, folder Draft, Gerald R. Ford Congressional Papers, GRFL. For a full listing, see document above.

5 Robert Stafford et al., "Press Release," May 7, 1968, p. 1, box D74, folder Draft, Gerald R. Ford Congressional Papers, GRFL.

6 Gerald Ford, "Radio-Television Script: A Military Draft Alternative," May 6, 1968, p. 1, box D74, folder Draft, Gerald R. Ford Congressional Papers, GRFL.

7 Ibid.

8 Department of Defense, *Modernizing Military Pay: Report of the First Quadrennial Review of Military Compensation*, vol. 1, *Active Duty Compensation* (Washington, DC: U.S. Government Printing Office, 1967), 26.

9 Rostker, *I Want You!*, 111. On the Hubbell Study, see 110–112.

10 Gerald Ford, "Radio-Television Script: A Military Draft Alternative," May 6, 1968, p. 1, box D74, folder Draft, Gerald R. Ford Congressional Papers, GRFL.

11 Ibid.

12 Ira Eaker, "Professional Army of Volunteers Urged," *Detroit News*, March 10, 1969.

13 Mark Hatfield, "The Draft Should Be Abolished," *Saturday Evening Post*, July 1, 1967.

14 Deborah Markovitz to Richard Nixon, January 5, 1969, box 11, folder WHCF: SMOF Martin Anderson All Volunteer Armed Force [4 of 4], White House Central Files, Staff Member and Office Files, Martin Anderson Files, RMNL.

15 Examples include James C. Miller III, ed., *Why the Draft? The Case for a Volunteer Army* (Baltimore: Penguin, 1968); Milton Friedman, "Why Not a Volunteer Army?" *New Individualist Review* 4, no. 4 (Spring 1967): 3–9; Sol Tax, ed., *The Draft: A Handbook of Facts and Alternatives* (Chicago: University of Chicago Press, 1967); and Milton

Friedman, "A Volunteer Army," *Newsweek*, December 19, 1966. For a fuller list of publications, see Edward Renshaw, "An Orderly End of the Draft," no date but provided as attachment to Renshaw's letter below to Arthur Burns on October 13, 1969, pp. 1–2, box A31, folder Volunteer Army (8), Arthur F. Burns Papers, GRFL.

16 Renshaw, "An Orderly End of the Draft," 1–2.

17 Ibid., 2.

18 Ibid.

19 Milton Friedman, "The Case for Abolishing the Draft—and Substituting for It an All-Volunteer Army," *New York Times Magazine*, May 14, 1967.

20 Edward Renshaw to Arthur Burns, October 13, 1969, p. 1, box A31, folder Volunteer Army (8), Arthur F. Burns Papers, GRFL.

21 On Nixon, see Richard Reeves, *President Nixon: Alone in the White House* (New York: Simon & Schuster, 2001).

22 Martin Anderson, "Memorandum to Richard Nixon, Re: An Outline of the Factors Involved in Establishing an All-Volunteer Armed Force," 1967, p. 3, box 11, folder WHCF: SMOF Martin Anderson All Volunteer Armed Force [2 of 4], White House Central Files, Staff Member and Office Files, Martin Anderson Files, RMNL.

23 For the ultimate representation of this sentiment, see Gates Commission, "Conscription Is a Tax," in *Report on an All-Volunteer Armed Force*, 23–33.

24 Martin Anderson, "Memorandum to Richard Nixon, Re: An Outline of the Factors Involved in Establishing an All-Volunteer Armed Force," 1967, p. 2, box 11, folder WHCF: SMOF Martin Anderson All Volunteer Armed Force [2 of 4], White House Central Files, Staff Member and Office Files, Martin Anderson Files, RMNL.

25 Ibid., 4.

26 Ibid., 1, 3, 4.

27 Ibid., 6.

28 Ibid., 4–6.

29 Annelise Graebner Anderson, "Ending the Draft: The Creation of an All-Volunteer Force," Nixon Legacy Forum, January 19, 2012, https://www.nixonfoundation.org/2012/01/rn-ends-the-draft-the-creation-of-the-all-volunteer-force/ (accessed June 21, 2022). For the article, see Robert B. Semple Jr., "Nixon Backs Eventual End of Draft," *New York Times*, November 18, 1967.

30 Lewis Hershey, "The Selective Service System during the Administration of President Lyndon B. Johnson, November 1963–January 1969, Volume I Administrative History," 1969, p. 39–40, box 1 Selective Service System, Volume I, Volume II, Parts I & II, folder Vol. I-Narrative History Preface–Chapter II, Administrative History, LBJL.

31 Selective Service System, "Its Concept, History and Operation," September 1967, p. 12, box 72, folder Selective Service System, "Its Concept, History and Operation," September 1967, RG 147, Entry 36, Selective Service System, Histories of the SSS, NARA.

32 *Congress and the Nation, 1969–1972*, 226.

33 Nick Thimmesch, "Proposals to End Draft," *Newsday*, February 6, 1969.

34 Ibid.

35 H. R. Haldeman, "Memorandum for: Mr. Flanigan," February 17, 1969, p. 1, box 1, folder WHCF: Subject Files EX FG 216 Selective Service System [Begin–7/31/1969], White House Central Files, Subject Files, FG 216 Selective Service System, RMNL.

36 Peter Flanigan, "Memorandum for Arthur Burns and John Ehrlichman," April 26, 1969, p. 2, box 1, folder WHCF: Subject Files EX FG 216 Selective Service System [Begin–7/31/1969], White House Central Files, Subject Files, FG 216 Selective Service System, RMNL.

37 Stephen Hess, "Memorandum for John Ehrlichman," May 7, 1969, p. 1, box 1, folder WHCF: Subject Files EX FG 216 Selective Service System [Begin–7/31/1969], White House Central Files, Subject Files, FG 216 Selective Service System, RMNL.

38 "Opposes End to Draft Law," *Chicago Daily News*, May 27, 1969.

39  Allan Marin to Richard Nixon, May 29, 1969, p. 1, box 1, folder WHCF: Subject Files EX FG 216 Selective Service System [Begin–7/31/1969], White House Central Files, Subject Files, FG 216 Selective Service System, RMNL. For another example of a scathing denunciation of Hershey, see Stuart Schwarzschild to Richard Nixon, August 6, 1969, p. 1, box 1, folder WHCF: Subject Files EX FG 216 8/1/1969–9/30/1969, White House Central Files, Subject Files, FG 216 Selective Service System, RMNL.
40  Jonathan Rose, "Ending the Draft: The Creation of an All-Volunteer Force," Nixon Legacy Forum, January 19, 2012, https://www.nixonfoundation.org/2012/01/rn-ends-the-draft-the-creation-of-the-all-volunteer-force/ (accessed June 21, 2022).
41  White House Press Secretary, "For Immediate Release: The White House," October 10, 1969, p. 1, box 1, folder WHCF: Subject Files EX FG 216 10/1/1969–12/31/1969, White House Central Files, Subject Files, FG 216 Selective Service System, RMNL.
42  Patrick Buchanan, "Memorandum to Richard M. Nixon," January 30, 1970, p. 1, box 1, folder WHCF: Subject Files EX FG 216 1/1/1970–2/15/1970, White House Central Files, Subject Files, FG 216 Selective Service System, RMNL.
43  Vincent Burke, "DiBona also Bows Out," *Los Angeles Times*, February 12, 1970; "Hershey Aide, a Retired Colonel, Named Acting Director of Draft," *New York Times*, February 17, 1970; "Ex-Educator Picked to Be Draft Director," *Los Angeles Times*, March 13, 1970.

# 4

# THE FIRST INDISPENSABLE STEP

## The Gates Commission

As President Nixon moved against Hershey, he simultaneously initiated a major component of the advent of the AVF that became known as the Gates Commission after its chair, Thomas S. Gates Jr., secretary of defense during the Eisenhower administration. Because the AVF was a high priority, Nixon quickly initiated action upon assuming the presidency to make it a reality. On March 27, 1969, Nixon created the President's Commission on an All-Volunteer Armed Force and appointed Gates its chair. The commission's sole mission was to advocate for the AVF and to determine how to create it[1] (Figure 4.1).

Nixon sought affirmation from a group of public servants, industry leaders, and military officers. In his personal invitation to prospective members, President Nixon made two things clear: his goal was the AVF, and he sought the commission's help to achieve it. "One of the serious problems troubling our country today, and, in particular, our young men, is compulsory military service," Nixon bemoaned. The draft had become an albatross—militarily, economically, socially, and especially politically. "After careful consideration of this problem, I have reached the conclusion that our national interest requires that we explore at once the specific steps that will need to be taken to enable us, once expenditures on Vietnam are substantially reduced, to move to an all-volunteer armed force." In order to accomplish his goal, however, Nixon enlisted high-profile commission members to make the case for the AVF.[2]

The assemblage represented a cross-section of American society, including notable economists, industry leaders, and military officers. Chaired by Gates, members were Thomas B. Curtis, former Republican congressional representative from Missouri; Frederick Dent, president of Mayfair Mills; Milton Friedman, professor of economics at the University of Chicago; Crawford Greenewalt, chair of the finance committee of E. I. duPont de Nemours; Alan Greenspan, chair of the board at Townsend-Greenspan economic consultants; Alfred Gruenther,

DOI: 10.4324/9781003035831-5

**FIGURE 4.1** Outgoing President Lyndon B. Johnson welcomes incoming President Richard M. Nixon to the White House on inauguration day. January 20, 1969

*Source*: Courtesy Lyndon B. Johnson Library.

former supreme allied commander; Stephen Herbits, Georgetown University law student; Theodore Hesburgh, president of the University of Notre Dame; Jerome Holland, president of the Hampton Institute; John Kemper, headmaster of Phillips Academy in Andover, Massachusetts; Jeanne Noble, vice president of the National Council of Negro Women; Lauris Norstad, former supreme allied commander; W. Allen Wallis, president of the University of Rochester; and Roy Wilkins, executive director of the National Association for the Advancement of Colored People (NAACP). William H. Meckling, executive director, led a sizeable commission staff, assisted by David J. Callard, deputy executive director, and four directors of research—Stuart Altman, Harry J. Gilman, David Kassing, and Walter Y. Oi.[3] The Gates Commission was diverse but from the outset demonstrated a heavy influence by economists, especially Friedman, Greenspan, and Oi. As a result, much of the ensuing discussion focused on economics.

From its inception, Nixon reinforced to the commission his ultimate end: "To achieve the goal of an all-volunteer force." In order to do so, however, he sought "the best advice we can obtain from eminent citizens and experts in many related fields of national endeavor."[4] As a result, Nixon clearly spelled out his "goal" for the group and clarified that to achieve it, he wanted the Gates Commission to provide both the roadmap to get there and their strong endorsement to build public support.

Once formed, the Gates Commission regularly met over the next ten months. From its initial gathering, its prestigious chair continually reinforced the president's guidance about the group's "basic purpose." He advised the group not to focus on such issues of draft reform as a lottery system, characterizing them as "a short-term solution," but rather to direct all their energies toward "a long-range plan which would move toward elimination of the draft."[5] Of course, Gates acknowledged that the group also "must consider the broader implications" of doing so. The group's charge, however, was clear: achieve the AVF.[6] Gates admitted that his commission was formed not to consider *whether* to move toward an AVF but rather to consider *how* to do so. This was a consequential distinction.

Even though the Gates Commission repeatedly convened, they encountered setbacks. President Nixon had hoped to receive their final report by early November. Such an optimistic goal—less than eight months to plan the AVF—proved unrealistic, even with all the staff support. The group informed the president that planning the AVF would take more time, estimating that their finished report would engender "a delay of about a month." To allow Nixon to make the necessary budget adjustments envisioned with a major pay raise for first-term servicemembers, the group provided the president its underlying economic rationale so that Nixon could begin the necessary planning for implementation. "In the interim, we feel it important that you have our views on current proposals for adjusting military pay," the commission revealed. "These bear significantly on the budget for Fiscal Year 1971 now being prepared."[7]

The Gates Commission revealed the crux of its work in its interim report to Nixon. The central pillar of the AVF had to be significant pay raises targeted at first-term servicemembers. "Our work demonstrates that a change in military pay is required to correct the severe financial disadvantage imposed on draftees and on volunteers in their first two years of service," the group revealed. "This correction will promote fairness and will also facilitate moving toward an all-volunteer force." The pay of first-term servicemembers significantly lagged civilian employment and had fallen farther behind over time because the draft had allowed the military services to meet their requirements without resolving this basic inequity. "Enlisted men in the first two years of service now receive little more than one-half as much in pay and benefits as their fellows in civilian life," the Gates Commission found.

After two years of service, they come far closer to receiving a sum equivalent to civilian pay. Since the draft was established in 1948, the pay of men with more than two years of service has risen by twice as large a percentage as the pay of new recruits.

The Gates Commission argued that correcting this fundamental pay imbalance would make the AVF possible and sustainable. Doing so would result in two tangible benefits—more volunteers and less turnover. In combination, these results would have the added benefit of lowering the overall costs of military personnel.[8]

Therefore, the main recommendation of the Gates Commission was to raise significantly the pay and benefits of first-term enlisted servicemembers. It was so important to them that they communicated it, unique among their recommendations, to the president even before they were done with their work, allowing Nixon the opportunity to craft a plan to implement pay raises. The Gates Commission argued that two specific benefits would accrue. First, the large increase in pay would incentivize more recruits to volunteer, thereby lessening or even eliminating the need for the draft in the short-term. Second, the combination of higher pay and a larger proportion of volunteers would increase retention over time, thereby lowering the number of new accessions required in the future and lessening the need for the draft in the long-term.

Throughout the lengthy deliberations of the Gates Commission, politics were omnipresent. The heightened U.S. involvement in the Vietnam War and the visceral unpopularity of the draft combined to form the primary political consideration. Stephen Herbits, the youngest representative and lone student on the commission, captured this dynamic. He pointed out that "the draft had become a focus for opposition" to escalation in the Vietnam War. Herbits connected the presence of the draft to an increased willingness by the previous Johnson administration to use military force to achieve foreign policy objectives. "It had been a great mistake for the country to 'back into' the war," Herbits maintained. President Johnson "had been able to quietly raise draft calls before the public was fully aware of what was going on." Some members, for example, Jerome Holland, saw other potential problems, primarily "that the nation might not maintain a volunteer force of sufficient size over a period of time and that it might be hard to reactivate the draft if everyone assumed it was only available for emergencies."[9]

The main political issue that the Gates Commission encountered was opposition to the draft. The Nixon administration had already received a great deal of criticism for the draft, even though it had proposed eliminating it and moving toward the AVF. As a result, the end of the draft and the advent of the AVF became two sides of the same coin. It was not so much that Nixon wanted an AVF in and of itself, but rather that he desperately wanted to end the draft. The ensuing discussion among the Gates Commission was largely driven by this fundamental political rationale. Over time, such economic reasons as increased pay and benefits appeared to buttress the AVF, but they primarily served to answer the question of how to implement it. The fundamental matter of why to do so was at its core the

**FIGURE 4.2** President Nixon greeting and talking to U.S. Army soldiers of the First Infantry Division in Dian, South Vietnam. July 30, 1969

*Source*: Courtesy Richard M. Nixon Library.

political motivation to end the draft because of the fierce antagonism that it provoked. The advent of the AVF, therefore, was the product of a specific time, place, and context—the 1960s, the Vietnam War, and a society divided over both that specific war and the increased use of the draft to wage it. Many important themes went unanswered or were not even discussed as a result, even with as robust an effort as the Gates Commission (Figure 4.2).

Retaining a standby draft was a major point of contention for the Gates Commission. Members balanced two seemingly contradictory impulses: their overriding desire to end the draft and their recognition that a standby draft might prove necessary. Members ensured that the president was not able to institute one alone. Instead, Congress would have to approve the draft in the future. William H. Meckling recorded that "there were three major reasons for requiring that Congress approve reactivation of the Selective Service System." Doing so would ensure prudent deliberation about its use, would prevent "undue pressure" on the president for its activation, and would entail a "relatively brief" lull before its employment. To these three rationales, Friedman added another, not surprisingly economic in nature. "Conscription was a tax," Friedman reasoned, and "taxes should be levied only by Congress." Friedman held that this compelling reason reinforced removing activation of the draft from the president's sole purview. "Congress had never delegated a discretionary power to tax another branch of the government," he declared.[10]

---

## Sidebar 4.1: Milton Friedman

Milton Friedman (July 31, 1912–November 16, 2006) was a prominent economist and won the Nobel Memorial Prize in Economic Sciences in 1976. Friedman was among a growing number of economists to use economic analysis during the 1960s to critique the draft. Over time, Friedman became one of the most influential economic advocates of the AVF. He served on President Nixon's Commission on an All-Volunteer Armed Force, colloquially known as the Gates Commission after its chair, Thomas S. Gates Jr., former secretary of defense in the Eisenhower administration. Friedman's work, especially his concept of the draft as a tax, became a central rationale for the AVF.

---

Friedman's concept of the draft as a tax became a central logic undergirding the transition. The idea repeatedly arose, characterizing the draft as a tax in time. The Selective Service System taxed draftees by forcing them to provide their time for military service, resulting in a significant economic opportunity cost. Friedman and the other members of the commission gave less thought, however, to the president's constitutional role as commander in chief. Certainly, the draft had to involve legislation, but it had always done so. Such was the case at that time and had been the case since World War I. Congress had recurrently endorsed the draft ever since. Congress had approved it at the same time that Friedman and the Gates Commission deliberated. Friedman acted as if the commission, and by extension the president, had no purview regarding manning the military through conscription when clearly that was not the case.

The Gates Commission also criticized "political costs" that encompassed "the draft's adverse effect on society." In addition to principled arguments against the draft based on libertarian and economic grounds, these confounding problems arose from the difficulties of enforcing it. Friedman argued that the AVF "would eliminate the conscientious objector problem; i.e., the necessity for investigating and judging what a person believes." In a related manner, the AVF would "free the courts and police from the responsibility of prosecuting people for failure to measure up to certain ideological standards." Friedman maintained that the draft had other "unfortunate social effects," including a "steady stream of exiles to Canada and the currently high rate of desertion in the armed forces."[11] Doing away with the draft would avoid this controversial activity and was therefore beneficial in the view of its members. In many ways, the Gates Commission looked at military service through a limited lens, one that conflated how to provide personnel for the U.S. military—in general and over time—with how to do so for the Vietnam War. Their implicit view was that if the United States moved toward the AVF, then it could get out of Vietnam and reduce reliance on the draft, thereby eliminating both.

The infusion of politics into the proceedings of the Gates Commission led to some interesting permutations. One was the hazy definition that the group applied to peacetime during the ongoing Cold War and intense fighting in Vietnam. In December 1969, as the group sought to conclude its work, Friedman acknowledged that all members concurred "that a peacetime force can and should be raised by voluntary means." Friedman also recognized, however, that "there was the problem of defining peacetime—which he thought should be construed to include such situations as the Vietnam War." Friedman based his argument on two factors. First, he argued that such a limited war as the one in Vietnam was not suitable for draftees. "History had shown," Friedman maintained, "that a nation cannot fight that kind of war with conscripted forces." Friedman extended his rationale beyond just the Vietnam War to total wars as well, although he did not press the group to agree with his broader premise. "The nation could fight a major war on an all-volunteer basis," Friedman proclaimed but acknowledged that "he was willing to set that argument aside and settle for agreement on a more limited basis."[12]

As a result, the Gates Commission pursued some tortured logic. At the end of 1969, the members agreed that such a situation should be considered peacetime, presumably because it was a limited hybrid war within the broader Cold War and not a total conventional conflict similar to World War II. But there was another flaw in this reasoning, which flatly assumed that enough volunteers would enlist to maintain adequate force levels for future wars. History had shown that this only worked in complete peacetime when force levels were quite low, not the Vietnam War example and not a total war with larger aims. When war had erupted throughout the twentieth century, there had simply not been enough volunteers, including in World War I and II, Korea, and Vietnam. That was the real conundrum. What to do about that challenge was the more difficult question, and the Gates Commission brushed it aside, confident that enough volunteers would enlist, both during peace and war, and that any use of force below total war should be considered peacetime.

## Major Critiques Considered by the Gates Commission

As the Gates Commission concluded its work, it sought to anticipate, crystalize, and counter major critiques of the AVF. The group had received detailed feedback from a wide array of supporters and those who deemed it either unfeasible or undesirable for a diverse array of reasons. Organizations that provided input included the Selective Service System, National Student Association, American Legion, Young Americans for Freedom, Scientific Manpower Commission, VFW, and NAACP, among many others. Not surprisingly, the most prominent critics of the AVF were Hershey, whose draft stood the most to lose, and veterans organizations. "The American Legion and VFW had taken their traditional position on an all-volunteer force," the Gates Commission revealed, "questioning the desirability of eliminating the draft and suggesting that such a move might be a threat to national security."[13]

As a result, the move toward the AVF became a major debate in American society, with various organizations taking divergent positions. Veterans groups, including the American Legion and VFW, were staunchly against it, arguing that the AVF would endanger national security by ending conscription and thereby lessening the prevalence of military service and availability of servicemembers. Student groups were generally supportive of the AVF, although varying in their degrees of effectiveness from "had not been very helpful" to "very articulate." Of special concern was the Gates Commission discounting of NAACP reservations, writing off its position as simply "the negative reactions of a few black leaders."[14]

The Gates Commission listened to input from social organizations and everyday citizens alike. It "considered carefully the many—and often contradictory—objections that have been made to a voluntary armed force" and responded to them throughout their deliberations and findings. Overall, however, the group found the objections to the AVF less than compelling. "Our firm conclusion," the Gates Commission maintained, "is that, while some have merit, most do not and none offset even in minor measure the great advantages of a volunteer force." The group countered the major critiques of the AVF, including potential "alienation of the military from the general public"; weakened civilian control of the military; armed forces that failed to represent American society, educationally, geographically, or racially; weakened patriotism; degraded "concern of the American people with foreign policy"; and a resultant climate of "military adventurism." Promising to explore each of these appraisals, the Gates Commission concluded, "Eternal vigilance continues to be the price of liberty. There are no short-cuts."[15] The Gates Commission made an adamant case for the AVF and against these prominent criticisms. Its members and staff had surveyed all possible options and had found the AVF to be the best one. Oftentimes, however, the group's assessment of alternatives proved fairly simple. Members dedicated little discussion about whether or not to implement the AVF. Instead, they exerted most effort on how to do so. This belied the Gates Commission's main contention that it had surveyed all factors and invited charges that the process predetermined the conclusion.

Most objections to the AVF centered on its impact on civil-military relations. Therefore, the Gates Commission spent most of its efforts on two related fronts: making the case for the AVF and countering objections against it. First, they articulated the economic feasibility and desirability of the AVF through their arguments on the hidden tax of the draft and the blatant inequity of artificially low pay, especially for first-term personnel. Second, they combated estimations that the AVF would damage U.S. civil-military relations. "The relationship between the military and society is at the heart of most objections to volunteer forces," the Gates Commission admitted. "Many of these objections reflect the traditional concern about civilian control of the military." Examples included the enhanced challenge of civilian control "over a 'professional' military"; the fear that the AVF would cause the military-industrial complex to "become even more powerful"; concern that the AVF might prove "a threat to our democratic way of life"; and the possibility that it would allow "policy makers to get into and stay in (un-popular) foreign wars." Admitting that "everyone has casual evidence or opinions about these considerations," the Gates Commission sought to "draw out the implications of these arguments as far as possible so they can be tested against history and the experience of other nations."[16]

The argument that the AVF would lead to alienation between the armed forces and society was rooted in the belief that the draft connected citizens to the military in two distinct and important ways. First, the draft selected citizens to serve in the military. Second, these draftees returned to civilian life after their service. Some observers argued that this constant flow of citizens, who other-wise would not have served, made the military representative of society, and, in turn, made society more conscious of military matters. While skeptical that the AVF would cause alienation, the Gates Commission admitted that "critics feel that the high turnover of manpower generated by the Selective Service System is a healthy phenomenon." The group explained that such a perspective rested on the notion that the "flow of men into and out of the armed forces" caused by the draft resulted in "a link between the services and civilian society." The reasoning was straightforward: the draft benefited both the military and society. "It is claimed that the constant inflow of civilian draftees with limited com-mitment to the military guards against the growth of a separate military ethos," the Gates Commission acknowledged. "The constant outflow of veterans, it is further claimed, to society makes society more informed, more patriotic, and more alert to threats to national life."[17] Therefore, one of the main arguments against the AVF was that it would lead to alienation, either of civilians from the military or vice versa. The Gates Commission discounted this argument but did not clearly articulate why it would not occur.

In response, the Gates Commission provided other advantages of ending the draft. One was eliminating the "channeling" ability that the Selective Service System maintained.[18] The draft not only allowed the system to compel young Americans to serve in the military, it also permitted it to provide deferments for certain categories and jobs. Channeling, therefore, granted the Selective Service System vast power far beyond military service. "Elimination of the draft will also reduce somewhat the military's influence over the use of manpower resources in the civilian sector," the Gates Commission explained. "The Selective Service System frankly acknowledges that it uses the draft to direct potential draftees into activities it regards as vital to the nation." The problems with such authority were manifold. For one, the Selective Service System implemented channeling with little oversight, "independent of any direct Congressional review." In addition, channeling proved quite inconsistent, often favoring the defense industry and discounting other work. The draft thereby had significant authority over the broader economy. The Gates Commission argued that the AVF "would end this practice, and to that extent limit the military's influence on the setting of priorities in America."[19] The Gates Commission highlighted that the Selective Service System had accrued vast power in America, deciding not only who would serve through the draft but also who would not through deferments. As these deferments proliferated and the Selective Service System pursued newer and more complex channeling, it grew more powerful. The Gates Commission argued that the AVF would end this inequitable arrangement and place military service back under more direct congressional control.

Another critique that the Gates Commission countered was that the AVF would not reflect American society—racially, economically, or both. These deliberations often centered on African American military service. In response, the Gates Commission contended that the AVF would prove representative. During heated, yet revealing, deliberations, Friedman contrasted "the increasing ratio of black draftees to black volunteers" and mused whether such a trend "reflected a declining black taste for the military." Gates pondered whether the difference between the lower enlistment rate and higher induction rate for African Americans, roughly 5 percent apart, reflected that "economic opportunities in civilian society are improving." At any rate, Gates concluded that "the traditional all-black army argument was turning out to be 100 percent wrong" and that trends indicated the reverse, declining preference for military service among African Americans, might actually be true. Commission members felt convinced that the Pentagon was committed to making significant strides regarding representation, including "a conscious effort to obtain more black officers." Of course, the Gates Commission itself was not immune to racism. General Gruenther questioned if "another reason why the proportion of blacks might actually decline was that the services would become more selective."[20]

There was animated debate within the Gates Commission regarding race, especially the potential impact of the AVF on African Americans and vice versa. The Gates Commission tried to counter growing publicity that the AVF would become heavily manned by African Americans, resulting in an "all-black army." While the racism of such assertions was clear, the group contemplated how the reverse was actually true at that time. African Americans had begun to question the value of military service in a generational shift. Older African Americans had seen military service as the leading edge to expanded civil rights in broader American society. There were tangible signs of progress throughout the desegregation of the U.S. military from World War II to the Korean War. The context of the Vietnam War—rapidly rising casualty rates among African Americans, especially in 1966 with great notoriety, and increased racial incidents within the military that local base and unit commanders tolerated, if not sanctioned—led many African Americans to question the desirability of military service in the mid- to-late 1960s.

At that time, African Americans represented 9.9 percent of all officers and enlisted and 11 percent of enlisted personnel, while their proportion in American society ranged from 13 to 16 percent, depending on the source. The "official" number was 13 percent, but some African American leaders claimed 16 percent was more accurate. These military service percentages had held steady since 1962. In 1968, however, African Americans were a higher percentage of the total Americans drafted (15.5 percent) and a lower percentage of the total Americans who volunteered (10.2 percent). These numbers revealed racial components of a draft system with very little African American representation on draft boards, leading to proportionally more African Americans drafted. This dynamic combined with a newfound questioning of the value of military service in the context of Vietnam War and the broader Cold War, leading to proportionally less African Americans volunteering. Such figures provided context to Gates's and Gruenther's comments given earlier. It was notable that Gates's instinct was that African Americans were less inclined to volunteer for military service due to heightened advantages in civilian society, which was very questionable in 1969, and that Gruenther's impulse was that it is simply due to higher standards, which demonstrated that the military, including advocates of the AVF, struggled with both structural and implicit racism.[21]

In the end, the only thing that they could agree on was that race would continue to be an important issue in ensuing debates over the AVF for a myriad of reasons. Of course, it proved quite difficult to ascertain a priori exactly what demographic alterations the AVF might entail. While the Gates Commission heavily focused on race, it largely ignored gender throughout its deliberations, which would prove quite ironic, given that one of the AVF's largest legacies would be to transform military service for women. "Clearly, the Gates Commission did not fully comprehend the positive impact that the all-volunteer force would have on the military itself," Bernard Rostker, director of the Selective Service System during the Carter administration, later remarked. "For example, it downplayed the dramatic effect it would have on participation of minorities and women."[22] Even so, race remained front and center. Alan Greenspan predicted that "a relatively high percentage of blacks might discourage whites from enlisting," while Harry J. Gilman, one of four directors of research for the commission, could only provide that "his best estimate of the percentage of blacks in a 2.5 million man all-volunteer force would be 13–14 percent, with an upper limit of 24 and a lower bound of 10 percent."[23]

As a result, the Gates Commission considered not only the AVF's impact on African Americans but also African Americans' bearing on the AVF. The Gates Commission was not simply trying to combat public assertions of an "all-black army" but worried that too many African Americans in the AVF might hurt its chances of success. Such sentiments revealed how racism, both implicit and explicit, and the very issue of race itself, permeated discussions of the AVF. It also demonstrated the wide range of predictions involved in a change of this magnitude. Even a group as informed on predictive analysis as the Gates Commission, with its coterie of leading economists and highly capable research staff, predicted demographic changes anywhere from 10 to 24 percent. Essentially, no one precisely knew what would happen, but they all agreed that this was a major change and a critical moment in American history.

## Outcome of the Gates Commission

As the Gates Commission concluded its work, the fundamental task before them was to transform military service from an obligation of citizens to their government to a professional vocation, with all the attendant expectations and benefits thereof.[24] "Instead," historian Beth Bailey observed, "they worked from two major assumptions: individual liberty is the most essential American value, and the free market is the best means to preserve it."[25] The Gates Commission concluded that two primary factors detracted from military service: the obvious compulsion associated with the draft and the artificially low pay that it perpetuated. "In recent years military service has been scorned and condemned by some Americans," the Gates Commission observed. "No doubt, the Vietnam War is partly responsible, but the draft has also contributed to the military's unpopularity." The Gates Commission determined that the reasons for such a demoralizing situation were simple: "Young men are inevitably skeptical about a career in an organization which has to use compulsion to obtain recruits. Moreover, the low pay implies that society places little value on a soldier."[26]

The Gates Commission urged that ending the draft and creating the AVF would ameliorate such negative sentiments and enhance military service, both practically and symbolically. Doing so would attract additional volunteers, enhance the American public's perception of military service writ large, and therefore make the AVF both desirable and sustainable. "The termination of the draft should immediately enhance the prestige of enlisted service," the Gates Commission resolved. "The knowledge that those in the armed forces have freely chosen to serve their country cannot but improve their image—in their own eyes as well as in the eyes of society." The Gates Commission was confident that significant increases in pay, especially for first-term servicemembers, would "go a long way toward improving the image of a military career." The group also outlined an enticing array of tangible benefits that the AVF would provide in the hopes of improving "the image of military life." These changes included consistent terms of service, vested retirement benefits, and optional lateral entry, among many others. As a result of such changes, the Gates Commission reasoned, "Military careers will become more professional and avoid the stigma of being an unpleasant task that some men must be forced to do temporarily."[27]

The Gates Commission altered the perception of military service as something entailing duty to one's country to one recognized career choice among many other professions. Ending compulsion in the form of the draft was the first step, and increasing military pay and benefits was the second. The changes, however, went well beyond simple compensation. It was a complete reorientation of military service from an obligation to a career. The "image of military life" had to be greatly improved, including resolving many quality-of-life issues. Their overall goal was to transform the image of military service to a viable career that became long-term rather than temporary, as was the case for many servicemembers under the shadow of the draft.

The Gates Commission made a forceful case, claiming that "our society has more to gain than to fear from an all-volunteer force." Members contended that the AVF aligned with U.S. history because it would rely on volunteerism during times of peace and use compulsion only as a last resort. The commission pointed out that before the initiation of the Cold War draft in 1948, the United States had only used the draft during major wars and quickly ended it once peace returned. The Gates Commission contrasted that history with the Cold War draft: "Only in the past twenty years has the United States used the draft to raise a standing military force." By comparison, the Gates Commission claimed that the lengthy U.S. experience of relying exclusively on volunteers prior to the Cold War draft had not generated any of the potential problems that critics of the AVF warned would result, including "a threat to civilian control," "a decline in patriotism," or "military adventurism," among many others. Instead, the Gates Commission concluded, "Our national experience strongly indicates that a volunteer force is likely to promote civilian control of the military, improve the quality of the armed forces, foster continued patriotism and help avoid military adventurism."[28]

The Gates Commission maintained that history was on its side. To some degree, they were right. They correctly pointed out that throughout most years of American history there was no draft. They did, however, apply a selective interpretation as it pertained to military service. In the twentieth century, when America became first a regional hegemon and then an international superpower, volunteers proved insufficient to fight the country's wars. There was no "rush of volunteers" in the major wars of the twentieth century. In World War I, the lack of sufficient numbers of volunteers triggered the creation of the Selective Service System. In World War II, conscription predated the war itself and led to the country's first peacetime draft. The Korean War instantly required conscription, while the Vietnam War likely would have proven unsustainable without it. The fact remained that every major war the United States fought in the twentieth century required conscription.[29]

On February 20, 1970, Thomas Gates provided President Nixon the commission's final report. He revealed,

> We unanimously believe that the nation's interests will be better served by an all-volunteer force, supported by an effective standby draft, than by a mixed force of volunteers and conscripts; that steps should be taken promptly to move in this direction; and that the first indispensable step is to remove the present inequity in the pay of men serving their first term in the armed forces.

Gates disclosed that the reasons for moving to the AVF would benefit both the U.S. military and American society. He detailed for Nixon the extensive work

**FIGURE 4.3**   Thomas S. Gates Jr. and Gerald R. Ford seated by the fireplace in the Oval Office. March 19, 1976

*Source*: Courtesy Gerald R. Ford Library

that the commission had undertaken, including official meetings, public consultations, military assessments, and technical studies. Gates also revealed that the group's recommendation was unanimous, even though Roy Wilkins had been unable to attend every meeting due to illness and did not sign the formal report.[30] Even though Wilkins had not participated in all the meetings, especially the last five wherein the commission finalized its major recommendations and revised its final report, he did "endorse the basic idea of moving towards an all-volunteer armed force"[31] (Figure 4.3).

Finishing its work, the Gates Commission advocated for the advent of the AVF and made three primary recommendations to achieve its advent. First, members stressed the critical importance of pay raises, urging that Nixon raise pay for first-term servicemembers "from $180 a month to $315 a month, the increase to become effective on July 1, 1970." Second, members advised that the Pentagon transform military service by instituting "comprehensive improvements in conditions of military service and in recruiting." Third, members sought to retain the Selective Service System in dormant form, "to be activated by joint resolution of Congress upon request of the President." This primary conclusion, create the AVF, and three enabling recommendations—increased pay, improved conditions, and inactivated draft—formed the basic contours of the Gates Commission's report.[32]

The Gates Commission unanimously recommended quickly moving toward the AVF. The group urged the Nixon administration to make the transition by July 1, 1971. The group envisioned that the AVF would comprise approximately

2.5 million personnel and total $3.2 billion in additional costs, with $2.7 billion of that total resulting from pay raises. The group admitted that an extra 75,000 volunteers would be necessary but envisioned that improvements to military life, along with enhanced recruiting and retention, could secure them.[33]

With the Gates Commission report in hand, the Nixon administration leveraged it as proof that the AVF was both desirable and viable and utilized the bona fides of the formidable group to portray it as something that the Gates Commission had recommended to the Nixon administration rather than vice-versa. "This report, which is unanimous and strongly supports the President's announced policy is only the beginning of a long and difficult process," Martin Anderson declared. "Now we have to sell this idea to the press, develop legislation and convince the Congress to pass it. In this process the members of the Commission, most of them of great distinction, can be extremely helpful—if they are properly motivated."[34]

## Pressure from the Political Right

Advocates of the AVF seized upon the Gates Commission report and exploited it to pressure the Nixon administration. One prominent politician to do so was Gerald R. Ford (R-MI), House minority leader. Ford pushed to have the group's recommendations implemented as soon as possible. "I fully concur with the President's Commission on an All-Volunteer Armed Force that we should move toward an all-volunteer military as quickly as possible," Ford declared. He agreed with the commission's recommendation to end the draft on June 30, 1971, and vowed that doing so "would not only be desirable but feasible." Ford promoted all the major proposals of the Gates Commission, including draft reform, pay raises, and the Total Force Concept. Harkening back to his longstanding commitment to end the draft, Ford left no ambiguity as to his overall design. "The only way to end *all* of the inequities in the draft is to end the draft itself," Ford proclaimed. He argued that President Nixon's Vietnamization plan made the AVF possible and declared that the group had performed a great service for the American public.[35]

With the Spiro T. Agnew and Watergate scandals that later embroiled the Nixon administration, Ford's subsequent selection as vice president proved crucial vis-a-vis the AVF because he was a longtime proponent and staunch advocate of it. When Nixon eventually resigned, the Ford administration was devoted to the AVF and its ultimate success. Having a successor less committed to the AVF could have proven disastrous during its difficult initial years, when many people doubted its survival and called for a return to the draft (Figure 4.4).

Other proponents emerged as well. Representative Marvin L. Esch (R-MI) joined 60 representatives from both sides of the aisle to introduce legislation to implement the AVF. This House bill mirrored its companion in the Senate supported by Goldwater and sought to end the draft and create the AVF by June 30, 1971. "As a long-time consistent supporter of an all-volunteer Army, I am very gratified that this sizable group of Congressmen from both sides of the aisle is

**FIGURE 4.4**    Gerald R. Ford and Melvin R. Laird talking at the White House. August 11, 1974

*Source*: Courtesy Gerald R. Ford Library.

introducing this bill," Esch declared. He went on to bemoan the congressional delays in reforming the draft and applauded efforts by the Nixon administration to move toward the AVF.[36]

As a result, a small but growing group of politicians to the right of Nixon advocated even more strongly for the AVF. This faction was gaining both numbers and strength. In the mid-1960s, it had been a much smaller group of fervent AVF proponents, including Ford and the five representatives who had written the book *How to End the Draft*. Their consistent advocacy had payed dividends and gained converts. They attempted to coopt the Gates Commission report and immediately translate it into law. Ford was a clear leader among this group. In addition, Senators Goldwater and McGovern supported the AVF. In contrast, Nixon sought the AVF but feared moving too quickly, lest it fail during the crucial transition and force a return to the draft. Nixon committed to make the transition in 1973, whereas this group clamored for it to occur in 1971.

Nixon worried that applying the Gates Commission recommendations either too rigidly or too precipitously might lead to complications, limit his options, and jeopardize the AVF. Other proponents, especially conservatives, saw no need to delay. Senators Barry Goldwater (R-AZ) and Mark O. Hatfield (R-OR) co-sponsored an amendment to the Fiscal Year 1971 defense procurement authorization bill that attempted to put the Gates Commission's recommendations directly into law. While garnering far more support than previous efforts to move toward the AVF, this measure floundered, not least because President Nixon refused to back it. The measure suffered defeat in an important roll-call vote, 35–52, held on August 25, 1970.[37]

As a result, Nixon faced swelling pressure from his right to move more hastily toward enactment. Goldwater and Hatfield wanted to launch the AVF in 1971, whereas Nixon sought to move toward the AVF more cautiously, eventually settling on 1973 for its advent. The result was a political conundrum for Nixon, its most vocal and visible champion. The president faced critics from both sides, including those who wanted to retain the draft and others who wanted to create the AVF sooner than he felt it prudent to do so. To complicate matters, there were also observers predisposed to the AVF—ideologically, economically, or militarily—but still quite doubtful that it was feasible, especially given its high costs and the fact that the Vietnam War still raged.

## Notes

1  *Congress and the Nation, 1969–1972*, 226.
2  Richard Nixon to prospective members of the Gates Commission, March 21, 1969, p. 1, box A31, folder Volunteer Army (8), Arthur F. Burns Papers, GRFL.
3  Gates Commission, *Report on an All-Volunteer Armed Force*, front matter.
4  White House Press Secretary, "Statement by the President Announcing a Commission on an All-Volunteer Armed Force," March 27, 1969, p. 1, box A31, folder Volunteer Army (8), Arthur F. Burns Papers, GRFL. For a complete membership list, see p. 2.
5  Gates Commission, "Minutes of the Meeting of the President's Commission on an All-Volunteer Armed Force," May 15, 1969, p. 2, box A31, folder Volunteer Army (7), Arthur F. Burns Papers, GRFL.
6  Thomas Gates to Carnegie Endowment for International Peace, September 8, 1969, p. 1, box A31, folder Volunteer Army (5), Arthur F. Burns Papers, GRFL. The Gates Commission sent this same letter to numerous organizations. For a full listing, see attachment, pp. 1–13.
7  Gates Commission to Richard Nixon, no date but presumably October 1969, p. 1, box A31, folder Volunteer Army (4), Arthur F. Burns Papers, GRFL.
8  Ibid.
9  Gates Commission, "Minutes of Seventh Commission Meeting," December 6, 1969, p. 8, box A31, folder Volunteer Army (1), Arthur F. Burns Papers, GRFL.
10  Ibid., 5.
11  Ibid., 12–13.
12  Ibid., 14–15.
13  Gates Commission, "Minutes of Fifth Meeting of the Commission," October 4, 1969, p. 17–18, box A31, folder Volunteer Army (4), Arthur F. Burns Papers, GRFL.
14  Ibid.
15  Gates Commission, "Introduction," December 8, 1969, pp. 4–5, box A31, folder Volunteer Army (3), Arthur F. Burns Papers, GRFL.
16  Gates Commission, "Discussion Paper and Preliminary Outline for the All-Voluntary Army Study," no date, pp. 11–12, box A31, folder Volunteer Army (7), Arthur F. Burns Papers, GRFL.
17  Gates Commission, "Chapter XII," December 24, 1969, pp. 11–12, box A31, folder Volunteer Army (2), Arthur F. Burns Papers, GRFL.
18  On channeling, see Rutenberg, *Rough Draft*, esp. 96–128.
19  Gates Commission, "Chapter XII," December 24, 1969, pp. 17–18, box A31, folder Volunteer Army (2), Arthur F. Burns Papers, GRFL.

20  Gates Commission, "Minutes of Fifth Meeting of the Commission," October 4, 1969, pp. 45–46, box A31, folder Volunteer Army (4), Arthur F. Burns Papers, GRFL.

21  Ibid., 43–44.

22  Bernard Rostker, "The Gates Commission: Right for the Wrong Reasons," in Bicksler, Gilroy, and Warner, *All-Volunteer Force*, 26.

23  Gates Commission, "Minutes of Fifth Meeting of the Commission," October 4, 1969, p. 47, box A31, folder Volunteer Army (4), Arthur F. Burns Papers, GRFL.

24  On benefits, see Mittelstadt, *Rise of the Military Welfare State*.

25  Bailey, *America's Army*, 33.

26  Gates Commission, "Chapter XII," December 24, 1969, pp. 25–26, box A31, folder Volunteer Army (2), Arthur F. Burns Papers, GRFL.

27  Ibid.

28  Ibid., 4–5.

29  One could extend this argument to the wars of the twenty-first century. There simply have not been enough volunteers. Instead of conscription, however, U.S. policymakers have resorted to other means, including stop loss, private contractors, expensive enlistment and reenlistment bonuses, and standards waivers.

30  Thomas Gates to Richard Nixon, February 20, 1970, in Gates Commission, *Report on an All-Volunteer Armed Force*, front matter.

31  Roy Wilkins to Richard Nixon, February 6, 1970, in Gates Commission, *Report on an All-Volunteer Armed Force*, front matter.

32  Gates Commission, *Report on an All-Volunteer Armed Force*, 10.

33  *Congress and the Nation, 1969–1972*, 226.

34  Martin Anderson, "Memorandum for Dwight Chapin, Subject: President's Commission on An All-Volunteer Armed Force," February 2, 1970, box 11, folder WHCF: SMOF Martin Anderson All Volunteer Armed Force [1 of 4], White House Central Files, Staff Member and Office Files, Martin Anderson Files, RMNL.

35  Gerald Ford, "News Release," February 21, 1970, p. 1, box D74, folder Draft, Gerald R. Ford Congressional Papers, GRFL.

36  Marvin Esch, "Press Release," August 5, 1970, p. 30, box D74, folder Draft, Gerald R. Ford Congressional Papers, GRFL.

37  *Congress and the Nation, 1969–1972*, 206.

# 5

# OUR COMMITMENT TO FREEDOM

## The AVF and Its Legacy

In spring 1970, prospects for the AVF had considerably improved, and the White House knew it. Martin Anderson explained to President Nixon and his key staff that the moment for the advent of the AVF was nigh. "Public opinion and the political situation appear to have changed dramatically since you first proposed the idea," Anderson explained. "At that time there was little interest in the Congress and only a small percentage of the public favored it." Anderson revealed that, in stark contrast, recent polling showed that "the public now prefers—52 percent to 38 percent—an all-volunteer force over a lottery draft." It was not just public acceptance that had shifted. Similar reverberations had occurred in the halls of Congress. Recent polling of roughly half of the House and one-third of the Senate revealed that among those members of Congress, "the all-volunteer plan was favored almost 2 to 1, although many doubted it could be accomplished until the situation in Vietnam improved."[1]

Such a sea change presented great possibility but also significant risk. The unpopularity of the draft had reached epic levels and proved difficult to control, even as the president reformed the draft's worst features and sought to abolish it outright. "A considerable sentiment is building in the country against the draft and it may even be difficult to get an extension of *induction* authority when *it* expires on July 1, 1971," Anderson warned Nixon. "An alarmingly high number of young men are simply not reporting for their physical examination or for induction." The primary complication was determining the critical moment to create the AVF. On the one hand, the Nixon administration feared that if it moved too soon, it might falter and fail, forcing a return to the draft. On the other, the Nixon administration worried that momentum was building so rapidly that it could force an end to the draft before the administration could create the AVF, leaving it without either the draft or the AVF. The complex vagaries of the ongoing Vietnam War proved a key factor. "Moreover, if the Vietnam situation winds down, the pressures for draft abolition will likely increase, thus making it very

DOI: 10.4324/9781003035831-6

difficult to maintain an armed force large enough to sustain our world-wide commitments," Anderson explained. "On the other hand, there are still forces, particularly among veteran's organizations, that support retention of the draft."[2] Navigating a course fraught with uncertainty proved difficult.

While the Nixon administration sensed a critical moment emerging in 1970 to achieve its ultimate goal of the AVF, it also balanced other important considerations. "There are numerous strategies and options available to you; among the basic issues are money and timing," Anderson advised Nixon.

> The achievement of an all-volunteer force sometime before the end of 1972 will require among other actions increasing military pay, primarily during the first two years of service, somewhere between $2.8 and $3.4 billion a year. The amount will depend on the level of the armed forces and the timing of the pay increase.[3]

The Nixon administration calculated the "net costs" to be about *"20 percent lower because of income taxes"* for the reason that military servicemembers would revert a portion of any pay increases back to the federal government in the form of personal income taxes.[4]

There was an intricate and delicate relationship between "money and timing." The Nixon administration needed to raise pay, especially for military personnel in their first two years of service, in order to redress longstanding pay inequities in those ranks, alter perceptions of the benefits of military service, and thereby attract additional volunteers. Such initial moves had to happen at the outset, even though there would be some lag between this initial move and the resulting new recruits. If the pay increases occurred too early, then critics would highlight how expensive it was, focus on how it was not immediately producing the necessary volunteers, and contend that it was not working and should therefore be scrapped. If the pay increases came too late, then there would not be enough volunteers by the time the draft ended, perhaps necessitating another extension. Detractors would certainly use that scenario to insist that the AVF was not viable. Anticipating and managing such complex considerations proved a most delicate balance.

Another volatile predicament was how to handle the draft. "Recent meetings with General Hershey and members of my staff who have been dealing with the problems of selective service convince me," Peter Flanigan explained, "that some sort of cosmetic reform of the current induction system is needed during this interim period prior to the introduction of an all-volunteer army." Even though the Nixon administration had already committed to ending the draft, it faced a difficult conundrum. The Vietnam War still raged, making some reliance on the draft in the short-term quite necessary. Closely connected to this issue and occurring at the same time, public antipathy toward the draft had reached all-time highs. Something had to be done. "Dissatisfaction is rampant with a system which appears to be riddled with inequities," admitted Flanigan. "I believe that there are several immediate changes which could be made at low political cost and with great benefit to the President's popularity among youth."[5]

## Draft Reform

There were many components of draft reform. The Nixon administration focused on four main efforts: creating a "youngest-first lottery selection system" instead of the current "oldest-first system," reinvigorating the membership of the National Selective Service Appeals Board with new appointees, moving General Hershey into retirement, and "possibly the delay of induction of graduate students until the end of the academic year in which they are called"[6] (Figure 5.1).

In doing so, the administration attacked the perceived inequities of the draft, especially for younger voters. The Nixon administration broke with the past, evidenced by distancing itself from Hershey and replacing the membership on the national appeals board, which Flanigan characterized as "unresponsive to this Administration."[7]

President Nixon advanced several related initiatives regarding draft reform. In fall 1969, he had reduced force levels in Vietnam so as to minimize the need for additional draft calls. By the end of 1969, Nixon had made dramatic changes to draft calls, eliminating them outright for the final two months of that year. Such a move was something that had not happened for some time and that many observers considered near impossible not long before. "Acting on the recommendation of the Secretary of Defense, the programmed draft calls for the months of November and December—32,000 for November and 18,000 for December—will be cancelled," President Nixon had proclaimed. "The draft call previously announced for the month of October will be phased out over the final quarter of the year." Such a dramatic

**FIGURE 5.1** President Nixon and Pat Nixon pose for an official state portrait by the stairway with Gen. Lewis B. Hershey and Mrs. Hershey before attending a state dinner honoring General Hershey. February 17, 1970

*Source*: Courtesy Richard M. Nixon Library.

move was made possible through deliberate efforts by the White House to reduce personnel requirements, largely through Nixon's policy of Vietnamization.[8]

Even though President Nixon had first sought to enact draft reform through Congress, the legislative branch proved a hesitant partner. By fall 1969, President Nixon had tired from the persistent lack of momentum in Congress for draft reform. "On May 13, I submitted legislation to the Congress," Nixon reminded members, "which would have removed from vulnerability to the draft all young men between the ages of 20 and 26, and which would provide for draft eligibility only those 19 years of age under a system of random selection." Nixon bemoaned the fact that in the intervening months, Congress had failed to act. In scolding Congress, the president hoped to propel legislation toward enactment. He would proceed alone if necessary, "although it will not accomplish the objective as clearly and as fairly as the legislation if it were passed."[9]

At 11:36 a.m. eastern daylight time on September 19, 1969, President Nixon, flanked by Secretary of Defense Laird in the Roosevelt Room, admonished Congress for inaction. The House of Representatives had approved a plan, but the Senate had refused to take up draft reform in fall 1969 before the end of its session. Therefore, Nixon moved forward on November 26, 1969, with Executive Order 11497 to implement the draft lottery system.[10] He also issued a presidential proclamation that announced the changes, reinforcing his public campaign for draft reform[11] (Figure 5.2).

**FIGURE 5.2**    President Nixon in the Oval Office during a meeting with Gen. William C. Westmoreland, former U.S. Military Assistance Command, Vietnam (MACV) commander and Secretary of Defense Melvin Laird. August 17, 1970

*Source*: Courtesy Richard M. Nixon Library.

President Nixon pronounced the "major revisions in the draft selection procedures" that his executive order enacted. In doing so, he revealed "how this new system will work" and disclosed how these changes would reform the "draft outlook for young men in 1970 under this system."[12] His first intermediate move was to institute the draft lottery, which addressed one of the harshest criticisms of the draft during the late 1960s, namely that it was patently unfair. Some observers countered that the lottery would not eliminate the underlying inequity. Instead, they maintained that the entire system was inextricably unjust for the reason that some youth were compelled to serve in the military and potentially die in an unpopular war while others escaped unscathed. Such critics pointed out that such fundamental inequities remained, regardless of whether the government chose inductees randomly or not.

President Nixon catalogued for the public the four "major improvements in draft selection procedures" that his executive order enacted forthwith. First, his draft reforms drastically shortened the "period of prime draft vulnerability, and the uncertainty that accompanies it," from seven years down to only one year by moving from oldest-first to youngest-first selection. Second, this reversal in selection age "established this vulnerability for a fixed time in each young man's life, which will be much less disruptive to him in terms of his personal planning." Third, it created a "fair and easily understandable" lottery process for all youth deemed by their local draft boards "available and qualified" for military service. Fourth, it sped up the examination process for registrants so that they could discern sooner if they were deemed "physically and mentally qualified" for military service, and by extension the draft.[13]

Therefore, President Nixon made key revisions to the draft prior to eliminating it. He reduced the twin clouds of vulnerability and uncertainty stemming from the draft's pervasive presence in the lives of American youth. Previously, the draft had hung over young men during a lengthy and formative period, almost a decade worth of angst depending on their individual circumstances. With President Nixon's draft reforms, that interval shrunk to only one year. This lessened the overall disruption to their lives and allowed far greater planning for such vital decisions as college, marriage, training, jobs, and careers. Nixon also boasted that the lottery system made the draft fair by using "random selection." He overplayed, however, the objective nature of the new system and discounted the subjectivity of local draft boards, which continued to classify whether a young man was "available and qualified" for military service and, by extension, the draft. Even with the new lottery system enacted, there was still a high degree of subjectivity throughout the process, regardless of Nixon's bold claims.[14]

The immediate reaction to President Nixon's draft reforms was quite positive. While many observers insisted that the only way to make the draft fair was to eliminate it altogether, removing the lengthy time that it pervaded their lives was an adjustment appreciated by youth and their families. The Associated Press remarked, "If the draft was after you before, it's probably still after you; but you won't have to wait as long, under President Nixon's new lottery system, to see if you get tagged."[15] While most draftees would have probably disagreed with this cavalier characterization of the draft as a game of tag, they undoubtedly would have applauded their reduced exposure to being "tagged." The lottery used birthdays first and then initials of names second, all done in random order, so that it theoretically used the same criteria for all potential inductees across the country.

Draft reform proved a popular endeavor. By January 1970, public polling indicated that 75 percent of the public approved of President Nixon's "recent draft lottery plan," while a slim majority of Americans now supported moving toward the AVF. Harris polling results published in the *Washington Post* revealed that 52 percent of Americans surveyed "would like to see the entire draft system scrapped and a volunteer army substituted for it," while only 38 percent opposed such a move and 10 percent were "not sure."[16] Nixon's two major moves on military personnel policy, first draft reform and then the advent of the AVF, proved more favored than not. In addition, the acceptance of both was growing. Draft reform turned out popular and boosted the AVF by demonstrating that significant change was possible.

On April 23, 1970, President Nixon announced additional draft reforms. Nixon halted occupational and paternity deferments and requested that Congress grant him the authority to cease student deferments. "None of these actions would affect individuals already holding deferment," reported the *Boston Globe*. President Nixon also reinforced his commitment to the AVF. He remarked that "his administration is on a course toward ending the draft altogether, and replacing it with an all-volunteer army." Nixon reiterated that his fundamental goal was not to rely on the draft at all but rather move toward the AVF. Nixon remarked, "From now on, the objective of this administration is to reduce draft calls to zero, subject to the overriding considerations of national security." The president made clear, however, that he did not plan to follow the Gates Commission's recommendation that "the changeover be effected next year."[17]

President Nixon's message reinvigorated proponents of the AVF in Congress. "President Nixon has taken a historic step toward eliminating the inequities of the present draft laws," Rep. Frank Horton (R-NY) declared. Horton hailed April 23, 1970, as "a landmark day in American history" in his speech on the House floor. Limiting deferments, ending the draft, and creating the AVF was something that Horton had longed to hear from a U.S. president.

> Today, for the first time since World War II, a President of the United States has sent to Congress a message in which he recommends legislation which will enable us to do just that—to rely on volunteers for the defense of our freedoms.[18]

## Challenges Confronting DOD

While the Nixon administration made the ultimate decision to implement the AVF, the herculean task of planning such a significant transition fell to the DOD. Many challenges confronted the Pentagon even though it had studied the possibility for some time. In addition to the DOD draft study from 1964 to 1966, it had launched another effort in 1969 known as Project Volunteer in Defense of the Nation (PROVIDE), or simply Project Volunteer.

The endeavor examined how the military services, especially the Army, could increase volunteers and thereby make the AVF feasible. "While conduct of the war in Vietnam remained their primary concern," historian Robert K. Griffith Jr. perceived, "Westmoreland and the Army staff devoted increasing attention to rebuilding the institution and restoring public and self-confidence in the organization."[19] Roger T. Kelley, assistant secretary of defense for manpower and reserve affairs, led the effort. Not wanting to cede control of his policy priority to Secretary Laird, Nixon placed the onus on the Gates Commission and demoted Project Volunteer to a subordinate role.[20] "In compliance with President Nixon's directive to the Department," Laird remarked, "Project Volunteer is prepared to provide staff assistance, information, and advice to the members of the Gates Commission."[21] Even though DOD had already launched Project Volunteer prior to the Gates Commission, the latter took precedence, primarily because of the seniority of its distinguished members, its publicity and congressional relations, and Nixon's insistence on privileging it over Project Volunteer.

The Pentagon also had to untangle the Vietnam War and the use of the draft to wage it. The tantamount obstacle was that draftees were primarily sent to Vietnam. "The situation appears unfair, but, viewed objectively, it also appears unavoidable," explained one DOD assessment. "The key factor is time." Draftees served a maximum of two years compared to volunteers who spent at least three years in the Army and four years in the Navy. Such a seemingly minor distinction was "of great consequence in a number of critical respects" to military assignments. The shorter time frame for draftees essentially ruled them out from noncombat overseas tours because they simply did not have enough time to complete basic training, authorized leave, and the noncombat overseas tour, which was two years in and of itself. "The Vietnam tour, however, being for only 12 months, falls well within the time span of a draftee's term of service," the Pentagon nonchalantly noticed. Military orders disallowed extensive specialized training for draftees for much the same reason. Such policies had been in effect since 1965 and remained a hurdle as implementation of the AVF drew closer. "A direct result has been that most of the 1.6 million men drafted since 1964 have served or are serving in Vietnam," revealed the Pentagon.[22]

Vietnam and the draft combined to form the perfect storm in terms of military manpower policy. A change that was meant to be a positive—shortening the standard two-year rotation policy to a new one-year standard for Vietnam in order to improve morale—resulted in increasing use of the draft to provide for the rapid rise in personnel sent to Vietnam. Assignment policies also meant that draftees by default usually went to Vietnam and rotated through Vietnam twice as fast as anywhere else. Such acceleration resulted in the need for more draftees on a regular basis and became a self-reinforcing relationship. It intimately connected the draft to the Vietnam War in a unique way. Therefore, the Pentagon had to find offsets for the loss of draftees in order to make the AVF feasible.

As the DOD planned implementation, the outlook was bleak. "The Army will need 212,000 new men, or about 18,000 a month, during the fiscal year 1972," reported the *New York Times*. Lt. Gen. Walter T. Kerwin Jr., Army deputy chief of staff for personnel, testified before Congress, "Noting that only 14,000 men volunteered each month last July through September, when the Selective Service Act had lapsed," and "estimated that the Army would fall short of its requirements by 4,000 men a month." Hadlai A. Hull, assistant secretary of the Army, echoed Kerwin's concern, and "told the committee that in the fiscal year 1973 the need for manpower would rise to 270,000, and that draft requirements would have to increase commensurately unless the hoped-for rise in volunteers took place."[23]

The Pentagon anticipated recruiting shortfalls, especially in the Army, with the transition from the draft to the AVF. Such numbers were significant: 4,000 per month compounded to 48,000 annually if sustained. As a result, there was concern that the AVF would not produce enough volunteers. The Pentagon's forecast looked even more dismal over time because requirements were rising and volunteers were dwindling. If Hull's predications proved accurate, the move to the AVF could more than double the monthly shortfall, from 4,000 per month in 1972 to 8,500 per month in 1973. Such a shortfall would be 102,000 too few volunteers for 1973 alone and just for the Army.

Unlike the Gates Commission, which had prominently grappled with race but largely ignored gender, military planners quickly identified women as the major offset for the loss of draftees. "Consideration was given to numerous factors relating to women in the service," Project Volunteer confirmed. "Resource availability will be high. By 1975 there will be over 13,000,000 women between the ages 18 and 24." While civilianization efforts formed another pillar of the Pentagon's planning for the AVF, recruiting of women proved more enticing. "The great value of this potential accrues from the flexibility and mobility women offer the service in responding to assignment requirements," Project Volunteer affirmed. "Unlike civilian employees, they are not subject to restrictions on transfer, movement overseas, overtime employment rights, and similar factors." Of course, military planners approached the issue from a patriarchal perspective that revealed a limited vision of women's participation in military service. "However, it must be recognized that women cannot replace soldiers on a space for space basis," Project Volunteer claimed. "Present assignment limitations, regulatory restrictions, and physical make-up of women preclude them from being freely substituted for men in short tour and other areas."[24]

Project Volunteer identified women as a potential offset with many advantages over civilian employees. Although Project Volunteer envisioned greatly expanding the utilization of women in terms of numbers, paternalism still constrained its conception of what was possible. The augmentation would be in limited roles only and certainly not in combat. In the Pentagon's calculus, additional recruiting of women enabled more men to serve in combat roles as the numbers of draftees first shrank and then disappeared entirely.

## Final Push from the Nixon Administration

In 1971, the Nixon administration prepared to make its final push for the AVF. As it did, two things remained evident. First, the movement was nearing its successful completion. Second, uncertainty about the timing lingered. On January 28, 1971, Nixon addressed Congress and made his case for the critical moment. "No one knows precisely when we can end conscription," Nixon conceded.

> It depends on many things—including the level of military forces that will be required for our national security, the degree to which the combination of military pay increases and enhanced benefits will attract and hold enough volunteers to maintain the forces we need, and the attitude of young people toward military service.

While recognizing that the draft was set to end on July 1, 1971, Nixon urged patience. "While I am confident that our plan will achieve its objective of reducing draft calls to zero," Nixon avowed, "even the most optimistic observers agree that we would not be able to end the draft in the next year or so without seriously weakening our military forces and impairing our ability to forestall threats to the peace." Nixon maintained that extending the draft one final time was "imperative" for national security but broke with precedent by urging Congress to extend it for only two years, to July 1, 1973, instead of the traditional four years. In return, Nixon promised that his administration "shall make every endeavor to reduce draft calls to zero by that time, carefully and continually reexamining our position as we proceed toward that goal."[25]

Recounting his many endeavors for the AVF since he launched his election campaign, Nixon emphasized, "Now, more than nine months later, I am even more strongly convinced of the rightness of these proposals." Nixon assured Congress and the American people that his goal endured and his commitment persisted. "Now, as then, the objective of this administration is to reduce draft calls to zero, subject to the overriding considerations of national security—and as long as we need the draft, to make it as fair and equitable as we can," Nixon stressed. He presented a litany of achievements demonstrating progress. "Average draft calls are now substantially lower than they were when this administration assumed office, and we have significantly improved the consistency and fairness of the draft system," Nixon claimed. "We shall continue these actions at an accelerated pace." At the same time, the president chided Congress for inaction and pleaded for its assistance. "However, to continue the progress that now is possible toward both goals—toward ending the draft, and in the meantime making it more nearly fair—legislative as well as Executive action will be needed," Nixon implored.[26]

The House of Representatives proved responsive to Nixon's overtures. Marvin L. Esch (R-MI) relayed to his constituents that the House "gave quick approval" to a compromise bill to extend the draft for two years. The Senate version, however, "became bogged down over a controversial 'rider' known as the

Mansfield Amendment." Senator Mansfield (D–MT), majority leader, demanded that Nixon recall all U.S. personnel from Vietnam nine months from the release of American POWs. Debate on the amendment slowed progress. "Finally the House and Senate conferees agreed upon compromise language that urges the President to negotiate an immediate cease-fire in Viet Nam and the withdrawal of all U.S. forces," taking into account the release of POWs. Esch welcomed this development but considered it "a watered-down version" of Mansfield's intent.[27] The House had passed an extension of the draft earlier in spring 1971, but the Senate took until that fall due to the Mansfield Amendment. Congress eventually worked out a compromise bill that extended the draft for two years until June 30, 1973. On August 4, 1971, the House voted in support 297-108. The Senate followed suit on September 21, 1971, by a vote of 55-30.[28]

As a result, the draft temporarily lapsed from July through September 1971 because the Senate disagreed over the Mansfield Amendment. In addition to the political machinations at play, the debate had an unintentional effect. The draft ceased for nearly three months. During this hiatus, a shortfall of volunteers in the Army tallied 4,000 per month. In summer and fall 1971, therefore, an unintentional test of the AVF occurred. The immediate result was not enough volunteers, especially in the Army. This unexpected development compounded angst that worse shortfalls awaited the AVF, slated to become permanent in summer 1973.

On September 28, 1971, President Nixon signed H.R. 6531. The bill "provided all these major draft reforms that the President had sought: a nationalized selection process that eliminated the local draft board quota system, discretionary authority for the President to suspend educational deferments and higher pay for lower-ranking personnel." The bill funded $2.4 billion in military pay raises, "weighted toward first-term enlistees and draftees and low-ranking officers." In the bill, Congress also stated its support of "an early end" to the Vietnam War, although such a sentiment was "a non-binding provision."[29] By fall 1971, Nixon achieved all his remaining draft reforms, including pay increases, nationalized selection process, and authority to stop educational deferments. He had already ended graduate deferments, occupational deferments, and paternity deferments.

Because of the hindrance caused by contentious debate in the Senate over the Mansfield Amendment, there occurred "almost a three-month interruption of the process of inducting young men into the armed services, the first time the draft had not been in effect since 1948." Throughout that interval, Curtis W. Tarr, newly minted director of the Selective Service System, assured Congress that "the nation could go for several months without inductions and without harm to its defense posture." The draft resumed its normal operation in November 1971.[30] The Mansfield Amendment and contentious debate over the 1971 draft law combined to create a brief lull in the draft for the first time in more than two decades. Tarr professed that he was not worried about an interruption of several months, although actual recruiting shortfalls belied his confidence.

In his final report as secretary of defense, Laird in 1972 detailed progress on the advent of the AVF. "Last year I reported that our manpower levels had been reduced to baseline strengths and that we intended to terminate our direct reliance on the draft by July 1, 1973," Laird reiterated. "We intend to meet that goal." Laird remained "confident" but admitted that "problems" remained. On the whole, Laird emphasized that "the quality of that force and improvements in its utilization under total force planning can improve overall capabilities and provide effective strength conducive to a generation of peace."[31]

By August 1972, the end of the draft was nigh. On August 28, President Nixon declared that the draft would cease for good by June 30, 1973. He also promised that "draftees will no longer be sent to Vietnam, unless they volunteer." During the campaign for the AVF, the White House had directed the Pentagon to reduce greatly its reliance on the draft. The results proved significant. "The Pentagon will draft less than 50,000 young men this year," the Republican National Committee (RNC) revealed, "down from 299,000 in 1968." Such a stark contrast revealed the interrelated nature of diminishing the draft in order to create the AVF. The Republican National Committee reported that Secretary Laird "hopes to stop draft inductions by December, about six months ahead of President Nixon's deadline for ending military conscription."[32]

Nixon, through Laird, continued to lower force levels, resulting in fewer than 50,000 draftees for all 1972. This total was a precipitous drop from six times as many draftees only several years prior. In addition, the Pentagon hoped to reduce draft calls to zero by December 1972 in anticipation of the advent of the AVF. Of significance, Nixon for the first time severed the intimate connection between draftees and Vietnam. Previously, based on the unique Vietnam rotation policy and the two-year draft term, almost all draftees went to Vietnam. Nixon ended this situation unless they volunteered. This dynamic, wherein almost all inductees went to Vietnam, was among the starkest inequities of the draft. In August 1972, Nixon removed it altogether.

The steady drop in draft calls during the Nixon administration provided further evidence that the AVF was possible. "The experience of the past three years seems to show that sufficient numbers of volunteers can be attracted to the armed forces to meet peacetime manpower needs," Nixon boasted. "In reaching this goal, we finally—28 years after World War II—have done what I said in 1968 we should do."[33] This achievement was the culmination of Nixon's efforts on the advent of the AVF. He had started his journey in 1968 as he campaigned for the presidency. Victorious in that election, he immediately embarked on his mission to end the draft and implement the AVF. Along the way, he had reformed some of the draft's many inequities and reduced the military's reliance on it. Nixon was now confident that the draft reforms his administration had enacted buttressed the creation of the AVF in 1973. There was little doubt that Nixon had greatly reduced reliance on the draft: draft calls were 299,000 in 1968; 289,000 in 1969; 163,000 in 1970; 98,000 in 1971; and 50,000 in 1972. This steep and steady reduction demonstrated remarkable progress toward the advent of the AVF in a relatively short timeframe.

In his final report as secretary of defense in 1972, Melvin R. Laird reflected on the campaign for the AVF. "Achieving the All-Volunteer Force, and eliminating reliance upon the draft," Laird maintained, "has been the principal objective we have focused on" in the area of military personnel. He explained that the advent of the AVF comprised many reinforcing efforts, including "establishing equitable and competitive levels of military pay, improving the quality of military recruiting, increasing the challenge of military jobs, civilianizing military jobs and expanding the role of women in the Services, and revitalizing the Reserve Forces—among others." Secretary Laird predicted that the AVF would "affect youth attitudes and the operation of DoD for many years to come, as it will influence the characteristics of our Armed Forces and how they are managed." He also reinforced that "the actions needed to ensure its long range effectiveness must continue to receive high priority attention"[34] (Figure 5.3).

**FIGURE 5.3**   Melvin R. Laird seated near the fireplace in the Oval Office. September 26, 1974

*Source:* Courtesy Gerald R. Ford Library.

Laird considered the advent of the AVF to be the Pentagon's, and by extension the Nixon administration's, signature achievement in terms of military personnel. He also articulated exactly how it came to be. Increased pay, heightened recruiting, improved quality of life in the military, use of civilians and women as offsets for the loss of draftees, and the Total Force Concept to replace draftees with the reserves and National Guard as the primary source of augmentation for the active force all proved pivotal.

---

## Sidebar 5.1: Total Force Concept

The Total Force Concept accompanied the advent of the AVF. Beforehand, draftees had served as the primary augmentation for active forces. When personnel requirements rose, so too did draft calls. In anticipation of the end of the draft, a new augmentation approach became necessary. The Total Force Concept ensured that the reserves and National Guard became the new primary augmentation mechanism. Once policymakers implemented the AVF, the concept became the Total Force Policy. The momentous change had both positive and negative implications. In the short-term, it made the AVF feasible and increased the capabilities of the reserves and National Guard. In the long-term, however, the later shift from a strategic to an operational reserve in response to the Iraq and Afghanistan Wars produced significant burdens, including repeat deployments, high operational tempo, and reduced dwell time.

---

### Early Impacts of the AVF

One of the most noticeable early impacts of the advent of the AVF was the creation of the Total Force Concept and increased reliance on the reserves and National Guard for military mobilization. Such a development was by design. Policymakers, especially President Johnson, had made the fateful decision to use the draft instead of reserves to wage the Vietnam War. With the end of the draft and the advent of the AVF on the horizon, such an arrangement was no longer feasible. Instead, the reserves and National Guard would have to fill the role previously assigned to the draft. "Our Reserve forces will play an increasingly important role," explained Laird, "for members of the National Guard and the Reserves of the several services—not draftees—will be the initial and primary source of augmentation of active forces in future emergencies."[35] The advent of the AVF created the Total Force Concept. Beforehand, draftees had been the primary augmentation of the active forces, while the reserves and National Guard were often seen as a safe haven from the draft. Johnson had not mobilized the reserves and National Guard throughout the Vietnam War but had utilized the draft every year that he was in office, upwards of 300,000 draftees in a single year.

The AVF turned this dynamic on its head by making the reserves and National Guard the primary augmentation of active forces.

The Total Force Concept, first announced as policy in August 1970 in anticipation of the AVF, "established that the Reserve Forces would be the initial and primary augmentation force for the Active Forces in the future." The result "revitalized" the reserves and National Guard in tangible ways, "rebuilding equipment inventories depleted during the Vietnam buildup of the Active Forces, improving readiness, redefining the roles and missions of the Reserve Forces, and educating the public and employers to the vital role of Reserve Forces." Secretary Laird promised that "further actions needed to ensure the combat effectiveness of Reserve Forces require a major continuing effort in the years ahead."[36] Prior to the AVF, the hedge for elastic force levels was the Selective Service System. Policymakers acquired most of the force through volunteers, roughly 80 to 90 percent. When force levels rose, however, they augmented it with approximately 10 to 20 percent draftees. For much of the Cold War, draftees were the only back-up plan. With the advent of the AVF, that contingency mechanism disappeared. What replaced it was the reserves and National Guard. These organizations henceforth played a much more prominent role in national defense. This change would have significant implications for the future use of the reserves and National Guard.

The Total Force Concept also began opening the reserves and National Guard to previously marginalized groups, including African Americans and women. "From June 30, 1971, through September 30, 1972," Melvin Laird recorded, "the number of blacks in the Guard and Reserve has increased by 70 percent from 16,792 to 28,472 and from 1.7 percent of total strength to 3.1 percent of total strength." While still paltry in terms of representation, such rapid change augured additional opportunities moving forward. In addition, Laird documented that women's participation held similar promise. "With the termination of the waiting list restrictions in the Fall of 1971, it has now become possible for the Guard and Reserve to pursue active recruiting of women. Near term goals have been established and significant progress is expected."[37] The reforms related to the Total Force Concept also began the process of ensuring that the reserves and National Guard would become more open to African Americans and women. African American representation was small but quickly growing. Although still paltry overall, largely due to discrimination within National Guard units, new opportunities seemed on the horizon. The opening to women was relatively new and would in time allow another set of prospects for women beyond those being expanded in the active forces.

Even with the advent of the AVF on the immediate horizon, a standby draft remained. On February 15, 1973, Byron V. Pepitone, acting director of the Selective Service System, explained to Gerald Ford how it worked. Pepitone divulged "a brief explanation of the plans for the Selective Service System and its employees as we move into the beginning phase of a standby system of operation." Induction authority would expire on July 1, 1973, necessitating a "considerable revamping of the System's operations," especially because funding and personnel cuts would logically follow. Even so, Pepitone relayed that the system would "continue to register and classify eligible young men" when necessary and "that the basic structure that we now have must continue to prevail; that is, the requisite national and state headquarters and the operating arm of the System embodied in its local boards."[38] The result was the standby draft. The Selective Service System still existed, albeit at greatly reduced funding, staffing, and locations. There were no active inductions, but registration could still occur in case of an emergency. The transition to the standby draft was the culmination of the advent of the AVF and moved the United States away from conscription. In doing so, it marked the conclusion of a critical moment in American history.

Induction authority expired on June 30, 1973. The underlying infrastructure for registration and classification remained, albeit it in greatly truncated form. As a result, the standby draft lay dormant in case of national emergency. The Military Selective Service Act required that

> the Selective Service System ... shall be maintained as an active standby organization with (1) a complete registration and classification structure capable of immediate operation in the event of a national emergency, and (2) personnel adequate to reinstitute the full operation of the system.

Even so, the Selective Service System dramatically shrunk, both in terms of its tangible assets and its dominant role in American society. Funding, boards, and personnel supporting the Selective Service System quickly contracted. The budget for the Selective Service System dropped from $83.5 million in FY 1973 to $55 million in FY 1974. Local draft board sites shrunk from 2,782 to only 925 over the same span. The number of employees fell by nearly half, from 7,403 in FY 1973 to 4,340 in FY 1974.[39] The advent of the AVF had finally arrived and with it, the draft receded into the shadows.

## The Legacy of the AVF

On July 1, 1973, newspapers around the country reported on the historic advent of the AVF. "At midnight last night, the President lost his authority to induct men into the armed services," William Claiborne, staff writer for the *Washington Post*, indicated. "For the first time in nearly a third of a century—and after more than 18 million American men have been conscripted into uniform—the draft has officially been ended." Claiborne waxed about all the changes wrought, including the absence of "'Greeting' letters," "pounding rubber stamps," and "legalized gambling events" through which young men's fate hinged on the draft's defining characteristics of notifications, boards, and lotteries.[40]

Other commentators were not so sure. On the same day, Ben A. Franklin of the *New York Times* took a pessimistic tone. He characterized the AVF as "one of the boldest policy and political gambles of the Nixon Presidency ... . And it is in trouble." Franklin pointed to mounting recruiting shortfalls, sharp criticism from military leaders, and heightened angst among policymakers and the public alike about a possible return to the draft. The reason was simple: there were not enough volunteers. Franklin charted how in January 1973 enlistees had barely surpassed requirements, totaling a meager 2.1 percent above the monthly goal. Recruits in each of the following six months fell short. Recruiters missed their February mark by 15 percent, their March target by 18 percent, their April objective by 15 percent, and their May aim by 30 percent. All indications had recruiters missing their June 1973 tally by another 30 percent.[41] Such was the inauspicious advent of the AVF. Throughout the remainder of the 1970s, the AVF slowly stabilized with some observers dubbing it a "success." Nevertheless, by the end of the decade concerns about its sustainability mounted and many observers feared that a return to the draft was necessary.[42] "A volunteer force is very fragile," acknowledged Bernard Rostker, director of the Selective Service System during the Carter administration. He later recalled that "the situation became very precarious" by the late 1970s.[43] Even President Nixon, foremost champion of the AVF, waivered. "I considered the end of the draft in 1973 to be one of the major achievements of my administration. Now, seven years later, I have reluctantly concluded that we should reintroduce the draft," he wrote in 1980.[44] In the five decades that followed, the AVF achieved many successes, produced numerous legacies, and encountered persistent challenges.

## Women in the Military

One of the most prominent legacies of the AVF has been women's heightened participation. Women have a long history of service in the U.S. military.[45] The advent of the AVF, however, fundamentally reshaped participation by and opportunities for women in the military. Beforehand, women comprised less than 2 percent of the military. Such meager representation remained consistent from 1948 until the creation of the AVF. Thereafter, the number of women in military service drastically rose. After fifty years of service of the AVF, the percentage of women in the military had climbed to more than 16 percent.[46]

By the 2000s, a major obstacle remaining for women in the military was access to combat arms. As a result, the issue of women in combat specialties loomed large after the first decade of the twenty-first century.[47] By 2013, Leon Panetta, secretary of defense, had announced a plan to remove the ban on women in combat assignments.[48] In August 2015, Captains Kristen Griest and Shaye Haver became the first women to graduate from Army Ranger School, illustrating the vast possibilities that newfound equal access provided.[49]

Panetta's successor, Ashton B. Carter, in December 2015 ended all restrictions on women serving in combat arms. At a Pentagon news conference on December 3, Carter announced the historic shift. "There will be no exceptions," the secretary of defense insisted.

They'll be allowed to drive tanks, fire mortars and lead infantry soldiers into combat. They'll be able to serve as Army Rangers and Green Berets, Navy SEALs, Marine Corps infantry, Air Force parajumpers and everything else that was previously open only to men.[50]

The order opened 220,000 military jobs to women, removing the last vestiges of formal gender barriers for specific positions within the military.

By January 2016, women made the transition into previously closed arenas. That year, Haver became the Army's first female infantry officer and in 2018 assumed command of a rifle company in the 82nd Airborne Division.[51] As a result, women played an increasingly larger, and much more visible, role in the new millennium, especially as it pertained to heretofore restricted jobs. The United Service Organizations (USO) revealed, "More than 300,000 women have served in Iraq and Afghanistan since 9/11, more than 9,000 have earned Combat Action Badges and today, women make up 16 percent of our nation's Armed Forces, serving in every branch of the U.S. military."[52]

Since 2000, women have also made long-overdue advances to the most senior leadership posts. One estimate found that the number of female generals and admirals during that time had doubled, increasing from 30 to 63 across all five military services.[53] High profile promotions included Gen. Ann Dunwoody in 2008 to lead U.S. Army Material Command, Adm. Michelle Howard in 2016 to serve as Vice Chief of Naval Operations and U.S. Air Force Gen. Lori Robinson that same year to head U.S. Northern Command, and Adm. Linda Fagan in 2022 to become commandant of the U.S. Coast Guard.[54] Even so, much work remains to be done. Lori Robinson and Michael E. O'Hanlon revealed that "only about 6 percent of four-star generals have been women even in the period after the glass ceiling was shattered."[55]

Sexual assault and sexual harassment continue to plague the U.S. military, despite repeated yet ineffectual efforts from the Pentagon and Congress to eradicate them. RAND estimated that 1 in 16 women experienced sexual assault and 1 in 4 women faced sexual harassment in military service, demonstrating that both remain "persistent problems in the services."[56] On February 26, 2021, Lloyd J. Austin III, secretary of defense, ordered an Independent Review Commission (IRC) on Sexual Assault in the Military, seeking an "impartial assessment" of how the military handles sexual assault and sexual harassment and recommendations for needed improvements. The IRC commenced its vital work on March 24 and issued its suggestions on July 2, 2021.[57]

## Current Status of the AVF

Since its advent in 1973, civilian and military leaders have reassessed the AVF, often pointing out strengths and weaknesses.[58] The same holds true today. The current AVF has held steady in terms of size and consists of 1.35 million active duty servicemembers, although analysts highlight that there are both strategic and budgetary pressures to reduce force structure moving forward. Mark F. Cancian, senior adviser with the Center for Strategic and International Studies (CSIS) International Security Program, characterized contemporary force structure as "staring into the abyss," largely because policymakers increasingly consider reducing personnel to fund technological improvements aimed at heightened competition with China.[59] Current end strength for the reserves and National Guard resides at 800,000 personnel, making today's AVF comprised 2.15 million servicemembers, active and reserve.[60] While these numbers are quite large, they represent a shrinking proportion of Americans who serve in the military. Less than three-quarters of one percent of the U.S. population serves in the military.

Demographically, the current AVF is predominately middle class. The middle three quintiles for household income are slightly overrepresented. In contrast, the top and bottom quintiles are underrepresented in the military, with the highest income level the most notably absent. One of the clearest differences between the AVF and American society regards gender. While the AVF profoundly changed both opportunities for women and their overall representation within military service, women still comprise only 16 percent of the AVF compared to 51 percent of U.S. society. The AVF is generally representative along racial and ethnic categories, although the extent varies, at times widely, among the various military services. Geographically, the AVF is not representative. States in the Northeast and on the West Coast are generally underrepresented based on their share of the overall population, while states in the South and Southwest are overrepresented.[61] More troubling, Douglas L. Kriner and Francis X. Shen have shown that casualties from America's wars have also proven geographically unrepresentative, although their incisive study extends well beyond the AVF.[62]

Another characteristic of the current AVF is that a large portion of recruits come from military families, by some estimates more than 60 percent in certain services.[63] Such a trend has generated the term "warrior caste" to describe families that have multigenerational military service. Amy Shafer revealed that as many as three out of four new recruits have at least one family member who served in the military. "These survey results coupled with the overall population percentage of veterans suggest that recruits with a direct military family connection are significantly overrepresented in today's U.S. military," she determined. "Indeed, the military family connection may be more significant than any other variable in determining the propensity to serve."[64] If such a trend were to slacken, or worse yet reverse, it would add significant strain to an already arduous recruiting environment.

## Contemporary Critiques of the AVF

From its very inception, the AVF received significant attention.[65] Contemporary critiques of the AVF, however, gained significant momentum in the post-9/11 era, especially as a result of the Iraq and Afghanistan Wars. In these two lengthy conflicts, often dubbed "forever wars," the AVF encountered much difficulty mobilizing and maintaining adequate force levels, let alone achieving significant and lasting results.[66] Such temporary fixes as private contractors, standards waivers, and stop loss all gained heightened attention as symptoms of a larger problem, questioning the overall viability and ultimate success of the AVF.[67]

Maj. Gen. Dennis Laich argued that the vast majority of Americans lack "skin in the game" when it comes to military service, thereby perpetuating a system that is fundamentally unfair, among other flaws. In doing so, Laich asked two searing questions: "Is the AVF fair, efficient, and sustainable?" and, even more troubling, "What if we had a war and no one showed up on our side?"[68] Laich maintained that the AVF failed on both counts, predominately because it is widely unfair, wholly inefficient, and largely unsustainable.[69]

Other persuasive voices decried the AVF as well. Andrew J. Bacevich characterized the overall implications of the AVF as a "breach of trust," grounding its advent in a visceral reaction to the Vietnam War that eroded civil–military relations. Bacevich lambasted the AVF as a remedy worse that the affliction it sought to cure. "Rather than offering an antidote to problems, the military system centered on the all-volunteer force bred and exacerbated them," Bacevich insisted. "It underwrote recklessness in the formulation of policy and thereby resulted in needless, costly, and ill-managed wars."[70]

Karl W. Eikenberry warned that the AVF militarized foreign policy in a unique and troubling way. He revealed that the AVF led to far more military deployments after its advent than before. Through a detailed examination, Eikenberry showed that the AVF deployed roughly five times more frequently than its predecessor, a development that he characterized as "worrisome."[71] Others reinforced the palpable and problematic emergence of a broader militarized foreign policy.[72]

Marybeth P. Ulrich contended that the AVF worsened the civil–military divide. Highlighting the insular nature of military service that it created, Ulrich characterized the prevailing view of military service among most Americans as something "that other people do." She maintained that the AVF widened the gap between civilian and military spheres within American society. "Perhaps the greatest impact of the trend of a military 'apart' from the society it serves is the loss of the common unifying experience of military service," Ulrich warned. "In a polarized social and political environment, opportunities to live, work, and depend on people from all parts of the country for a higher purpose are increasingly rare."[73]

Others highlighted significant concerns regarding its sustainability. Michael Runey and Charles Allen catalogued the myriad and compounding challenges related to recruiting, stemming from both social and political changes in American society. Runey and Allen demonstrated that a mere 4 percent of the available military-age youth in the United States are both "willing and qualified" to serve in the military. The result is that the "talent pool" necessary to sustain the AVF has dramatically shrunk. "Divergent military, societal, and political forces risk the AVF's future viability," cautioned Runey and Allen. "Although America likes its volunteer force, the military is attempting to drive it to higher quality through recruitment even as society is showing it will not sustain the military's steady call for volunteers."[74] Such varied and persistent critiques of the AVF highlight some of its trials moving forward.

## Contemporary Relevance of the AVF

Even in the aftermath of the Iraq and Afghanistan Wars, the AVF remains most relevant.

As part of the Fiscal Year 2017 National Defense Authorization Act (Public Law 114–328), Congress created the National Commission on Military, National, and Public Service, a modern-day successor to the Marshall and Gates Commissions. Congress tasked this newest commission with recommending "methods to increase participation" in various forms of service "in order to address national security and other public service needs of the Nation."[75]

With eleven commissioners chaired by Joseph J. Heck, U.S. Army major general and former representative for Nevada's 3rd congressional district, the commission held 25 public meetings and hearings with more than 100 speakers in 42 cities across the country. The commission engaged more than 500 organizations and received input from more than 4,300 citizens during the course of its work from 2017 to 2020. It released its interim report on January 23, 2019, outlining its progress and remaining work.[76]

The commission issued its final report on March 25, 2020. Members recommended expanding registration with the Selective Service System, most notably to women. The commission advised that "the time is right" to include women from the ages of 18 to 26 in registration. "This is a necessary and fair step, making it possible to draw on the talent of a unified Nation in a time of national emergency," the commission maintained.[77]

Timing is everything, and the release of the commission's final report in March 2020 was significant. The onset of a global pandemic and subsequent disruptions muted its reception. The commission disbanded in September 2020, although Congress continued to debate and consider the major recommendations contained in its final report as the pandemic subsided.[78] As the largest evaluation of American military service in some time, the commission reinforced the continued relevance of the AVF as it neared its fiftieth anniversary.

## Reflections After 50 Years of Service

The AVF was born during a critical moment in American history. A disliked war coalesced with an even more unpopular draft to force policymakers to rethink American military service in a way that they had avoided for a generation. Richard Nixon, sensing a political opportunity, seized on the issue with a determination that was nothing short of zealous. The result was the advent of the AVF. Its creation solved many problems. Over time, however, it has generated complications all its own.

After fifty years of service, three general themes emerge regarding the AVF. First, national security exists within a political arena. Policymakers, civilian and military alike, assess the international security environment and ensure that the United States fulfills a constructive role in it. They do so, however, with political considerations never far afield. While the specific policies, in this case the advent of the AVF, vary over time, the nature of this profound relationship remains constant. Second, military policies reverberate into American society. The AVF was no different. Decisions meant to address policy concerns had important corollaries, some intended and others not. Third, civil–military relations lie at this vital intersection. Finding the appropriate balance between national security on the one hand and individual liberty on the other is a constant struggle. It is essential, however, to ensure that policy, politics, and society coexist in a way that betters each one. Understanding those crucial linkages—that perennial military matters exist within a political milieu and that their implications reverberate into American society—demonstrates that civil–military relations remains a promising, and vital, field of study.

Looking ahead, additional challenges for the AVF remain on the horizon. The massive transition from the Global War on Terror and the Iraq and Afghanistan Wars to a renewed era of great power competition, especially with China, augurs fresh requirements and new priorities that will have significant impacts on the AVF. Emerging technologies, including artificial intelligence, cyber warfare, and un-manned vehicles on land, air, and sea all require intense research, development, and funding. They also demand that the military services reconceptualize their force structure, recruiting, and retention, thereby shifting from traditional models of yesteryear to incorporate new ideas relevant to future developments. In addition, such original theaters of competition, and likely conflict, as space and the artic are opening up in newfound ways. The newly minted Space Force and the U.S. Marine Corps Force Design 2030 are but two examples that the perennial questions of who serves and how they do so remain as vital today as they always have been.[79]

In this sense, the advent of the AVF is but one critical moment in American history in a much larger saga regarding finding the appropriate answers to these twin questions, not just militarily, but politically, economically, and socially. Therefore, the advent of the AVF is both a critical moment in American history and one moving forward. Constantly reevaluating its strengths and weaknesses, all with the intent to improve it, remains as relevant today as when the Gates Commission undertook its pivotal work. As the Gates Commission discussed the fundamental vision of "Protecting the Free Society," they reiterated, "Without endangering the nation's security, the means of defense should support the aims of the society."[80] Indeed. The future of the AVF will no doubt be just as complicated as its advent, seeking to balance national security with individual liberty in American democracy. Finding that equilibrium has always been, and will remain, one of the perennial challenges of protecting free society.

## Notes

1 Martin Anderson, "Memorandum for Kenneth Belieu, John Ehrlichman, Peter Flanigan, General Haig, Roger Kelley, Henry Kissinger, Secretary Laird, Robert Mayo, James Schlesinger; Subject: Draft Memorandum on All-Volunteer Armed Force," March 17, 1970, p. 1, box 11, folder WHCF: SMOF Martin Anderson All Volunteer Armed Force [1 of 4], White House Central Files, Staff Member and Office Files, Martin Anderson Files, RMNL. This memorandum circulated to all key staff and then to President Nixon. It was ultimately for Nixon. Harris had directed the public polling

in January 1970, and *Christian Science Monitor* had conducted the congressional polling in November 1969.

2  Ibid., 2.

3  Ibid.

4  Ibid., 12.

5  Peter Flanigan, "Memorandum for Arthur Burns and John Ehrlichman," April 26, 1969, p. 1, box 1, folder WHCF: Subject Files EX FG 216 Selective Service System [Begin–7/31/1969], White House Central Files, Subject Files, FG 216 Selective Service System, RMNL.

6  Ibid.

7  Ibid., 2.

8  White House Press Secretary, "Statement by the President on Draft Reform," September 19, 1969, p. 1, box D74, folder Draft, Gerald R. Ford Congressional Papers, GRFL.

9  Ibid.

10  Richard Nixon, "Executive Order 11497," November 26, 1969, p. 1, box A31, folder Volunteer Army (5), Arthur F. Burns Papers, GRFL.

11  Richard Nixon, "Random Selection for Military Service: A Proclamation by the President of the United States of America," November 26, 1969, p. 1, box A31, folder Volunteer Army (5), Arthur F. Burns Papers, GRFL.

12  White House Press Secretary, "New Draft Selection System Fact Sheet," November 26, 1969, p. 1, box A31, folder Volunteer Army (5), Arthur F. Burns Papers, GRFL.

13  Ibid., 1–2.

14  Ibid.

15  Associated Press, "Draft Lot Cuts Wait to Year," November 28, 1969, p. 1, box D74, folder Draft, Gerald R. Ford Congressional Papers, GRFL.

16  Louis Harris, "The Harris Survey: 52 percent Favor Volunteer Army Plan," *Washington Post*, January 26, 1970.

17  "New Draft Plan Cuts Deferments," *Boston Globe*, April 24, 1970.

18  Office of Congressman Frank Horton, "Horton Supports President's Draft Reforms in House Speech," April 23, 1970, p. 1, box D74, folder Draft, Gerald R. Ford Congressional Papers, GRFL.

19  Griffith, *Army's Transition*, 25. On Project Volunteer, see 29–46.

20  On early tension between Nixon and Laird over the AVF, see Taylor, *Military Service and American Democracy*, 112–113.

21  Melvin Laird, "The First Five Months: Problems and Progress," June 27, 1969, p. 8, box A76, folder Laird—First Five Months, 1969, Melvin R. Laird Papers, GRFL.

22  Ibid., 3–4.

23  Dana Adams Schmidt, "Army Needs 212,000 Men in '72; Draft Requirement Is Uncertain," *New York Times*, October 20, 1971, p. 1, box D74, folder Draft, Gerald R. Ford Congressional Papers, GRFL.

24  Lee Doyle to Martin Anderson, March 18, 1970, attached to the letter is U.S. Army, "PROVIDE: Project Volunteer in Defense of the Nation, Volume I, Executive Summary" and "PROVIDE: Project Volunteer in Defense of the Nation, Volume II, Supporting Analysis," pp. 15–16, box 41, folder WHCF: SMOF Martin Anderson AVAF-Project Volunteer, White House Central Files, Staff Member and Office Files, Martin Anderson Files, RMNL.

25  White House Press Secretary, "Message to the Congress of the United States," January 28, 1971, p. 2, box D74, folder Draft, Gerald R. Ford Congressional Papers, GRFL.

26  Ibid., 1.

27  Marvin Esch, "Washington Report," October 7, 1971, p. 1, box D74, folder Draft, Gerald R. Ford Congressional Papers, GRFL.

28  Washington Campus News Service, "Draft Returns for Two Year Encore," September 1971, pp. 1–2, box D74, folder Draft, Gerald R. Ford Congressional Papers, GRFL.

29  *Congress and the Nation, 1969–1972*, 213.

30  Ibid., 225.

31  Melvin Laird, "Final Report as Secretary of Defense," 1972, p. 17, box A76, folder Laird—Final Report as Secretary of Defense (Draft), 1972, Melvin R. Laird Papers, GRFL.

32  Republican National Committee Research Division, "Factbook Update: Draft," September 1, 1972, p. 1, box D74, folder Draft, Gerald R. Ford Congressional Papers, GRFL.

33  James McCartney, "U.S. Plans to Replace Draft with Volunteers by July '73: Switch Tied to Bonus and Skill Pay," p. 13A, box D74, folder Draft, Gerald R. Ford Congressional Papers, GRFL.

34  Melvin Laird, "Final Report as Secretary of Defense," 1972, section "Manpower and Reserve Affairs," p. 1, box A76, folder Laird—Final Report as Secretary of Defense (Draft), 1972, Melvin R. Laird Papers, GRFL.

35  Melvin Laird, "Final Report as Secretary of Defense," 1972, p. 11, box A76, folder Laird—Final Report as Secretary of Defense (Draft), 1972, Melvin R. Laird Papers, GRFL.

36  Melvin Laird, "Final Report as Secretary of Defense," 1972, section "Manpower and Reserve Affairs," p. 2, box A76, folder Laird—Final Report as Secretary of Defense (Draft), 1972, Melvin R. Laird Papers, GRFL.

37  Ibid., 6.

38  Byron Pepitone to Gerald Ford, February 15, 1973, p. 1, box 49, folder Draft, Robert T. Hartmann Papers, GRFL.

39  "Fact Sheet: Selective Service Operations," February 14, 1973, p. 1, box 49, folder Draft, Robert T. Hartmann Papers, GRFL.

40  William Claiborne, "But Selective Service Lives On," *Washington Post*, July 1, 1973.

41  Ben Franklin, "Lag in a Volunteer Force Spurs Talk of New Draft," *New York Times*, July 1, 1973.

42  John Finney, "Volunteer Force Called a Success," *New York Times*, February 14, 1975; Warren Rogers, "The All-Volunteer Army's Bleak Future," *Washington Post*, August 6, 1978; Richard Halloran, "Carter Draft Plan Urges Registration of Men and Women," *New York Times*, February 9, 1980.

43  Bernard Rostker, "Ending the Draft: The Creation of an All-Volunteer Force," Nixon Legacy Forum, January 19, 2012, https://www.nixonfoundation.org/2012/01/rn-ends-the-draft-the-creation-of-the-all-volunteer-force/ (accessed June 21, 2022).

44  Richard Nixon, *The Real War* (New York: Simon & Schuster, 1980), 201.

45  See Tanya L. Roth, *Her Cold War: Women in the U.S. Military, 1945–1980* (Chapel Hill: University of North Carolina Press, 2021); William A. Taylor, "From WACs to Rangers: Women in the U.S. Military since World War II," *Marine Corps University Journal*, Special Issue: Gender Integration (2018): 78–101; Tanya Biank, *Undaunted: The Real Story of America's Servicewomen in Today's Military* (New York: NAL Caliber, 2014); Heather Marie Stur, *Beyond Combat: Women and Gender in the Vietnam War Era* (Cambridge: Cambridge University Press, 2011); Kara Dixon Vuic, *Officer, Nurse, Woman: The Army Nurse Corps in the Vietnam War* (Baltimore: Johns Hopkins University Press, 2010); and Department of Defense, *Report of the Task Force on Women in the Military* (Washington, DC: U.S. Government Printing Office, 1988).

46  Council on Foreign Relations, "Demographics of the U.S. Military," July 13, 2020, https://www.cfr.org/backgrounder/demographics-us-military (accessed May 17, 2022). See esp. the graph, "Percentage of Female Enlisted Recruits, 1970–2018."

47  See Kristy Kamarck, "Women in Combat: Issues for Congress," *Congressional Research Service Report*, August 18, 2015; David Burrelli, "Women in Combat: Issues for Congress," *Congressional Research Service Report*, May 9, 2013; and Megan MacKenzie, "Let Women Fight: Ending the U.S. Military's Female Combat Ban," *Foreign Affairs* 91, no. 6 (November/December 2012): 32–42.

48  Elisabeth Bumiller and Thom Shanker, "Equality at the Front Line: Pentagon Is Set to Lift Ban on Women in Combat Roles," *New York Times*, January 24, 2013.

49  Taylor, "From WACs to Rangers," 78–79, 96–97.

50  Matthew Rosenberg and Dave Philipps, "All Combat Roles Now Open to Women, Defense Secretary Says," *New York Times*, December 3, 2015, https://www.nytimes.com/2015/12/04/us/politics/combat-military-women-ash-carter.html (accessed May 17, 2022).

51  Steve Beynon, "The Rise of Female Commanders in Combat Arms," *Stars and Stripes*, August 15, 2020, https://www.stripes.com/theaters/us/the-rise-of-female-commanders-in-combat-arms-1.641418 (accessed May 20, 2022).

52  USO, "Over 200 Years of Service: The History of Women in the U.S. Military," March 1, 2022, https://www.uso.org/stories/3005-over-200-years-of-service-the-history-of-women-in-the-us-military (accessed May 17, 2022).

53  Richard Sisk, "Number of Female Generals, Admirals Has Doubled since 2000, Report Finds," April 17, 2019, *Military.com*, https://www.military.com/daily-news/2019/04/17/number-female-generals-admirals-has-doubled-2000-report-finds.html (accessed May 20, 2022).

54  Adam Linehan, "Meet the Highest Ranking Female General in US History," *Task and Purpose*, May 16, 2016, https://taskandpurpose.com/news/meet-highest-ranking-female-general-us-history/ (accessed May 20, 2022); Patricia Kime, "Coast Guard Admiral Becomes First Woman to Lead a US Military Branch," *Military.com*, May 12, 2022, https://www.military.com/daily-news/2022/05/12/coast-guard-admiral-becomes-first-woman-lead-us-military-branch.html (accessed June 21, 2022).

55  Lori Robinson and Michael O'Hanlon, "Women Warriors: The Ongoing Story of Integrating and Diversifying the American Armed Forces," *Brookings*, May 2020, https://www.brookings.edu/essay/women-warriors-the-ongoing-story-of-integrating-and-diversifying-the-armed-forces/ (accessed May 20, 2022).

56  Joie Acosta, Matthew Chinman, Amy Shearer, "Countering Sexual Assault and Sexual Harassment in the U.S. Military: Lessons from RAND Research," *RAND Research Report*, 2021, https://www.rand.org/pubs/research_reports/RRA1318-1.html (accessed May 20, 2022).

57  Independent Review Commission on Sexual Assault in the Military, "Hard Truths and the Duty to Change," July 2, 2021, 3, https://media.defense.gov/2021/Jul/02/2002755437/-1/-1/0/IRC-FULL-REPORT-FINAL-1923-7-1-21.PDF/IRC-FULL-REPORT-FINAL-1923-7-1-21.PDF (accessed May 29, 2022).

58  On government reevaluations, see Congressional Budget Office, *The All-Volunteer Military: Issues and Performance* (Washington, DC: Congressional Budget Office, 2007); Janice Laurence, *The All-Volunteer Force: A Historical Perspective* (Washington, DC: Office of Under Secretary of Defense (Force Management Policy), 2004); Les Aspin, *All Volunteer: A Fair System; a Quality Force* (Washington, DC: U.S. Government Printing Office, 1991); and Military Manpower Task Force, *A Report to the President on the Status and Prospects of the All-Volunteer Force* (Washington, DC: U.S. Government Printing Office, 1982).

59  Mark F. Cancian, "U.S. Military Forces in FY 2022: Peering into the Abyss," *Report of the CSIS International Security Program*, March 2022, v.

60  Cancian, "U.S. Military Forces in FY 2022," 6, see esp. Table 1.

61  Council on Foreign Relations, "Demographics of the U.S. Military," July 13, 2020, https://www.cfr.org/backgrounder/demographics-us-military (accessed May 17, 2022). On the highest income bracket, see Roth-Douquet and Schaeffer, *AWOL*.

62  Douglas L. Kriner and Francis X. Shen, *The Casualty Gap: The Causes and Consequences of American Wartime Inequalities* (Oxford: Oxford University Press, 2010).

63  Robinson and O'Hanlon, "Women Warriors."

64  Amy Schafer, "Generations of War: The Rise of the Warrior Caste and the All-Volunteer Force," *CNAS Report*, May 8, 2017, 6, https://www.cnas.org/publications/reports/generations-of-war (accessed May 20, 2022). See also Mark Thompson, "Here's Why the U.S. Military Is a Family Business," *Time*, March 10, 2016, which reports even higher percentages across the military services (Army 79 percent, Navy 82 percent, Marine Corps 77 percent, and Air Force 86 percent).

65  On initial analysis, see Felix Moos, "History and Culture: Some Thoughts on the United States All-Volunteer Force," *Naval War College Review* 26, no. 1 (July 1973): 16–27; Jack Butler, "The All-Volunteer Armed Force: Its Feasibility and Implications," *Parameters* 2, no. 1 (Summer 1972): 17–29; and Morris Janowitz, "Volunteer Armed Forces and Military Purpose," *Foreign Affairs* 50, no. 3 (April 1972): 427–443.

66  For example, see Edward Halperin, "Are America's Endless Wars Partly the Result of Our All-Volunteer Military?" *The Defense Post,* October 29, 2021, https://www. thedefensepost.com/2021/10/29/endless-wars-volunteer-military/ (accessed May 16, 2022).

67  Laich, *Skin in the Game,* 54–74. On private contractors, see 54–61. On standards waivers, see 62–67. On stop loss, see 70–74.

68  Laich, *Skin in the Game,* 9, xiii.

69  For reporting on Laich's views and other appraisals, see Todd South, "All-Volunteer Force Can't Meet Pentagon's Future Needs, Advocates Warn," *Army Times,* April 5, 2021, https://www.armytimes.com/news/your-army/2021/04/05/all-volunteer-force-cant-meet-pentagons-future-needs-advocates-warn/ (accessed May 16, 2022).

70  Bacevich, *Breach of Trust,* 13.

71  Karl W. Eikenberry, "Reassessing the All-Volunteer Force," in *The Modern American Military,* ed. David M. Kennedy (Oxford: Oxford University Press, 2013), 217.

72  On militarization of U.S. foreign policy at a broad level, see Robert Gates, "The Overmilitarization of American Foreign Policy," *Foreign Affairs* 99, no. 4 (July/August 2020): 121–132 and Gordan Adams and Shoon Murray, eds., *Mission Creep: The Militarization of US Foreign Policy* (Washington, DC: Georgetown University Press, 2014).

73  Marybeth P. Ulrich, "Mind the Civil-Military Gap: The Republic Depends on All Citizens," *The Hill,* January 29, 2019, https://thehill.com/opinion/national-security/427385-mind-the-civil-military-gap-the-republic-depends-on-all-citizens/ (accessed May 17, 2022).

74  Michael Runey and Charles Allen, "An All-Volunteer Force for Long-Term Success," *Military Review* 95, no. 6 (November–December 2015): 92–100, see esp. Figure 1 on 97, https://www.armyupress.army.mil/Portals/7/military-review/Archives/English/ MilitaryReview_20151231_art016.pdf (accessed May 16, 2022).

75  Kristy Kamarck, "The Selective Service System and Draft Registration: Issues for Congress," *Congressional Research Service Report,* August 18, 2021, 18–21, quote on 18, https://sgp.fas.org/crs/misc/R44452.pdf (accessed May 16, 2022).

76  National Commission on Military, National, and Public Service, *Interim Report: A Report to the American People, the Congress, and the President* (Washington, DC: U.S. Government Printing Office, 2019).

77  National Commission on Military, National, and Public Service, *Inspired to Serve: The Final Report of the National Commission on Military, National, and Public Service* (Washington, DC: U.S. Government Printing Office, 2020).

78  Nicole Ogrysko, "One Year Later, Commission's Proposals for Improving Military, Public Service May Get a Serious Look," *Federal News Network,* March 11, 2021, https:// federalnewsnetwork.com/congress/2021/03/one-year-later-commissions-proposals-for-improving-military-public-service-may-get-a-serious-look/ (access May 20, 2022).

79  U.S. Space Force, "About the United States Space Force," https://www.spaceforce. mil/About-Us/About-Space-Force/ (accessed May 17, 2022) and U.S. Marine Corps, "Force Design 2030," March 2020, https://www.hqmc.marines.mil/Portals/142/ Docs/CMC38%20Force%20Design%202030%20Report%20Phase%20I%20and%20II. pdf?ver=2020-03-26-121328-460 (accessed May 17, 2022).

80  Gates Commission, *Report on an All-Volunteer Armed Force,* 5.

# Documents

# DOCUMENT 1

## Marshall Commission, "Introduction and Summary of Conclusions," February 1967

## I. Introduction and Summary of Conclusions

Sweeping changes have come to our society since the system for selecting men for induction into the Armed Forces was established a quarter of a century ago.

Among them are two which work with opposite effect on the manpower situation: A dramatic population growth has increased the supply of eligible men available for military service. But changes in military technology and transitions in strategic concepts have at the same time modified manpower requirements for national security. Of the nearly 2 million men now reaching draft age each year, our Armed Forces are likely to need only from half to one-third of them, varying with the circumstances. And of those, only a portion must be selected for non-voluntary induction. (The range in recent years has been from 10 to 40 percent, depending on the total size of the force level.) The problem which results, and which confronted this Commission, as one member expressed it for all the others, is: Who serves when not all serve?

It is an enduring problem, but floodlighted today by the war in Vietnam. The echo of American battle fire impels, as it always should, the hard probe for better solutions.

The Commission saw as its overriding obligation the necessity to search for a method of manpower procurement which would assure the Armed Forces' ability to acquire the men they need, under any circumstances, to protect the nation's security and meet its commitments; and at the same time function as uniformly and equitably as possible with due regard for the problems and the rights of the individuals into whose lives it must intrude.

Following the mandate of its charter, the Commission examined proposals ranging from elimination of all compulsory service to compulsion for all.

Aware of the spirit of social concern that animates much of young America today, the Commission considered whether other programs such as the Peace

Corps and VISTA, elevating society and benefiting the participants alike, could be developed and serve as substitutes for military service.

It made a thorough study of the Selective Service System as it presently works—the entire system, from the policies that guide its nationwide operation to the actual functioning of its local draft boards; the procedures by which men are examined, classified, and readied for induction; the variety of deferments and exemptions, and the factors which influence them; the appeals machinery; the people's attitude toward the system itself.

It reviewed the administrative procedures governing enlistment into the Army Reserve and National Guard which have subjected those components to wide and often legitimate public criticism.

Its search directed Commission attention to serious defects in our national life. Of each group of men coming to draft age each year, from one-fourth to one-third of those examined are found ineligible for service because of educational or health deficiencies or both; almost 700,000 potential draftees were found unqualified to serve in the last fiscal year. A total of 5 million men between the ages of 18½ and 34 who have been examined for the draft are today considered ineligible to serve. The Commission studied the implication of these figures as they affect the national security and reveal weaknesses in our society.

In pursuit of the answers to all the questions it faced, the Commission sought to hear the nation's voice. It invited the opinions of more than 120 organizations across the country, reflecting every sector of the society; a group of college student leaders; some 250 editors of student newspapers; each of the more than 4,000 local draft boards and the 97 appeal boards; many prominent private citizens; every Governor, the head of every appropriate Federal department and agency, the mayors of a number of cities. Answers came from many of these sources. The Commission had access to and studied the testimony and data provided in Congressional hearings. Members conferred with political leaders and college presidents and representatives of the poor. Observers attended and reported on three national conferences on the draft. The Commission listened to specialists who spoke on particular points of law and military need, management procedures and the values of social programs. And finally it had letters, which it gratefully acknowledges, from people across the land who voiced their suggestions, their convictions, their resentments, and their hopes.

But seeking to know the national mind was not, of course, enough. In the diversity of its interests, the nation does not think with one mind, or speak with one voice. To meet its responsibility, the Commission had to find its own answers, based on its own comprehension of issues that involve both the national welfare and the rights of the individual.

After long and careful deliberation, those answers are presented here in summary form, and discussed in detail in the body of this report.

*To provide a flexible system of manpower procurement which will assure the Armed Forces' ability to meet their national security commitments under all foreseeable circumstances, the Commission recommends:*

1.  **Continuation of a selective service system. (See ch. II.)**

*To make the controlling concept of that system the rule of law, rather than a policy of discretion, so as to assure equal treatment for those in like circumstances, the Commission recommends:*

2.  **A consolidated selective service system under more centralized administration to be organized and operated as follows:**

A.  National headquarters should formulate and issue clear and binding policies concerning classifications, exemptions, and deferments, to be applied uniformly throughout the country.

B.  A structure of eight regional offices (aligned for national security purposes with the eight regions of the Office of Emergency Planning) should be established to administer the policy and monitor its uniform application.

C.  An additional structure of area offices should be established on a population basis with at least one in each state. At these offices men would be registered and classified in accordance with the policy directives disseminated from national headquarters. (The Commission sees the possibility of 300–500 of these offices being able to answer the national need.)

1.  The use of modern data-handling equipment, as well as the application of uniform rules, would facilitate processing, registration, and classification.

2.  Under appropriate regulations, registrants would change their registration from one area office to another as they changed their permanent residence.

D.  Local boards, composed of volunteer citizens, would operate at the area office level as the registrants' court of first appeal.

E.  These changes should be made in the organization of the local boards:

1.  Their composition should represent all elements of the public they serve.

2.  The maximum term of service should be 5 years.

3.  A maximum retirement age should be established.

4.  The President's power to appoint members should not be limited to those nominated by the governors of the states.

5.  Women should be eligible to serve.

F.  The entire appeals process should be made uniform and strengthened in the following ways:

1.  The registrant should be able to appeal his classification to his local board within 30 days instead of the 10 days presently stipulated.

2.  Local boards should put their decisions in writing so appeal boards will have the benefit of the record in making their decisions, and the registrant will be able to know the reasons for the decision.

3.   Appeal boards should be collocated with the eight regional offices, although operate independently of them. The National Selective Service
(Presidential) Appeal Board would remain as presently constituted.

4.   Appeal agents should be readily available at the area offices to assist
registrants in making appeals.

5.   An adequate number of panels should be established, above the local
board level, for the specific purpose of hearing conscientious objector cases on an expedited basis. (See ch. IV.)

*To remove widespread public ignorance concerning the operations of the Selective Service
System, the Commission recommends:*

**3.   Both the registrant and the general public should be made fully ac-
quainted with the workings of the improved system and the registrant's
rights under it, in these ways:**

A.   Easily understandable information should be prepared in written form
and made available to all registrants each time they are classified.

B.   An adviser to registrants should be readily available at the area office to
inform and counsel registrants who need assistance with registration and
classification problems.

C.   Public information procedures regarding the entire system should be
made more effective by national headquarters. (See ch. IV.)

*To reduce the uncertainty in personal lives that the draft creates, and to minimize the disruption
it often causes in the lives of those men who are called, the Commission recommends:*

**4.   The present "oldest first" order of call should be reversed so that the
youngest men, beginning at age 19, are taken first. (See ch. V.)**

*To further reduce uncertainty and to insure fairness in the selection of inductees from a large
pool of eligible men, when all are not needed, the Commission recommends:*

**5.   Draft-eligible men should be inducted into service as needed ac-
cording to an order of call which has been impartially and randomly
determined. The procedure would be as follows:**

A.   At age 18, all men would register, and as soon as practicable thereafter
would receive the physical, moral, and educational achievement tests and
evaluations which determine their eligibility for military service according to Department of Defense standards. (This universal testing
would meet social as well as military needs.

B.   Those found to be qualified for service (I-A) who would reach the age of 19
before a designated date would be included in a pool of draft eligibles. Those
men reaching 19 after that date would be placed in a later draft-eligible pool.

C. The names of all men in the current draft-eligible pool would be arranged in an order of call for the draft through a system of impartial random selection.

D. For a specified period (a year, or possibly less), men in the pool would undergo their maximum vulnerability to the draft. Induction, according to the needs of the Department of Defense throughout that period, would be in the sequence determined by the impartial and random process.

E. When the specified period of maximum vulnerability had elapsed, an order of call would be determined for a new group of men, and the remaining men in the previous pool would not be called unless military circumstances first required calling all of the men in the new groups. (See ch. V.)

6. **No further student or occupational deferments should be granted, with these exceptions:**

A. Under appropriate regulations which will safeguard against abuses, students who are in school and men who are in recognized apprentice training when this plan goes into effect will be permitted to complete the degrees or programs for which they are candidates. Upon termination of those deferments they will be entered into the random selection pool with that year's 18-year-olds.

B. Thereafter, men who are already in college when they are randomly selected for service would be permitted to finish their sophomore year before induction.

C. Men who undertake officer training programs in college should be deferred, provided they commit to serve in the Armed Forces as enlisted men if they do not complete their officer programs. (These represent majority decisions; a minority of the Commission favors continued student deferment.)

D. Hardship deferments, which defy rigid classification but which must be judged realistically on individual merits, would continue to be granted.

7. **Study should begin now to determine the feasibility of a plan which would permit all men who are selected at 18 for induction to decide themselves when, between the ages of 19 and 23, to fulfill that obligation. Inducements would be offered to make earlier choice more attractive, and the option of choice could always be canceled if manpower needs were not met. If the feasibility of this plan is confirmed, the plan should be put into effect as soon as possible. (See ch. V.)**

*To broaden the opportunities for those who wish to volunteer for military service, the Commission recommends:*

8. Opportunities should be made available for more women to serve in the Armed Forces, thus reducing the numbers of men who must involuntarily be called to duty. (See ch. II.)

9. The Department of Defense should propose programs to achieve the objective, insofar as it proves practicable, of accepting volunteers who do not meet induction standards but who can be brought up to a level of usefulness as a soldier, even if this requires special educational and training programs to be conducted by the armed services. (See ch. VIII.)

*To remove the inequities in the enlistment procedures of the Reserve and National Guard programs, the Commission recommends:*

10. Direct enlistment into Reserve and National Guard forces should not provide immunity from the draft for those with no prior service except for those who enlist before receiving their I-A classification.

11. If the Reserves and National Guard units are not able to maintain their force levels with volunteers alone, they should be filled by inductions. Inductions would be determined by the same impartial random selection system which determines the order of call for active duty service. (See ch.VI.)

*The Commission supports recommendations presented to it by the National Advisory Commission on Health Manpower and the Department of State:*

12. A national computer file of draft eligible health professionals should be established to assist selective service area offices to place their calls for doctors and dentists and allied professions so as to cause minimum disruption in the medical needs of the community.

13. Policies governing the drafting of aliens in the United States should be modified in the following ways to make those policies more equitable and bring them into closer conformity with the country's treaty arrangements:

   A. All nonimmigrant aliens should be exempt from military service.
   B. Resident aliens should not be subject to military service until 1 year after their entry into the United States as immigrants.
   C. One year after entry, all resident aliens should be subject to military draft equally with U.S. citizens unless they elect to abandon permanently the status of permanent alien and the prospect of U.S. citizenship.
   D. Aliens who have served 12 months or more in the Armed Forces of a country with which the United States is allied in mutual defense activities

should be exempted from U.S. military service, and credit toward the U.S. military service obligation should be given for any such service of a shorter period. (See ch. VII.)

In arriving at the recommendations presented herein, the Commission considered other propositions which it rejected. Among them were:

1.  Elimination of the draft and reliance on an all-volunteer military force.

Although there are many arguments against an exclusively volunteer force, the decisive one, the Commission concluded, was its inflexible nature, allowing no provision for the rapid procurement of larger numbers of men if they were needed in times of crisis. (See ch. II.)

2.  A system of universal training.
    In the context in which the Commission studied it, universal training is a program designed by its proponents to offer physical fitness, self-discipline and remedial training to great numbers of young Americans—and not a substitute for the draft. The Commission concluded that:

    A.  Such a program cannot be justified on the grounds of military need, and
    B.  Compulsion is not a proper means of accomplishing the worthwhile objectives of rehabilitation. (See ch. II.)

The problem of men rejected for service for health and educational deficiencies, to which universal training is directed, is one which presents the country with a tragedy of urgent dimensions. Recommendations in this report will, the Commission hopes, help to alleviate this problem. The proposal to examine all 18-year-old men (recommendation 5A, p. 6) will help in identifying the problems and obtaining assistance for those rejected. (See ch. VIII.) The proposal to permit men failing to meet induction standards to volunteer for service and receive special training (recommendation 9, p. 7) will also be of value. But the larger part of this problem is imbedded in the conditions of the rejected men's lives, such as discrimination and poverty. It is essential to the future of the country that further steps be taken to correct those conditions before they can grow—as they are growing now—into a national shame and a threat to the nation's security. (See ch. VIII.)

3.  A system of compulsory national service; and along with that,

4.  Volunteer national service as an alternative to military service.

The Commission found first of all that there are difficult questions of public policy—and a lack of constitutional basis—involved in compulsory national service. Second, it concluded that no fair way exists to equate voluntary service programs with military service.

Volunteer national service must, then, be considered on its own merits as a separate program unrelated to military service. That there is a spirited interest in such service today is abundantly clear. But the needs which such service would meet and the way in which programs would be administered and financed are matters which are still inconclusive. The Commission received no clear or precise answers to the questions it raised concerning them. The Commission is sensitive to the spirit which motivates the desire for national service, and it suggests further research to define the issues more clearly, together with public and private experimentation with pilot programs. (See ch. IX.)

5. Recognition as conscientious objectors of those opposed to particular wars (instead of war in any form).

There is support within the Commission for this proposal. However, a majority of the Commission opposes it. The Commission majority believes, moreover, that the recent Supreme Court decision in *U.S. v. Seeger* offers sufficient guidance in defining the standards of the conscientious objector's position. That decision interprets the statute's requirement that conscientious objection be based on religious training and belief, to include "a given belief that is sincere and meaningful [and] occupies a place in the life of its possessor parallel to that filled by the orthodox belief in God of one who clearly qualifies for the exemption." (See ch. V.)

There remains another point to be made in this summary:

The Commission gave careful study to the effect of the draft on and its fairness to the Negro. His position in the military manpower situation is in many ways disproportionate, even though he does not serve in the Armed Forces out of proportion to his percentage of the population. He is underrepresented (1.3 percent) on local draft boards. The number of men rejected for service reflects a much higher percentage (almost 50 percent) of Negro men found disqualified than of whites (25 percent). And yet, recent studies indicate that proportionately more (30 percent) Negroes of the group qualified for service are drafted than whites (18 percent)—primarily because fewer Negroes are admitted into Reserve or officer training programs. Enlistment rates for qualified Negroes and whites are about equal, but reenlistments for Negroes are higher: Department of Defense figures show that the rate of first-term reenlistments is now more than double that of white troops. Negro soldiers have a high record of volunteering for service in elite combat units. This is reflected in, but could not be said to be the sole reason for, the Negro's overrepresentation in combat (in terms of his proportion of the population): Although Negro troops account for only 11 percent of the total U.S. enlisted personnel in Vietnam, Negro soldiers comprise 14.5 percent of all Army units, and in Army combat units the proportion is, according to the Department of Defense, "appreciably higher" than that. During the first 11 months of 1966, Negro soldiers totaled 22.4 percent of all Army troops killed in action.

There are reasons to believe, the Commission finds, that many of the statistics are comparable for some other minority groups, although precise information is not available. Social and economic injustices in the society itself are at the root of inequities which exist. It is the Commssion's [sic] hope that the recommendations contained in this report will have the effect of helping to correct those inequities.

Source: Marshall Commission, *In Pursuit of Equity*, Chapter I, pp. 3–10.

# DOCUMENT 2

## Marshall Commission, "The Need for the Draft," February 1967

### II. The Need for the Draft

The first question is the fundamental one: Is selective service necessary? In arriving at its conclusion—in the affirmative—the Commission gave careful consideration to two alternatives which have received wide public attention: A defense establishment manned entirely by volunteers, and a system of universal training.

### An All-Volunteer Force

Even with the draft law, the effort of military recruitment policy has traditionally been directed toward filling as much of the manpower requirement as possible with volunteers, and depending on the draft only to supplement the numbers needed. Volunteers have contributed two-thirds of the military force since 1950. With limited exceptions, the Navy, Marines, and Air Force have used volunteers almost entirely. And in periods of relative quiet, when draft calls have been low, most of the entrants into the Army itself have been volunteers. To be sure, a high proportion of all these volunteers in all the services—about four out of 10 in the years before Vietnam, according to Department of Defense estimates—are motivated by the existence of the draft. But the basic emphasis on volunteer service is clear nonetheless.

Changing world conditions could result in a future period—similar to those in the past—when draft calls are low, or conceivably nonexistent. Short of that hopeful development, there are undoubtedly actions within the range of control of the Armed Forces themselves which can encourage more enlistments and reduce the numbers of draftees necessary.[1]

Among those is the possibility of making more military positions available to women. Particularly at a time when manpower demands are great—such as the present—there is a disturbing paradox in this circumstance: Women willing to volunteer for military duty exist in far greater numbers than the services will accommodate; but at the same time there are undoubtedly military tasks suitable for women which are being filled by men who have to be involuntarily inducted. The Commission has been advised that the Department of Defense is currently reviewing its entire program of utilizing women in uniform. Out of that review, the Commission hopes, will come decisions which will benefit young men and young women alike and increase the effectiveness of the military services.

The Commission looked into the proposition that voluntary service could be sufficiently encouraged to eliminate the need for the draft altogether. Resistance to the draft has been voiced in various conferences held across the country, and in some of the correspondence addressed to the Commission. The National Council of Churches forwarded a resolution taken by its general board that inducements to volunteer be stepped up sufficiently so that the Selective Service Act could eventually be abolished. And the United States Youth Council, a coordinating body for 35 youth organizations, reported to the Commission that in a survey of its members "the issue of the voluntary army raised the virtues of voluntarism in a democratic society and the evils of conscription more than any other question or series of questions." Of those of its members responding to the survey, the council said, 61 percent favored a volunteer army.

But the Youth Council itself, although it recommended the reduction of "compulsion to its minimum," stopped short of suggesting abolition of the draft, for it recognized a basic conflict, revealed in its own survey: It candidly acknowledged that 58 percent of its respondents—almost as many as those who would depend on voluntarism—indicated that they personally would not volunteer.

And this of course is the basic fact. Since 1940—except for a very short period after World War II—a draft law has been necessary precisely because there have not been enough volunteers to meet military manpower needs.[2] Those needs are determined by national security requirements and military commitments.

Moreover, world conditions change, and those changes can modify the magnitude of military commitments and needs. An exclusively voluntary system would preclude the ability to meet changing demands.

An exclusively volunteer system would be expensive—although the Department of Defense gives no solid estimate of how much such a system would cost. And some members of the Commission see unfortunate social consequences in an all-volunteer military force sustained only by financial incentive. Such an establishment, motivated not by the concept of service, but by the lure of greater reward than the members' skills could command elsewhere, could easily—it is feared—become a mercenary force unrepresentative of the nation.

But more important than these considerations is the fact that an exclusively voluntary system, with no provision for selective service, would permit no flexibility for crisis. The sudden need for greater numbers of men would find the nation without the machinery to meet it. To a Commission deliberating grave issues of life and death in an atmosphere created by just such a sudden need, this is of overriding significance.

It was this stark and uncontested fact which was the most persuasive in forging the Commission's conviction that the nation must now, and in the foreseeable future, have a system which includes the draft. Only with such a flexible system can the military services be assured of their ability always to have the numbers of men necessary to fulfill the mission demanded of them for the nation's security.

## Universal Training

Immediately after World War II, universal military training was widely supported in this country as a means of making available a large pool of trained manpower should the nation have to mobilize again the massive land armies of World War II. Changes in the technology of war, resulting in basic changes in military concepts and requirements, have eliminated that need.

Today, the idea commands attention once again. Expressions in favor of it have been presented to the Commission from veteran and other prominent organizations, several Governors and other political leaders. In today's context, however, it is better understood as a system of universal training—without the "military"—for it is proposed for reasons other than those which were its direct purposes two decades ago. One of the most forceful and carefully reasoned of the universal training proposals to be submitted to the country for consideration is that of former President Eisenhower.[3]

General Eisenhower does not suggest that the program he envisions would replace the draft or eliminate the need for it. It would not even be directly related to the military's manpower needs. It would be a universal system of military, physical, and remedial training, administered by the Defense Department mainly because of its facilities and resources, and given for 1 year to all young men, except those disqualified for serious physical or mental reasons, and those who chose to volunteer for service in the Armed Forces. (A draft—eventually of universal training "graduates"—would still be required to fill the manpower needs not taken care of by volunteers.) In effect, the Eisenhower program would be an extensive training and educational program for all of America's male youth, and he sees its values as the opportunity to promote physical fitness and self-discipline, provide remedial instruction for those who need it, and instill a patriotic sense of duty and love of country.

The men directly affected by this program would be, of course, those—varying from half to two-thirds of the eligible population—who do not now see military service. And those who would be affected most greatly would be that large number rejected for educational deficiencies or physical disabilities.

With his proposed programs of rehabilitation which would benefit those currently rejected, General Eisenhower and others who have voiced their alarm over the size and condition of this group call attention to a matter which the Commission believes is of deep and urgent concern to the nation. Indeed, those distressing statistics—the nearly 700,000 who were found ineligible for service last year, and the 5 million men between the ages of 18½ and 34 who have now accumulated in the inventory of the disqualified—bear the seeds of the destruction of our society.

There is within the Commission some support for universal training as a method of correcting this situation—and, in the process, providing the country with trained and disciplined citizens who would be valuable to their communities in the event of nuclear attack. (The Eisenhower proposal views this as an additional advantage of a universal training program.)

But the Commission was obliged to test universal training—as every other proposal before it—against its strictly confined charter to determine only the most fair and workable way of providing the nation with its military manpower needs. Universal training would not answer that problem. The Commission, as a whole, rejected universal training because there is no military requirement for it; and and [sic] in the absence of a military requirement, the Commission concluded that although the grimly serious problem posed by the men disqualified for Armed Forces duty must be solved, compulsory service should not be the means for its correction. (The Commission, however, decided that otherwise disqualified men who volunteer for service should be given the benefit of special training; see page 57.)

## Summary of Recommendations

1.  **A draft law should be continued to provide the nation with a flexible system of manpower procurement which will assure the Armed Forces' ability to meet their national security commitments under all foreseeable circumstances.**
2.  **Opportunities should be made available for more women to serve in the Armed Forces, thus reducing the number of men who must involuntarily be called to duty.**

Source: Marshall Commission, *In Pursuit of Equity*, Chapter II, pp. 11–16. This document does not include three charts from the original report.

# DOCUMENT 3

## Marshall Commission, "Profile of the Present System," February 1967

### III. Profile of the Present System

The United States has outgrown its Selective Service System.

That System has operated with high standards of integrity and dedication through wars and warlike peace for a quarter of a century. Those who have held the System's operation in their hands surely merit the nation's gratitude—from the thousands of citizens who have contributed their service on the local draft boards across the country to the distinguished official who for so long has given the System its leadership, Lt. Gen. Lewis B. Hershey. Moreover, it is still a flexible instrument for providing the country's military manpower needs. But world conditions have produced new circumstances in which needless inequities and confusion are generated under the System among the men who must donate part of their lives to serve the nation's security.

### The Way It Works Now

For all practical purposes, the Selective Service System in operation today dates back to legislation passed in 1940. It is, then, virtually the same as that which guided the country's gigantic manpower procurement during World War II.

Its basic functioning organism is the local board. There are more than 4,000 of them across the country, ranging in size and character from one in Hinsdale County, Colo., with a total registration of 28, to the 68 boards which share responsibility for New York City, handling an average of more than 20,000 registrants each.[4] Each board is composed of three or more members—citizens who volunteer their time and service. Officially they are appointed by the President on nomination by the Governor of the State. The appointive power has in practice been delegated to the Director of Selective Service by Executive Order of the

President. The board's records are kept by a clerk—usually a woman—who works either full or part time.

Every young man reaching the age of 18 is required to register with the local board in his area. On the basis of information he supplies, and other information, he is classified by the board. (Chart 4 describes the various Selective Service classifications.) Unless the local board gives the registrant a deferment or an exemption, it places him in the I-A (or I-A-O or I-O) category. It can also grant a IV-F for "obvious" physical defects, but usually that determination is made on the basis of subsequent examinations to which all I-A's (and conscientious objectors) are subjected. Those examinations determine the registrant's physical status, educational level and moral qualifications according to standards set by the Department of Defense.

A registrant dissatisfied with his classification (or someone acting on his behalf) can request a change through his appeal board. There are 96 appeal boards, at least one for each judicial district; and above these is a National Selective Service Appeal Board, which makes the final decision on all appeals to the President.

The file of a man who appeals goes to the appeal board considering his case. With that exception, however, a registrant's records remain under the jurisdiction of the local board which classifies him initially, wherever his travels, study or occupation take him.

A national headquarters—directed by General Hershey—supervises the operation of the entire System, and between the national office and the local boards are 56 State headquarters (one for each possession, Puerto Rico, and the District of Columbia as well) which administer the act at that level. The State director, like the local board members, is appointed by the President on the nomination of the Governor.

The local boards, in making their classifications, and the appeal boards in their proceedings, are guided by information from both these headquarters.

The national headquarters, on receiving manpower calls from the Department of Defense, prorates them to the states, usually according to the number of men classified I-A in each state, after allowing for expected rejections.[5] The states in turn divide them into quotas for their local boards. The boards fill their quotas from among the most eligible of their I-A's—current policy is delinquents first,[6] then volunteers for induction, then 25-year-olds, followed by those downward in age to 19—and order them for induction into the Armed Forces.

## The Personnel

The national and state headquarters are heavily oriented toward the military. Commissioned officers of the Armed Forces occupy most of the executive positions at the national level. State directors and their key staffs are usually Reserve or National Guard officers on active duty.

The members of the local boards are all male (as the regulations now demand), mostly veterans, and almost exclusively white: a 96.3-percent response to a Commission questionnaire in October 1966 indicates that only 1.3 percent of

16,632 local board members are Negro,[7] 0.8 percent are Puerto Rican, 0.7 percent Spanish American. There are 38 members (0.2 percent) who are Oriental, and 16 (0.1 percent) American Indians.

The average age is 58. One-fifth of all the board members are over 70, and of these, 400 are over 80; 12 are between 90 and 99.

Almost half have served on their local boards more than 10 years; 1,335—8 percent of those responding—have served more than 20 years.

The majority (67 percent) have served on active military duty—41 percent in World War II, another 17 percent in World War I, and the remainder in Korea and at other times.

As compared with the general population of the same age, local board members are well educated; about one-third of them are college graduates, contrasted with less than 10 percent of the population's comparable age group.

Seventy percent are in white-collar occupations. Of these, more than 20 percent are professional men. A majority (15 percent) of the rest are farmers. Craftsmen, service workers, semiskilled workers and laborers are represented on local boards in far smaller proportions (less than 25 percent) than their representation in the general population.[8]

## The Problems

When the 1940 Selective Training and Service Act was being deliberated, the local board concept was described in congressional hearings in terms of its vitality and fairness: "An eligible citizen chosen to serve is selected by a board composed of his neighbors who live in the same community in which he lives." General (then Major) Hershey, testifying before the Senate committee, pointed out that "* * * we are only seeking * * * about 1 million out of 11,500,000, so there has got to be an equity decision. Somebody has got to decide which one of the 11 is to be taken, and I do want to impress upon all the fact that * * * the choice is being made by the neighbors of the man * * *." That concept was actually first envisioned in the period after the Civil War—which had seen violent public reaction to the draft—when a report recommended that future conscription be placed in the hands of local boards composed of "civilian neighbors." It has thus survived for a century. In its budget justification for fiscal 1967, Selective Service characterized the local boards as "little groups of neighbors on whom is placed the responsibility to determine who is to serve the nation in the Armed Forces and who is to serve in industry, agriculture, and other deferred classifications." And in one of its recent communications to local boards, the national office told them: "Because of its comparatively long association with a registrant and knowledge of what he has done, the local board is relatively well-qualified to evaluate his ability to perform."

However universally valid this personalized concept might have been in the past, only in rural areas does it appear to be true today. Urban board members usually work in anonymity—and indeed seem to look upon that anonymity as an advantage. Rarely it would seem do those on such a board actually know the men whom they are classifying on the basis of their records—and vice versa. After taking an extensive look into local board operations in one state, a team of researchers reported to the Commission: "Very little evidence exists to suggest that the fact of drafting by local boards has more than symbolic significance, if that, in urban settings."

A group of nine college students who took soundings on campuses across the country on matters relating to the draft met with the Commission to report their findings. The fallacy of the personalized concept of the local draft board was high on their list of topics of interest. Identity of local board members, one of them reported, "is one of the best guarded secrets in America." There was no doubt that he spoke the sentiments of his colleagues, although another expressed it more moderately: "The idea that the draft boards are a group of your neighbors sitting in judgment or consideration of your fate is not a workable real plan right now. No one seems to know who the members of his draft board are. The few exceptions, the people who do know, tend to come from small towns." This anonymous character of the boards can of course be overstated. A registrant always has the right to request a personal appearance before his board—if, for instance, he wishes to seek a reclassification—so long as he makes his request within 10 days of his classification notice. But the point is clear that board operations are not usually intensely personal.

In utilization of office space, many urban boards themselves have moved away from the strictly "neighborhood" approach and toward an informal sort of consolidation. In Baltimore, the Commission learned, 17 boards operating in that area all keep their records and meet in one centrally located building. The eight boards in San Antonio do the same thing; in fact, this appears to be the practice among more than half the metropolitan boards of the country.

Each of these boards has its own clerk who handles the records for her board—although there is inevitably some sharing of the workload among them. The clerk is an important part of any board's operation. There is a tendency on the part of many young registrants to overestimate this importance, to assume, as one of the college students told the Commission, that "the draft board members are rubberstamp machines and the clerks actually have the power to say who gets what deferment, who is I-A, who gets inducted." The "anonymity" of the boards is perhaps one reason for this impression; even more likely however is the method of board operation. Many board members have heavy professional and business duties. They usually meet in the evening to make their classification decisions. A registrant seeking information by phone or in person would no doubt find the clerk the only person on hand. The more efficient she is, the more authoritative her answers may appear to the registrant. The assumption which results is understandable, but misleading. Evidence before the Commission indicates that board members around the nation are deeply aware of their responsibilities and conscientious in the discharge of them.

The fact does remain, however, that the clerk's role is a highly important one. Inevitably, much of a board's work is routine. (Some 17 percent of the boards responding to a Commission survey indicated that 90 percent or more of the classification decisions made in their September 1966 meeting were virtually automatic.)[9] Although the board itself does the classifying, a good clerk can make the board's job considerably easier. Perhaps the most important of her tasks—certainly from the registrant's point of view the most critical—is the routine preparation of cases for board review and decision, which in practical effect amounts to an initial classification. The clerks usually are highly regarded by their boards. Many of them also have long years of experience in and familiarity with the System, some dating from World War II days. Despite the importance of their work, however—and although they are subject to civil service rules—their salaries are set by the state directors and especially in smaller towns and rural areas are considerably below that of most Federal workers. (The woman who coordinates the work of all the clerks of those 17 Baltimore boards has been with the Selective Service System 21 years and her pay is the equivalent of that earned by a recent college graduate in the civil service with 2 years' experience.)

But there is a wide variation in the way in which local boards view the routine aspect of their work; it ranges from that previously noted 17 percent who say they actually have to review in detail only 10 percent of their cases, to another 7 percent who say they have to review virtually all cases in detail. This reflects the System's absence of uniformity as it operates throughout the country. The wide range in the workloads of local boards, determined by their size, obviously contributes to the lack of uniformity.

A good deal of the variation is dictated by social and economic factors.[10] For men with different educational backgrounds, there is a substantial degree of difference in their chances of entering military service. Men with less than an eighth-grade education, and Negro high school dropouts are less likely to enter because more of them fail the written examination. On the other hand, graduate and professional students are much less likely to see active duty because many of them continue their student deferments until they are 26, fathers, or can receive occupational deferments. (See chart 5.)

High-income areas usually have a high proportion of student (II–S) deferments; a study in one state pursued this circumstance further and showed that boards in high-income areas had the lowest proportion of registrants serving or having served in the Armed Forces. Low-income slum areas have the greatest number of men rejected for service. And there is a direct relationship between those two statistics: In the state subjected to intensive study, the board with the highest percentage of rejectees also had the lowest number of student deferments. That area was also 50 percent Negro.

The Negro's position in the total military manpower picture—both his service and his ineligibility for service—is a matter deserving attention. His participation is in several ways inequitable. It is an inequity which is difficult to pinpoint specifically, for its manifestations are the results of the handicaps under which the Negro has struggled in this country, and reflect social and economic injustices which are older by far than the operation of the Selective Service System.

The Negro does not serve in the Armed Forces out of proportion to his representation in the population as a whole. But far greater percentages of Negroes than whites are rejected for service.[11] Department of Defense estimates showed that of all those examined almost 50 percent of nonwhite men aged 26–29 years in 1964 had been found unfit for service as opposed to almost 25 percent of the white male population of the same age group.[12] (See chart 6.) The percentage of Negroes considered qualified for service was thus considerably smaller than the similar percentage of whites. Nevertheless, 30.2 percent of that qualified Negro group was drafted, whereas only 18.8 percent of the qualified whites were. (See chart 7.) This is primarily because of two factors: (1) Fewer Negroes are admitted into Reserve programs. The 1964 study showed Reserve duty experience for 2.8 percent of all nonwhites in the age group reviewed, and 5.4 percent of those qualified for military service, compared with 15.5 percent of all comparably aged whites, and 20.6 percent of the whites qualified. (The Reserve problem is discussed later in this report.) (2) Fewer Negroes get into officer programs—little more than 0.2 percent of that total nonwhite group and less than 0.4 percent of those qualified, contrasted with 3.3 percent of all the whites and 4.3 percent of the qualified whites in the group studied.[13]

Enlistment rates are about equal for qualified white and Negro men. However, Negroes already in the service reenlist at a substantially higher rate than do white servicemen—their first term reenlistment rates have been more than double that of whites in recent years, according to Department of Defense figures. The Report of the U.S. Commission on Civil Rights in 1963 concluded that this "suggests that Negro servicemen believe on balance that the Armed Forces offer them greater career opportunities than they can find in the civilian economy." The Negro soldier has a record of heavy volunteering in elite combat units. (Some airborne divisions, which rely exclusively on volunteers, are 24 percent Negro.) The possible attractiveness of a relatively nonsegregated society which primarily measures ability cannot be said, however, to be the sole reason for the Negro's heavy representation in combat units. The same educational deficiencies which disqualify the Negro for service in such large numbers continue to work their effect inside the service as well; fewer Negroes even among those eligible for service are admitted to jobs requiring technical skills; sometimes the path leading to an infantry division is the only one entirely open. Approximately 20 percent of all personnel assigned to combat occupations throughout the Army are Negro.

The overall proportion of Negroes in relation to all enlisted personnel in Vietnam is only 11 percent; but their percentage in the Army units there is 14.5 percent; and their representation in Army combat units is, according to the Defense Department, "appreciably higher" than that. Current figures are not available, but as of late 1965, 22.8 percent of the enlisted men in combat units in Vietnam were Negro. The casualty figures reflect this. During the first 11 months of 1966, Negro soldiers comprised 22.4 percent of all Army troops killed in action.

The Commission considers that there is reason to believe that many of the statistics relating to the Negro would be comparable for some other minority groups, although specific information to establish this is not available.

In determining the number of men who will be required for the draft, enlishment [sic] rates are a variable factor, influencing the decision. Among 240 local boards surveyed in a sample study, there was a range between 19 who had to induct 40 percent of their I-A registrants during a particular period of time, and 4 who inducted only 10 percent of their like group. Such variable factors not only help to decide the numbers to be drafted, but have, as well, a distinct influence on determining who among the I-A's will be selected; 90 percent of the boards in the States of Washington and Alabama—but none of the boards in Connecticut—had to induct married men during the first 5 months of 1966.[14] (Married men without children are I-A, but lower in the order of call than unmarried I-A's.)

Not all the variability is the result of socio-economic factors, however. Examination of records from a national sample of 199 local boards shows a wide range of board action on reclassification—which is about four-fifths of the System's workload—with some boards never reclassifying men with deferments in effect and others moving men into I-A when their deferments had not expired. (Some 27 percent of the registrants whose records were surveyed had this happen.)

About half reclassified into II-A were in neither a critical occupation nor an essential industry as defined by the Department of Labor.[15]

Much of the System's uneven performance relates to the lack of standardization in the guidance the local boards receive.

That guidance comes to them in the form of regulations (signed either by the President or the National Director), operations bulletins, local board memoranda, and several other forms of information. The state directors also receive these, along with others specifically designed for them alone; and the State directors themselves pass instructions to the local boards on matters that are of particular importance in their areas. But because the System offers wide latitude for critical judgment by the boards themselves, this profusion of guidance does not always articulate a clearly defined policy to the board. Moreover, boards across the country (and sometimes within individual States) receive varying amounts of, and sometimes directly conflicting, guidance on the same subject.

In 1966, 39 state headquarters issued 173 directives, bulletins, or memoranda to their local boards dealing with deferment policies. This means of course that some states sent no such guidance; of those that did, several sent only 1 or 2, several 7 or 8, and 1 headquarters dispatched 13. More than half of the directives of these treated the subject of student deferment.[16]

The student deferment issue is the source of a great deal of confusion. The only legal requirement relating to student deferments is the one (I-S) which obliges local boards to permit college students called for induction to finish their current academic year before reporting for duty. (It also permits high school students to finish their high school education if they do so before their 20th birthday.) However, most college deferments (II-S) are those which local boards can, at their discretion, give to men whose studies they judge to be in the national interest.

The variety of guidance sent out on this subject last year reveals that a student's immediate future can be influenced by his state headquarters' interpretation of national policy, for that advice was not uniform, and indeed entirely contradictory in some instances. Some offices instructed their local boards to use as a basis for their determination college qualification test scores and information concerning a student's rank in class—both of which, after several years of disuse, were revived in 1966 with the year's larger draft calls. Other state headquarters specifically told their boards that those criteria were only advisory and could be ignored. In some states, a man must carry 12 semester hours in order to qualify as a full-time student; others put the cutoff point at 15 hours; and still other offices told their boards to accept the school's definition of a full-time load.

Some state headquarters would advise giving a student deferment (II-S) to an individual in a business, trade, or vocational school. Others say the II-S classification is inappropriate but that an I-S (the statutory permission for students to finish their academic year) can be given. And one state headquarters advised that such a man could qualify for an occupational (II-A) deferment.

The same pattern of variation is generally true of appeal boards. Sometimes, those within a single state may make completely opposite decisions on comparable cases.[17]

Appeal boards do not always see issues from the same perspective as do local boards, which may suggest nothing more than a zealous regard for their appellate function. But there is one interesting conflict which is locked into a peculiar condition of the Selective Service System—one which was deliberately intended. Although a registrant cannot change his local board if he moves, a man with an occupational deferment can use the appeal board in the area of his employment. A local board is, of course, sensitive to the social and economic factors in its own community. Surely it would be consistent with human nature for its members to prefer to tap someone who has moved away when they have to dip into their previously deferred pools. So this picture emerges: A man now living in another city, denied an extension of his occupational deferment by his local board, takes his case to the appeal board which serves his new community; and it, sensitive to the economic factors in its own area, reverses the decision of the local board. It does not always happen that way, but appeal boards in industrial centers reinstating occupational deferments taken away by local boards in other areas present the most striking study of appeal board disagreement with local board action. In no other case are so many local board decisions reversed. From the perspective of the appeal boards, it is a rational procedure; local boards do not always consider it so.

There is a pronounced disparity in the workloads of appeal boards across the country. In one state, four boards handled an average of more than 3,000 cases each during the last fiscal year; for another state during the same period, the entire number processed totaled 25. Geography accounts for some of this. Some states have three appeal boards for 250,000 registrants; others, one for 450,000. Characteristics of the respective region are also pertinent. Registrants from urban states generally make more appeals, while southern and mountain states have the lowest proportions.[18]

But probably also some part of the low incidence of appeals in some states is indicative of a failure to inform registrants of their appeal rights. This is not conclusive, but neither is it by any means clear that all registrants are informed of those rights. The Selective Service System contains more than 8,000 advisers, whose task is to assist men at the time of their registration (by providing information, answering questions, and so forth), and some 4,000 appeal agents to aid registrants who wish to appeal. These men, like the board members themselves, are not compensated. They are also the most elusive components of the entire System. The research team which reported the results of its intensive one-state study told the Commission: "The clear fact is * * * that appeal agents are almost totally inactive. Most board members barely know who their appeal agent is and cannot recall when he was last in the office. Clerks freely admit that their appeal agents have checked no files, seen no registrants, made no appeals in years. What advising of registrants there is, must be done by clerks or by an occasional private attorney. Most registrants are probably quite unaware that there are appeal agents in the System." The team concludes: "We doubt that this is peculair [sic] to our State." The Commission, on the evidence presented to it, shares that doubt. The condition appears to be uniform throughout the System—indeed, perhaps, it is its most uniform characteristic.

Finally, there is—not surprisingly—a decided variation in individual attitudes. Almost a fourth of the surveyed—and responding—local board members gave as their opinions that a student's self-support in college should be an important factor in determining his deferment; an equal number thought it should not be considered at all. Members of appeal boards differ in their attitudes toward graduate school, and in the weight they assign to a student's course of study.[19] And 55 percent of the local board members of one state believe conscientious objectors should not be deferred at all.

To the Commission, all of these factors together strongly describe a critical need for policy uniformity through the application of clear regulations consistently applied. And the Commission's survey shows that many local board members themselves agree.

Source: Marshall Commission, *In Pursuit of Equity*, Chapter III, pp. 17–29. This document does not include four charts from the original report.

# DOCUMENT 4

## Martin Anderson to Richard Nixon, "An Outline of the Factors Involved in Establishing an All-Volunteer Force," July 4, 1967

### Memorandum

To: Richard Nixon

From: Martin Anderson

Re: An Outline of the Factors Involved in Establishing an All-Volunteer Armed
    Force

> "The compulsory draft is far more typical of totalitarian nations than of
> democratic nations. The theory behind it leads directly to totalitarianism. It
> is absolutely opposed to the principles of individual liberty which have
> always been considered a part of American democracy."
>
> *Senator Robert A. Taft, 1940*

Drafting the youth of our country constitutes two years of involuntary servitude to
the State. It is inimicable [sic] to the basic principles of freedom that are the moral
foundations of our Republic. It has been tolerated reluctantly only because it has
been thought to be absolutely necessary to preserve and protect the national security of the United States.

Recent studies of new information by reliable experts now show that it is
within our grasp to eliminate this last vestige of involuntary servitude without
weakening the security of our country in the slightest; to the contrary, we would
actually strengthen our security.

The key to this bold, progressive step forward in the cause of freedom lies in
the ultimate establishment of a modern, highly-trained armed force of competent
professionals, staffed completely by volunteers.

## A. ADVANTAGES OF ALL-VOLUNTEER ARMED FORCE

1. Moral

   a. Two years of involuntary servitude to the State, even for military service, is an abrogation of men's rights and establishes the principle that man's life is at the disposal of the State.

   b. The elimination of the draft would eliminate the contradiction inherent in defending individual rights and reluctantly supporting the draft.

2. National Security

   a. The establishment of an all-volunteer armed force would strengthen the military security of the U.S.

   b. A highly trained, motivated team of professionals, skilled in the technical aspects of modern warfare is—man for man—a far more effective defense force.

   c. Drafted men resent being conscripted, they often do just enough to "get by." Their resulting inexperience lowers the effectiveness of our military forces. In battle it may even constitute a threat to the safety of career soldiers.

   d. Fully 93 percent of draftees leave the military as soon as possible; their expensive training is largely wasted. A much higher percentage of volunteers will make the military a career, and utilize their valuable skills in the defense of the country.

3. Economic

   a. Contrary to the general impression created by the Department of Defense and the media, the annual monetary cost of moving forward to an all-volunteer armed force (including a truly ready volunteer reserve) is in the range of $5 to $7 billion. This is three to four percent of the current level of annual expenditures of the federal government.

      1. The higher reenlistment rate characteristic of a volunteer armed force means that far fewer men are need [sic] annually. This would result in lower training costs and a reduction of the number of men required for training purposes.

      2. To achieve an all-volunteer military, pay and allowances would have to be increased about 68 percent for enlisted men during their first tour of duty. To maintain balance the pay and allowances of current career men should be increased about 17 percent.

   b. During his first tour of duty an enlisted man earns an annual income equivalent to $2,400. This is far below the so-called poverty level, far less than that guaranteed to civilians by minimum wage laws.

1.  If policement [sic], FBI agents, or CIA personnel were paid similar wages, it would be "necessary" to draft them also. It is only fair that men in the military be paid reasonable wages.

c.  It has been estimated that enlisted men could earn at least $3,600 a year in civilian jobs. Thus, they pay a hidden tax of $1,200 a year—twice that paid by the average taxpayer.

d.  More effective recruitment techniques and more effective utilization of manpower under the stimulus of an all-volunteer force would result in significant cost savings.

1.  The existence of the draft tends to create a dependence on its use, and leads to a slackening of recruitment efforts.
2.  Today we only spend $1 on manpower research in the military for every $300,000 spent on weapons related research.
3.  More realistic mental and physical recruitment standards would further reduce costs. Men could be classified according to their mental and physical abilities and assigned to appropriate jobs.

4.  Political

a.  Clearly explained and understood, it is likely that most Americans would support an all-volunteer armed force.

1.  The attainment of both increased military protection and increased personal freedom should gain support from Republicans, Independents and Democrats, from Conservatives and Liberals.
2.  1,700,000 career military men and their families would enjoy increased pay, prestige and dignity.
3.  Upwards of 20,000,000 young men and their families and friends would have the uncertainty associated with the draft removed. They would be able to plan their futures—civilian or military—and make their own choices.

5.  Social

a.  With an all-volunteer armed force no income group, no racial group, no educational group, would bear an unjust proportion of coercion; no coercion would exist.
b.  A well-paid career in the armed forces would be viewed as an attractive opportunity. It would provide well-paying, important work that many young people would be proud to have.

B.  OBJECTIONS TO AN ALL-VOLUNTEER ARMED FORCE

1.  The National Security Would be Threatened

a. The opposite is true—an experienced all-volunteer armed force is a far more effective defense team than a partially drafted one. Today, 43 percent of our Army is composed of men with less than one year's experience.

2. Not Enough Men Will Volunteer

a. During the transition to an all-volunteer armed force the draft would be maintained until the increases in pay, and other changes, had increased the level of volunteers to the point where the draft is unnecessary. There is no risk involved.

b. Stand-by draft provisions, for use in extreme emergencies, would be developed and maintained.

3. We Can't Do It While the Vietnam War Continues and the Federal Government Incurs a $30 billion Deficit

a. In view of the intensity of the pressures of Vietnam on our whole military establishment, and the dangerous $30 billion deficit the Johnson Administration will incur in fiscal 1968, the implementation of an all-volunteer armed force should be postponed until the major fighting stops in Vietnam and the economy is sound.

4. A Volunteer Force Lacks Flexibility for Quick Response

a. A volunteer career armed force would be backed up by a large volunteer ready reserve, composed of well-trained, experienced men, committed to fight on short notice.

b. Draftees take months to induct, and more months to train. A volunteer ready reserve would be far more flexible, and more effective, than hastily trained teen-agers [sic].

5. It Would Cost Too Much

a. The costs are not prohibitive. Clearly $5 to $7 billion a year is within our economic reach. Moreover, significant savings would result from lower turnover of military personnel and lower training costs.

6. There is Increased Danger of a Military "Take-over"

a. Any possibility of a military take-over would initiate in the top ranks of the officer corps. Today's officer corps are composed solely of volunteers, and the transition to an all-volunteer armed force would affect only the lower ranks of the enlisted men.

7. We Should Not be Defended by "Mercenaries"

a. A career military man is not a mercenary. A mercenary is a man who fights for anyone—regardless of nationality or ideology or moral conviction—for money.

8. Everyone Has a Duty to Serve

   a.   No one has any obligation to serve the State involuntarily, even in the military.

   b.   Even if we maintain the draft, less than half of our men will ever be likely to serve in the military.

9. You Couldn't Get Men Qualified in Special Skills

   a.   This is a technical manpower problem that has been solved admirably by our Navy, our Air Force, our Marines, and our officer corps in all brances [sic] of the armed services, who rely almost exclusively on volunteers. The appropriate adjustments in pay and other incentives could be made for jobs that are relatively difficult to fill.

10. We Would be Defended by an All-Negro Armed Force

   a.   Any reluctance to be defended by Negroes per se is over racism.

   b.   An all-Negro armed force is physically impossible. Even in the highly unlikely event that all qualified Negroes volunteered, the majority of the armed forces would still be white.

   c.   It is possible that a relatively higher percentage of Negroes would enlist voluntarily, but they would only do so if they found it to their advantage.

11. In Time of Extreme Danger Men Would Not Volunteer, Regardless of Pay

   a.   If there was a serious threat to the security of the U.S., men would certainly be motivated to fight to defend their lives, their families and their property. In all likelihood there would be more volunteers than could be effectively assimilated into an effective fighting force.

C.  SUMMARY

Because it is moral and fair, because it increases our national security, and because it is economically feasible, we should give high priority to the goal of establishing an all-volunteer armed force with fair, decent wages that will offer the young men of our country the opportunity to participate in its defense with dignity, with honor and as free men.

Source: Martin Anderson, "Memorandum to Richard Nixon, Re: An Outline of the Factors Involved in Establishing an All-Volunteer Armed Force," July 4, 1967, pp. 1–7, box 2, Martin Anderson Donated Collection, RMNL, https://www.nixonfoundation.org/wp-content/uploads/2012/01/An-Outline-of-the-Factors-Involved-in-Establishing-an-All-Volunteer-Armed-Force-by-Martin-Anderson.pdf (accessed August 31, 2021).

# DOCUMENT 5

## Presidential Candidate Richard Nixon, "The All-Volunteer Armed Force," October 17, 1968

I speak tonight about a matter important to us all, but especially to young Americans and their parents.

I refer to compulsory military service—or, as most of us know it, "the draft."

We have lived with the draft now for almost 30 years. It was started during the dark uncertainty before the Second World War, as a temporary, emergency measure. But since then we have kept it—through our ordeals in Korea and Vietnam, and even in the years of uneasy peace between.

We have lived with the draft so long, in fact, that too many of us now accept it as normal and necessary.

I say it's time we took a new look at the draft—at the question of permanent conscription in a free society.

If we find we can reasonably meet our peacetime manpower needs by other means—then we should prepare for the day when the draft can be phased out of American life.

I have looked into this question very carefully. And this is my belief: once our involvement in the Vietnam war is behind us, we move toward an all-volunteer armed force.

This means, that just as soon as our reduced manpower requirements in Vietnam will permit us to do so, we should stop the draft and put our Selective Service structure on stand-by.

For the many years since World War II, I believed that, even in peacetime, only through the draft could we get enough servicemen to defend our nation and meet our heavy commitments abroad. Over these years it seemed we faced a Hobson's choice: either constrict the freedom of some, or endanger the freedom of all.

But conditions have changed, and our needs have changed. So, too, I believe, our defense manpower policies should change.

Tonight, I would like to share with you some of the reasons why I think this is so.

First, let me talk about what we cannot do.

First of all, we must recognize that conditions in the world today require us to keep a powerful military force. Being prepared for war is our surest guarantor of peace. While our adversaries continue to build up their strength, we cannot reduce ours; while they continue to brandish the sword, we cannot lay aside our shield.

So any major change in the way we obtain military manpower must not keep us from maintaining a clearly superior military strength.

In the short run, we need also to recognize the limits imposed by the war in Vietnam. However we might wish to, we can't stop the draft while we are in a major war.

What we can do—and what we should do now—is to commit ourselves as a nation to the goal of building an all-volunteer armed force.

The arguments about the draft center first on whether it's right, and second, on whether it's necessary.

Three decades ago, Senator Robert Taft declared that the draft "is absolutely opposed to the principles of individual liberty which have always been considered a part of American democracy."

I feel this way: A system of compulsory service that arbitrarily selects some and not others simply cannot be squared with our whole concept of liberty, justice and equality under the law. Its only justification is compelling necessity.

The longer it goes on, the more troublesome are the questions it raises. Why should your son be forced to sacrifice two of the most important years of his life, so that a neighbor's son can go right along pursuing his interests in freedom and safety?

Why should one young American be forced to take up military service while another is left free to make his own choice?

We have all seen, time and time again, how hit-or-miss the workings of the draft are. You know young people, as I do, whose lives have been disrupted first by uncertainty, next by conscription. We all have seen the unfairness of the present system.

Some say we should tinker with the present system, patching up an inequity here and there. I favor this too, but only for the short term.

But in the long run, the only way to stop the inequities is to stop using the system. It does not work fairly—and, given the facts of American life, it just can't.

The inequity stems from one simple fact—that some of our young people are forced to spend two years of their lives in our nation's defense, while others are not. It's not so much the way they're selected that's wrong, as it is the fact of selection.

Even now, only about 40 percent of our eligible young people ever serve. As our population grows, and the manpower pool expands, that percentage will shrink even further. Ten years ago about a million men become of draft age each year. Now there are almost two million.

There has also been a change in the armed forces we need. The kinds of war we have to be prepared for now include not only conventional war and nuclear war, but also guerrilla war of the kind we are now experiencing in Vietnam.

In nuclear war, huge ground armies operating in massive formations would be terribly vulnerable. That way of fighting, where nuclear weapons are in use, is a thing of the past.

An all-out non-nuclear war, on the other hand—that is, what we knew before as large-scale conventional war—is hard to see happening again.

Of course, a sudden Soviet ground attack from Eastern Europe could mix Soviet forces with the populations in the West and thereby prevent swift resort to nuclear weapons.

But even in this situation a massing of huge ground units would be impossible because of their nuclear vulnerability. So again, even this kind of struggle would break up into smaller unit actions.

In a guerilla war of the Vietnam type, we face something else entirely. Here we need a highly professional, highly motivated force of men trained in the technique of counterinsurgency. Vietnam has shown us that success in such wars may depend on whether our soldiers are linguists and civil affairs specialists, as well as warriors. Also, the complex weapons of modern war demand a higher level of technical and professional skill.

Of course, we will still need conventional forces large by standards of only a few decades ago to guard our vital interests around the world. But I don't believe we will need them in such quantity that we cannot meet our manpower needs through voluntary enlistments.

Conscription was an efficient mechanism for raising the massive land armies of past wars. Also, it is easier—and cheaper—simply to order men into uniform rather than recruiting them. But I believe our likely military needs in the future will place a special premium on the services of career soldiers.

How, then, do we recruit these servicemen? What incentives do we offer to attract an adequate number of volunteers?

One kind of inducement is better housing, and better living conditions generally. Both to recruit and to retain the highly skilled specialists the services need, military life has to be more competitive with the attractions of the civilian world.

The principal incentives are the most obvious: higher pay and increased benefits.

The military services are the only employers today who don't have to compete in the job market. Supplied by the draft with the manpower they want when they want it, they've been able to ignore the laws of supply and demand. But I say there's no reason why our military should be exempt from peacetime competition for manpower, any more than our local police and fire departments are exempt.

A private in the American army is paid less than $100 a month. This is a third of the minimum wage in the civilian economy. Now to this we should add food, uniforms and housing which are furnished free. Taken all together, a single young man can probably get by on this. But it's hardly competitive with what most people can earn in civilian life. Even with allowances, many married servicemen in enlisted ranks have actually been forced to depend on relief payments to support their families.

These pay scales point up another inequity of the draft system. Our servicemen are singled out for a huge hidden tax—the difference between their military pay and what they could otherwise earn. The draftee has been forced by his country not only to defend his neighbors but to subsidize them as well.

The total cost of the pay increases needed to recruit an all-volunteer army cannot be figured out to the dollar, but authoritative studies have suggested that it could be done for 5 to 7 billions of dollars more a year.

While this cost would indeed be heavy, it would be increasingly offset by reductions in the many costs which the heavy rate of turnover now causes. Ninety-three percent of the Army's draftees now leave the service as soon as their time is up—taking with them skills that it costs $6,000 per man to develop. The net additional annual cost of shifting to an all-volunteer armed force would be bound to be much less.

It will cost a great deal to move to a voluntary system, but unless that cost is proved to be prohibitive, it will be more than worth it.

The alternative is never-ending compulsion in a society consecrated to freedom. I think we can pay a great deal to avoid that.

In any case, in terms of morale, efficiency and effectiveness, a volunteer armed force would assuredly be a better armed force.

Today, 7 out of every 10 men in the Army have less than two years' military experience. As an Army chief of personnel put it: "As soon as we are able to operate as a unit, the trained men leave and we have to start all over again."

A volunteer force would have a smaller turnover; it would be leavened by a higher percentage of skilled, motivated men; fewer would be constantly in training; and fewer trained men would be tied down training others.

The result would be, on the average, more professional fighting men, and less invitation to unnecessary casualties in case of war.

The same higher pay scales needed to get more volunteers would also strengthen incentives for career service. I am sure the spirit and self-confidence of the men who wear the nation's uniform would be enhanced.

In proposing that we start toward ending the draft when the war is over, I would enter two cautions:

First, its structure needs to be kept on stand-by in case some all-out emergency requires its reactivation. But this can be done without leaving 20 million young Americans who will come of draft age during the next decade in constant un-certainty and apprehension.

The second caution I would enter is this: the draft can't be ended all at once. It will have to be phased out, so that at every step we can be certain of maintaining our defense strength.

But the important thing is to decide to begin, and at the very first opportunity to begin.

Now, some are against a volunteer armed force because of its cost, because they're used to the draft and hesitant to change. But three other arguments are often raised. While they sound plausible, I say they don't stand up under examination.

The first is that a volunteer army would be a black army, so it is a scheme to use Negroes to defend a white America. The second is that a volunteer army would actually be an army of hired mercenaries. The third is, a volunteer army would dangerously increase military influence in our society.

Now, let's take these arguments in order:

First, the "black army" one. I regard this as sheer fantasy. It supposes that raising military pay would in some way slow up or stop the flow of white volunteers, even as it stepped up the flow of black volunteers. Most of our volunteers now are white. Better pay and better conditions would obviously make military service more attractive to black and white alike.

Second, the "mercenary" argument. A mercenary is a soldier of fortune—one who fights for or against anyone for pay. What we're talking about now is American soldiers, serving under the American flag. We are talking about men who proudly wear our country's uniform in defense of its freedom. We're talking about the same kind of citizen armed force America has had ever since it began, excepting only the period when we have relied on the draft.

The third argument is the threat of universal military influence. This, if ever it did come, would come from the top officer ranks, not from the enlisted ranks that draftees now fill—and we already have a career officer corps. It is hard to see how replacing draftees with volunteers would make officers more influential.

Today all across our country we face a crisis of confidence. Nowhere is it more acute than among our young people. They recognize the draft as an infringement on their liberty—which it is. To them, it represents a government insensitive to their rights—a government callous to their status as free men. They ask for justice—and they deserve it.

So I say, it's time we looked to our consciences. Let's show our commitment to freedom by preparing to assure our young people theirs.

Source: Richard Nixon, "The All-Volunteer Armed Force," October 17, 1968, pp. 2–10, box 3, Martin Anderson Donated Collection, RMNL, https://www. nixonfoundation.org/wp-content/uploads/2012/01/Candidate-Nixon-Statement-on-an-All-Volunteer-Force.pdf (accessed August 25, 2021).

# DOCUMENT 6

## Melvin Laird, "The First Five Months: Problems and Progress," June 27, 1969

### People

How to attract and retain an adequate number of people with needed intelligence and skills is a first priority problem of the armed forces and always will be.

At present we require 1,050,000 accessions from civilian life in the course of a year to maintain the strength level of the regular and reserve forces. Approximately one-quarter of these are provided by the Selective Service system. One-half are volunteers who are motivated by the existence of the draft.

Our needs after Vietnam for personnel are not clear. If we assume that the size of the Armed Forces will level off at the pre-Vietnam level of 2,650,000, past experience leads us to believe that we would still need the draft to supply about 100,000 of the 750,000 new accessions that would be required annually.

The objective of the Nixon administration is to end reliance on the draft as a source of military manpower as soon as this step can be taken without endangering national security. Toward this end, the President has appointed a distinguished Commission on an All-Volunteer Armed Force, chaired by former Secretary of Defense Thomas Gates. This Commission will make its recommendations on the steps needed to abolish conscription and move toward a completely volunteer military force in November of this year.

At the time of the appointment of the Gates Commission, the Department of Defense had already begun a study of its own on this subject called Project Volunteer. The Department's study is headed by Roger Kelley, Assistant Secretary for Manpower and Reserve Affairs. In compliance with President Nixon's directive to the Department, Project Volunteer is prepared to provide staff assistance, information, and advice to the members of the Gates Commission.

Since at best some time will elapse before any transition from conscription to an all-volunteer force can be made, the Administration has proposed to Congress important changes in the Selective Service system in the interest of greater efficiency and equity. These changes, in summary, provide for reversing the order of call so that 19 year-olds rather than 26 year-olds will be the first to be inducted, determining the order of induction by lottery or random selection of birth dates, and limiting the period of maximum vulnerability to the draft for any individual to a period of one year [...] .

In order to attract and retain the kind of personnel the armed forces will need in the years ahead, reform of the system of military compensation is a matter of high priority. This becomes even more important if we are to seek to fill our personnel requirements completely from volunteers.

A pay reform proposal was put together which was a modification of the earlier comprehensive Hubbell Pay Plan. Our hopes of making such a system effective as of July 1, 1969, could not be realized. Consequently, we decided for the next fiscal year to stand pat with the 12.6 per cent [sic] increase in basic pay scheduled to go into effect on July 1 of this year under existing law.

We shall seek to make military pay reform effective as of July 1, 1970. Our existing proposal is now undergoing review by an outside organization and may be modified in the light of its recommendations or those which the Gates Commission will offer in November.

Source: Melvin Laird, "The First Five Months: Problems and Progress," Armed Forces Staff College, Norfolk, VA, June 27, 1969, pp. 7–10, box A76, folder Laird – First Five Months, 1969, Melvin R. Laird Papers, GRFL.

# DOCUMENT 7

## William Brehm, "Ongoing, Planned and Other Actions to Reduce Reliance on the Draft," July 12, 1969

DEPARTMENT OF THE ARMY
OFFICE OF THE ASSISTANT SECRETARY
WASHINGTON, D.C. 20310

MEMORANDUM FOR THE ASSISTANT SECRETARY OF DEFENSE (MANPOWER AND RESERVE AFFAIRS)

SUBJECT: Ongoing, Planned and Other Actions to Reduce Reliance on the Draft

At Inclosure [sic] 1 is the Army's detailed response to the Project Volunteer Committee request for action-oriented items.

The Army is working on both sides of this problem. That is, we are seeking to minimize active-duty requirements; and we are seeking ways to make active duty and reserve duty more attractive. The ongoing and planned actions reported are a part of our continuing effort to maximize volunteering and retention. These merely need additional emphasis or redirection of effort and can be accomplished within existing constraints. The other actions—outside existing resource constraints—are regarded as essential to the early attainment of an all-volunteer Army.

### Active-Duty Requirements

We are seeking to limit the Army's active-duty personnel requirements in two ways. First, we are holding the size of the division force equivalent (DFE) at 48,000 spaces, despite strong and understandable pressure for increases for aviation units, signal units, and forward air defense weapons. Second, we are reviewing the distribution of elements within the DFE in order to provide no more than the minimum essential active forces. The remaining force structure will be placed in the reserve components, thus saving both active manpower and costs.

## Attractiveness of Military Duty

The types of actions proposed for the long-term which are oriented toward the individual cover these areas:

1. Image
2. Professional development
3. Personal pride and satisfaction
4. Compensation.

The steps suggested for dealing with these issues may appear prosaic when stated briefly. It is the implementation, however, that must be dramatic and innovative. We intend that it shall be so, but we will need budgetary and legislative assistance.

The prerequisite to improvement in the enlistment and retention area is a sharp improvement in the image which the public has of the Armed Services. Service life, active and reserve, must not only be an accepted and honorable vocation, but a respected and attractive career. To this end, I am recommending a large increase in the Recruiting Command's advertising budget—now. We spend $8.5 billion annually on military pay and allowances, but only $3 million on recruiting advertising. I am proposing a better than tenfold increase in this advertising budget in order to let advertising do for the Army what it has done successfully for American business. A factual description of the positive benefits of Army careers must be conveyed to prospective recruits and their families.

Most of the items recommended for further consideration are what might be labeled product improvement as opposed to advertising. We cannot successfully advertise a product which retains some of the present deficiencies. Many of these deficiencies have become traditionalized and institutionalized as the result of long-term budgetary limitations. To change the "Beetle Bailey" image to a "Steve Canyon" image will require more than advertising. It may require eliminating the repetitive rounds of KP, trash collecting, and latrine scrubbing that intrude on the soldiers' military training and development. Young men are not going to be persuaded that we consider their time and talents valuable if we squander them on janitorial or custodial duties. A college student who was told that he would have to mop the hallways, scrub washrooms, police grounds, and work in the cafeteria for no additional compensation because alumni donations were falling off would soon matriculate at another school. This part of the current problem is amenable to monetary solution.

Additional money would also enable the Army to conduct more realistic, although more expensive, training for active and reserve units. This would include use of the most modern equipment and conduct of maneuvers and weapons firing which would increase effectiveness as well as morale and a sense of professionalism.

To further provide for increased emphasis on raising the professional quality of the Army, I propose a multi-faceted program designed to achieve individual improvement and increased self-esteem. Career patterns provide for advancement to top enlisted, warrant, or officer grades. A comprehensive three-level non-commissioned officer educational development program is pending implementation, however, much of the enlisted and warrant officer advancement is achieved without benefit of formal schooling or training at the supervisory level. Movement into warrant and commissioned status remains somewhat limited. Therefore, I would propose a close examination of the personnel areas in which additional enlisted and warrant officer supervisory training is required. At present, OCS provides the major avenue of movement from enlisted to officer status. More opportunities and incentives can be offered to increase the aspirations and possibilities of qualified individuals to move from enlisted to warrant or commissioned status through special education programs. One program of this type is included in the attached list of recommendations. Providing adequate funds and manpower spaces to satisfy existing civil schooling requirements would provide incentive for thousands of officers and enlisted men. The combination of increased pride in personal achievement and better opportunities for individual development should result in improved retention, motivation, quality and public image.

Qualitative and quantitative improvement in family housing and barracks has been a long-term goal. To provide the desired impact it could involve architectural design competition based on attractiveness as well as economy and should be publicized. The quality of these homes and barracks should be suitable for coverage in Sunday newspaper supplements and homemakers magazines. The extraordinary attention given to the "Habitat" apartment constructed for the Montreal Exposition is an example of how housing design can become a news feature.

With the reduction of extraneous non-military duties and with a more liberal attitude on allowing compensatory time off for extra duty hours, time may become available for the forms of vocational and educational activities which will further enhance the attractiveness of Service life.

These kinds of ideas together with the pay studies would give us the means to push out in four directions: image building, increasing personal and family satisfaction, improving professional career development, and improving pay and other emoluments which comprise the total compensation package.

William K. Brehm

1 Inclosure [sic]

as

## ONGOING, PLANNED AND OTHER ACTIONS
## TO REDUCE RELIANCE ON THE DRAFT

1.  The following actions ongoing or planned are designed to reduce reliance on the draft and can be accomplished within existing budgetary and legislative constraints.

a.    Recruiting.

    1.    Bring the U.S. Army Recruiting Command to authorized strength on a priority basis assigning the highest quality personnel available.

    2.    Evaluate the effect of the "Project 100,000 Program" on the quality composition of the Army and develop appropriate enlistment standards which will increase the eligible manpower pool.

    3.    Develop and undertake a program to counsel personnel prior to separation on the benefits and advantages of a career in the reserve components.

b.    Career Planning and Personnel Management.

    1.    Disseminate career guidance information to all potential reenlistees including a proposed DA Pamphlet on enlisted career planning.

    2.    Increase the number of authorized spaces to provide for career counselors down to battalion level and provide them adequate training for effective counseling.

    3.    Monitor and evaluate enlisted assignments based on the individual's MOS(s), job performance, and career needs through an automated process.

    4.    Continue efforts to centralize all enlisted promotions above grade E-4.

    5.    Reexamine all manning documents and designate spaces that are suitable for substitution with women (AR 1-45).

c.    Working Conditions and Morale.

    1.    Direct command attention toward more effective personnel utilization to insure that individuals are not required to be present for duty for an unreasonable number of hours during the work week.

    2.    Provide enlisted personnel the same freedom of movement during non-working hours presently enjoyed by officers.

    3.    Improve job satisfaction by directing command attention to the continuing problem of oversupervision of officers and non-commissioned officers.

    4.    Direct more effective use of NCO councils with attention to those areas which would provide immediate improvement of the conditions of enlisted service.

d.    Dependent Services.

    1.    Distribute a revised pamphlet to explain medical care services, facilities, civilian programs such as Civilian Health and Medical Program of the Uniformed Services (CHAMPUS) and rights of dependents to medical care.

    2.   Improve civilian appreciation of the Army, its problems, and its contribution to our national heritage through a series of exchange visits, briefings, orientations, and publications.

    3.   Encourage and provide for junior enlisted wives to take part in the activities of the military community.

    4.   Designate follow-on assignments for married service members ordered to unaccompanied overseas tours and enable eligible families to move to follow-on assignment in advance of service member when quarters are available.

    5.   Furnish to all married personnel who are eligible for dependent housing and are on orders for an unaccompanied tour, a current list of installations having on-post housing available for dependents, with instructions on how to obtain quarters.

2.   The following are other actions for consideration outside existing budgetary and legislative constraints to reduce reliance on the draft. Where available, annual cost estimates follow the action.

   a.   Pay and Allowances.

    1.   Increase entry pay to a level commensurate with the pay the soldier's civilian counterpart earns.

    2.   Establish an attractive and competitive career pay schedule, using the "Hubbell Pay Study" as a basis.

    3.   Change the amount of the family dislocation allowance to provide advance payment of one-half of one month's base pay, tax free, in lieu of one month's quarters allowance ($16.5 million additional annual cost for current force).

    4.   Increase the amount of family separation allowance to $2.50 a day ($81.9 million additional annual cost for current force).

    5.   Change maximum dependent travel pay from total of 18¢ a mile to 6¢ per mile per family member, regardless of age ($4.3 million additional annual cost for current force).

    6.   Provide a cost of living allowance for high cost CONUS areas.

   b.   Recruiting.

    1.   Authorize the U.S. Army Recruiting Command to expend funds required for the conduct of a massive advertising campaign to attract volunteers ($36,058,964).

    2.   Transfer control of the recruiting school to USAREC at a location deemed most advantageous and economical.

    3.   Offer the following types of enlistment options commensurate with the needs of the service.

> a.   In-service training for and assistance in obtaining a civilian job after discharge in exchange for a three-year enlistment (cost $1,000 per man).
>
> b.   Post-service, all expense paid technical/vocational schooling for a three-year enlistment.
>
> c.   Four-year all expense paid post-service college education for a four-year enlistment (cost $2,083 per man per year).
>
> d.   Guaranteed assignment to high skill jobs for which trained for the entire period of enlistment.
>
> e.   A limited number of assignments to the geographic area of the enlistee's choice for the entire period of a three-year enlistment.
>
> f.   Higher entry grades for civilian-acquired skills usable in the Army (cost reduced by elimination of AIT).

4.   Provide Army recruiters with inducements and benefits that will enable them to afford living on the civilian economy and motivate them to strive for outstanding performance.

c.   Women's Army Corps.

1.   Increase the strength of the Women's Army Corps (WAC) from 1,100 officers and 12,400 enlisted women to 2,000 officers and 22,400 enlisted women.

2.   Concurrent with 2c(1) above, construct additional facilities at the WAC Training Center and rehabilitate living space at 60 installations Army-wide ($8,200,000 = one-time cost).

d.   Morale.

1.   Increase Servicemen's Group Life Insurance (SGLI) from $10,000 to $20,000 ($122,052,000).

2.   Provide servicemen on unaccompanied tours in overseas areas, with R&R not chargeable as leave or chargeable leave in CONUS. Transportation at government expense to be furnished in both cases.

3.   Provide for non-emergency withdrawal of 10 percent soldier deposit in any overseas area (i.e., 5 percent interest rate applied to accounts drawn against in less than a twelve-month period).

4.   Provide free mail service to all servicemen overseas and those hospitalized in CONUS ($4.9 million additional annual cost for current force).

5.   Provide direct-hire civilian employees to perform KP details at Army service schools with eventual expansion to all non-combat areas ($77.4 million FY 70 and $134.7 million FY 71 for current force).

6.   Provide monetary compensation for all leave lost each year.

7.   Broaden opportunities for selected enlisted personnel to obtain in-Service college education leading to baccalaureate degree and commission.

e.   Housing.

1.   Increase the amount of leased civilian community housing in the vicinity of posts where inadequate on-post quarters exist until adequate on-post quarters are provided. Number of units required should be based on peacetime force levels ($175 per month per unit).

2.   Construct additional on-post quarters to meet quantitative and qualitative requirements ($1 billion one-time cost).

3.   Authorize increased weight allowance for household goods based on rank and number of dependents.

4.   Improve present barracks living conditions to provide a measure of privacy and attractiveness ($2,900 per unit plus 15 percent for support facilities).

5.   Establish a policy that senior NCO quarters and housing will be comparable to that of junior officers.

6.   Upon PCS reimburse military homeowner for closing cost or similar expenses incident to the purchase of a new residence or sale of old residence in CONUS, territories or possessions, if a loss is incurred.

7.   Guarantee resale by the government of service member's home, if homeowner is unable to sell.

f.   Reserve Components.

1.   Examine the feasibility of increasing reserve component benefits to authorize eligibility for educational benefits of the GI Bill.

2.   To reduce reserve reliance on the draft, support legislation of the following incentives or benefits.

a.   Authorize credit for reserve component retirement pay purposes, all inactive duty points earned for participation at training assemblies (HR 6008).

b.   Extend the Servicemen's Group Life Insurance to reservists for periods of active duty or active duty for training of 30 days or less (HR 6016).

c.   Extend the proficiency pay program to cover enlisted reserve component personnel (HR 6009).

d.   Authorize reserve component personnel medical care equivalent to that of active duty personnel for injuries, accidents, and disease incurred while participating in inactive duty training or active duty for 30 days or less ($353,000) (HR 3342).

e.   Authorize quarters allowance to U.S. Army Reserve and National Guard members (REP) on active duty for more than 30 days (HR 2722).

f.   Provide benefits to families of members of reserve components whose service exceeded 20 years but who died before retirement eligibility.

g.  Authorize retirement of reserve component personnel at age 50 rather than age 60.

g.  Medical Service.

1.  Support legislation establishing an Armed Forces Medical Academy ($56,300,000 for basic sciences only).
2.  Expand the current AMEDS procurement and training programs.
3.  Increase manpower authorization of Army medical/dental units to at least match current dependent requirements.
4.  Liberalize the granting of statements of non-availability of medical care when clinic loads warrant and/or civilian care for dependents is preferred.
5.  Adjust pay of medical officers to approximate the pay received by their civilian contemporaries.
6.  Support pending legislation that would provide medical and dental scholarships as an incentive for Army service.

Source: William Brehm, "Memorandum for the Assistant Secretary of Defense (Manpower and Reserve Affairs), Subject: Ongoing, Planned and Other Actions to Reduce Reliance on the Draft," July 12, 1969, pp. 1–4, enclosure pp. 1–6, box C1, folder All-Volunteer Documents 10–15, Melvin R. Laird Papers, GRFL.

# DOCUMENT 8

## Gates Commission, "Protecting the Free Society," February 20, 1970

Since the founding of the republic, a primary task of the government of the United States has been to provide for the common defense of a society established to secure the blessings of liberty and justice. Without endangering the nation's security, the means of defense should support the aims of the society.

The armed forces today play an honorable and important part in promoting the nation's security, as they have since our freedoms were won on the battlefield at Yorktown. A fundamental consideration that has guided this Commission is the need to maintain and improve the effectiveness, dignity, and status of the armed forces so they may continue to play their proper role.

The Commission has not attempted to judge the size of the armed forces the nation requires. Instead, it has accepted a range of estimates made for planning purposes which anticipate maintaining a total force in the future somewhere between 2,000,000 and 3,000,000 men.

We unanimously believe that the nation's interests will be better served by an all-volunteer force, supported by an effective standby draft, than by a mixed forces of volunteers and conscripts; that steps should be taken promptly to move in this direction; and that the first indispensable step is to remove the present inequity in the pay of men serving their first term in the armed forces.

The United States has relied throughout its history on a voluntary armed force except during major wars and since 1948. A return to an all-volunteer force will strengthen our freedoms, remove an inequity now imposed on the expression of the patriotism that has never been lacking among our youth, promote the efficiency of the armed forces, and enhance their dignity. It is the system for maintaining standing forces that minimizes government interference with the freedom of the individual to determine his own life in accord with his values.

The Commission bases its judgments on long-range considerations of what method of recruiting manpower will strengthen our society's foundations.

The Commission's members have reached agreement on their recommendations only as the result of prolonged study and searching debate, and in spite of initial division. We are, of course, fully aware of the current and frequently emotional public debate on national priorities, foreign policy, and the military, but are agreed that such issues stand apart from the question of when and how to end conscription.

To judge the feasibility of an all-volunteer force, it is important to grasp the dimensions of the recruitment problem in the next decade. If conscription is continued, a stable mid-range force of 2.5 million men (slightly smaller than pre-Vietnam) will require 440,000 new enlisted men per year. To maintain a fully voluntary stable force of the same effective strength, taking into account lower personnel turnover, we estimate that not more than 325,000 men will have to be enlisted annually. In recent years about 500,000 men a year have volunteered for military service. Although some of these volunteered only because of the threat of the draft, the best estimates are that at least half—250,000 men—are "true volunteers." Such men would have volunteered even if there had been no draft, and they did volunteer in spite of an entry pay that is roughly 60 percent of the amount that men of their age, education, and training could earn in civilian life.

The often ignored fact, therefore, is that our present armed forces are made up predominately of volunteers. All those men who have more than four years of service—38 percent of the total—are true volunteers; and so are at least a third of those with fewer than four years of service.

The return to voluntary means of raising and maintaining our armed forces should be seen in this perspective. With true volunteers now providing some 250,000 enlisted men annually, a fully volunteer force of 2.5 million men can be achieved by improving pay and conditions of service sufficiently to induce approximately 75,000 additional young men to enlist each year from the 1.5 million men who will annually turn 19 and who will also meet the physical, moral, and mental requirements. A voluntary force of 3.0 million men would require 400,000 enlistments each year, or 150,000 additional volunteers from the 1.5 million eligible 19-year-olds. Smaller forces would require fewer than 75,000 additional volunteers annually. Reasonable improvements in pay and benefits in the early years of service should increase the number of volunteers by these amounts.

In any event, such improvements are called for on the ground of equity alone. Because conscription has been used to provide raw recruits, the pay of men entering the services has been kept at a very low level. It has not risen nearly as rapidly as the pay of experienced military personnel, and it is now about 60 percent of comparable civilian pay. Similarly, the pay of first-term officers has not been kept in line with the pay of more experienced officers, or with comparable civilians.

Correcting this inequity for first-term enlisted men and first-term officers will add about $2.7 billion to the defense budget in fiscal 1971. Regardless of the fate of the draft, the Commission strongly recommends elimination of this discrimination against first-termers.

If the Commission's recommendations are put into effect for fiscal 1971, they will entail a budget increase of an estimated $3.3 billion for the following expenditures:

| | |
|---|---|
| Basic pay increase (Billions) | $2.68 |
| Proficiency pay | .21 |
| Reserve pay increase | .15 |
| Additional medical corps expense | .12 |
| Recruiting, ROTC, and miscellaneous | .08 |
| | $3.24 |

The additional proficiency pay is required to attract individuals in the first term with special skills and talents. The additional reserve pay extends the increase in pay provided for the active-duty forces to the reserves, and is called for as a step toward a voluntary reserve. The additional outlay for a voluntary medical corps is for increased pay to medical officers, for medical student fellowships, and, where possible, for contracting with civilian physicians to provide medical services now rendered by military physicians.

Because most of this budget increase takes the form of personal income, $540 million of it will be recovered by the Treasury in federal income tax collections. The net increase in the budget in fiscal 1971, after taking these tax collections into account, will be $2.7 billion.

The Commission recommends that these additional funds be provided effective July 1, 1970. We believe, on the basis of our study, that the increased pay and other recommended improvements in personnel management will provide enough additional volunteers during the transition to achieve an all-volunteer force by July 1, 1971.

When force levels are stabilized, the additional expenditures needed in the transition to a voluntary force will be partly offset by savings engendered through lower turnover and a reduction in the number of persons in training status.

Combining the expenditures to eliminate the present inequity for first-termers, and other steps necessary to move to an all-volunteer force with the savings that will accrue, the Commission estimates that the added budget required to maintain a fully voluntary force on a stable, continuing basis is:

$1.5 billion for a 2,000,000-man force
$2.1 billion for a 2,500,000-man force
$4.6 billion for a 3,000,000-man force

These are net amounts, reflecting the personal income tax collections that would be recovered.

Although the *budgetary expense* of a volunteer armed force will be higher than for the present mixed force of volunteers and conscripts, the *actual cost* will be lower. This seemingly paradoxical statement is true because many of the costs of manning our armed forces today are hidden and are not reflected in the budget. Men who are forced to serve in the military at artificially low pay are actually paying a form of tax which subsidizes those in society who do not serve. Furthermore, the output of the civilian economy is reduced because more men serve in the military than would be required for an all-volunteer force of the same strength. This cost does not show up in the budget. Neither does the loss in output resulting from the disruption in the lives of young men who do not serve. Neither do the costs borne by those men who do not serve, but who rearrange their lives in response to the possibility of being drafted. Taking these hidden and neglected costs into account, the actual cost to the nation of an all-volunteer force will be lower than the cost of the present force.

The Commission has attempted to allow for the uncertainties of the future. In the event of a national emergency requiring a rapid increase in the number of men under arms, the first recourse should be to ready reserves, including the National Guard. Like the active duty forces, these reserves can and should be recruited on a voluntary basis. Whatever advantages may be claimed for it, conscription cannot provide emergency forces: it takes many months of training for civilians to become soldiers. However, to provide for the possibility of an emergency requiring a major increase in forces over an extended period, we recommend that machinery be created for a standby draft, to take effect by act of Congress upon the re-commendation of the President.

The draft has been an accepted feature of American life for a generation, and its elimination will represent still another major change in a society much buffeted by change and alarmed by violent attacks on the established order. Yet the status quo can be changed constructively and the society improved peacefully, by responsible and responsive government. It is in this spirit that the Commission has deliberated and arrived at its recommendations. However necessary conscription may have been in World War II, it has revealed many disadvantages in the past generation. It has been a costly, inequitable, and divisive procedure for recruiting men for the armed forces. It has imposed heavy burdens on a small minority of young men while easing slightly the tax burden on the rest of us. It has introduced needless uncertainty into the lives of all our young men. It has burdened draft boards with painful decisions about who shall be compelled to serve and who shall be deferred. It has weakened the political fabric of our society and impaired the delicate web of shared values that alone enables a free society to exist.

These costs of conscription would have to be borne if they were a necessary price for defending our peace and security. They are intolerable when there is an alternative consistent with our basic national values.

The alternative is an all-volunteer force, and the Commission recommends these steps toward it:

1.   Raise the average level of basic pay for military personnel in the first two years of service from $180 a month to $315 a month, the increase to become effective on July 1, 1970. This involves an increase in total compensation

(including the value of food, lodging, clothing, and fringe benefits) from $301 a month to $437 a month. The basic pay of officers in the first two years should be raised from an average level of $428 a month to $578 a month, and their total compensation from $717 a month to $869 a month.

2. Make comprehensive improvements in conditions of military service and in recruiting as set forth elsewhere in the report.

3. Establish a standby draft system by June 30, 1971, to be activated by joint resolution of Congress upon request of the President.

Source: Gates Commission, *Report on an All-Volunteer Armed Force*, Part I, Chapter 1, pp. 5–10.

# DOCUMENT 9

## Gates Commission, "The Debate," February 20, 1970

"We have lived with the draft so long," President Nixon has pointed out, "that too many of us accept it as normal and necessary." Over the past generation, social, political, and economic arrangements have grown up around conscription that touch our lives in a great many ways. The elimination of the draft will inevitably disrupt these arrangements and may be disturbing to some. But beyond these narrow, often overlooked interests lie broader considerations which have prompted defenders of conscription to argue that an all-volunteer armed force will have a variety of undesirable political, social, and military effects.

In our meetings we have discussed the opposing arguments extensively. As our recommendations disclose, we have unanimously concluded that the arguments for an all-volunteer force are much the stronger. Yet, there can be no question of the sincerity and earnest conviction of those who hold the views we have rejected. In fairness to them, and to acquaint the nation with both sides of the issues, this chapter summarizes the main arguments raised against the volunteer force and offers answers to them. In succeeding chapters (noted in parentheses) these arguments are taken up in detail.

A general point should be made here. The elimination of conscription admittedly is a major social change, but it will not produce a major change in the personnel of our armed forces. The majority of men serving today are volunteers. And many who are now conscripted would volunteer once improvements were made in pay and other conditions of service. Therefore, the difference between an all-volunteer force and a mixed force of conscripts and volunteers is limited to that minority who would not serve unless conscripted and who would not volunteer in the absence of conscription. An all-volunteer force will attract men who are not now conscripted and who do not now volunteer but who will do so when military service imposes less of a financial penalty than it currently does.

Contrary to much dramatic argument, the reality is that an all-volunteer force will be manned largely by the same kind of individuals as today's armed forces. The men who serve will be quite similar in patriotism, political attitudes, effectiveness, and susceptibility to civilian control. The draft does not guarantee the quality of our armed forces, and neither will voluntarism. There are no simple solutions or shortcuts in dealing with the complex problems that must always concern us as a free people.

Arguments against an all-volunteer force fall into fairly distinct, though sometimes overlapping, categories, one of which is feasibility. Summarized below are some of the main objections under this heading.

*Objection 1:*   An all-volunteer force will be very costly—so costly the nation cannot afford it.

*Answer:*   The question of how much the armed forces cost is confused with the question of who bears those costs. It is true that the budget for a voluntary force will generally be higher than for an equally effective force of conscripts and volunteers; but the cost of the voluntary force will be less than the cost of the mixed force. This apparent paradox arises because some of the costs of a mixed force are hidden and never appear in the budget.

Under the present system, first-term servicemen must bear a disproportionately large share of the defense burden. Draftees and draft-induced volunteers are paid less than they would require to enlist without a draft. The loss they suffer is a tax-in-kind, which for budget purposes is never recorded as a receipt or an expenditure. We estimate that for draftees and draft-induced volunteers the total tax amounts to $2 billion per year; an average of $3,600 per man. If government accounts reflected as income this financial penalty imposed on first-term servicemen, it would become clear that a voluntary force costs less than a mixed force. One example of real cost savings that will accrue is the reduction in training costs as a result of the lower personnel turnover of a voluntary force.

Conscription also imposes social and human costs by distorting the personal life and career plans of the young and by forcing society to deal with such difficult problems as conscientious objection (chapter 3).

*Objection 2:*   The all-volunteer force will lack the flexibility to expand rapidly in times of sudden crises.

*Answer:*   Military preparedness depends on forces in being, not on the ability to draft untrained men. Reserve forces provide immediate support to active forces, while the draft provides only inexperienced civilians who must be organized, trained, and equipped before they can become effective soldiers and sailors—a process which takes many months. The Commission has recommended a standby draft which can be put into effect promptly if circumstances require mobilization of large numbers of men. History shows that Congress has quickly granted the authority to draft when needed (chapter 10).

Others contend that an all-volunteer force will have undesirable political and social effects. Some of these objections are given below.

*Objection 3:*   An all-volunteer force will undermine patriotism by weakening the
traditional belief that each citizen has a moral responsibility to serve his country.

*Answer:*   Compelling service through a draft undermines respect for government
by forcing an individual to serve when and in the manner the government
decides, regardless of his own values and talents. Clearly, not all persons are
equally suited to military service—some are simply not qualified. When not
all our citizens can serve, and only a small minority are needed, a voluntary
decision to serve is the best answer, morally and practically, to the question of
who should serve (chapters 3 and 12).

*Objection 4:*   The presence of draftees in a mixed force guards against the growth
of a separate military ethos, which could pose a threat to civilian authority,
our freedom, and our democratic institutions.

*Answer:*   Historically voluntary service and freedom have gone hand in hand. In the
United States and England, where voluntarism has been used most consistently,
there is also the strongest tradition of civilian control of the military. There are
responsibilities to be met in maintaining civilian control, but they must be exercised
from above rather than at the lowest level of the enlisted ranks. They reside in the
Halls of Congress, and in the White House as well as in the military hierarchy.

In either a mixed or volunteer force, the attitudes of the officer corps are the pre-
ponderant factor in the psychology of the military; and with or without the draft,
professional officers are recruited voluntarily from a variety of regional and socio-
economic backgrounds. It is hard to believe that substituting a true volunteer for a
draftee or a draft-induced volunteer in one of every six positions will so alter the military
as to threaten the tradition of civilian control, which is embodied in the Constitution
and deeply felt by the public. It is even less credible when one considers that this
substitution will occur at the lowest level of the military ladder, among first-term enlisted men and officers, and that turnover of these first-term personnel in an all-
volunteer force will be approximately three-fourths of that in a comparable mixed force.

The truth is, we already have a large professional armed force amounting to
over 2 million men. The existing loyalties and political influence of that force
cannot be materially changed by eliminating conscription in the lowest ranks
(chapter 12).

*Objection 5:*   The higher pay required for a voluntary force will be especially
appealing to blacks, who have relatively poorer civilian opportunities. This,
combined with higher re-enlistment rates for blacks, will mean that a
disproportionate number of blacks will be in military service. White enlistments
and re-enlistments might decline, thus leading to an all-black enlisted force.
Racial tensions would grow because of white apprehension at this development
and black resentment at bearing an undue share of the burden of defense. At the
same time, some of the most qualified young blacks would be in the
military—not in the community where their talents are needed.

*Answer:*    The frequently heard claim that a volunteer force will be all black or all this or all that simply has no basis in fact. Our research indicates that the composition of the armed forces will not be fundamentally changed by ending conscription. Negroes presently make up 10.5 percent of the enlisted forces, slightly less than the proportion of blacks in the nation. Our best projections for the future are that blacks will be about 14 percent of the enlisted men in a conscripted force totaling 2.5 million officers and men, and 15 percent in an all-volunteer force of equal capability. For the Army, we estimate that the proportion of blacks will be 17 percent for the mixed force and 19 percent for the voluntary force as compared to 12.8 percent in the Army today. To be sure, these are estimates, but even extreme assumptions would not change the figures drastically.

If higher pay does make opportunities in an all-volunteer force more attractive to some particular group than those in civilian life, then the appropriate course is to correct the discriminations in civilian life—*not* to introduce additional discriminations against such a group.

The argument that blacks would bear an unfair share of the burden of an all-volunteer force confounds service by free choice with compulsory service. With conscription, some blacks are compelled to serve at earnings below what they would earn in the civilian economy. Blacks who join a voluntary force presumably have decided for themselves that military service is preferable to the other alternatives available to them. They regard military service as a more rewarding opportunity, not as a burden. Denial of this opportunity would reflect either bias or a paternalistic belief that blacks are not capable of making the "right" decisions concerning their lives (chapter 12).

*Objection 6:*    Those joining an all-volunteer force will be men from the lowest economic classes, motivated primarily by monetary rewards rather than patriotism. An all-volunteer force will be manned, in effect, by mercenaries.

*Answer:*    Again, our research indicates that an all-volunteer force will not differ significantly from the current force of conscripts and volunteers. Maintenance of current mental, physical, and moral standards for enlistment will ensure that a better paid, volunteer force will not recruit an undue proportion of youths from disadvantaged socioeconomic backgrounds. A disproportionate fraction of the 30 percent presently unable to meet these standards come from such backgrounds, and these men would also be ineligible for service in an all-volunteer force. Increasing military pay in the first term of service will increase the attractiveness of military service more to those who have higher civilian earnings potential than to those who have lower civilian potential. Military pay is already relatively attractive to those who have very poor civilian alternatives. If eligible, such individuals are now free to enlist and, moreover, are free to remain beyond their first term of service when military pay is even more attractive.

Finally, how will "mercenaries" suddenly emerge in the armed forces as a result of the better pay and other conditions of service? The term "mercenary" applies to men who enlist for pay alone, usually in the service of a foreign power, and precludes all other motives for serving. Those who volunteer to serve in the armed forces do so for a variety of reasons, including a sense of duty. Eliminating the financial penalty first-term servicemen presently suffer, and improving other conditions of service, will not suddenly change the motives and basic attitudes of new recruits. Also, can we regard as mercenaries the career commissioned and noncommissioned officers now serving beyond their first term? (chapter 12).

*Objection 7:*   An all-volunteer force would stimulate foreign military adventures, foster an irresponsible foreign policy, and lessen civilian concern about the use of military forces.

*Answer:*   Decisions by a government to use force or to threaten the use of force during crises are extremely difficult. The high cost of military resources, the moral burden of risking human lives, political costs at home and overseas, and the overshadowing risk of nuclear confrontation—these and other factors enter into such decisions. It is absurd to argue that issues of such importance would be ignored and the decision for war made on the basis of whether our forces were entirely voluntary or mixed.

To the extent that there is pressure to seek military solutions to foreign policy problems, such pressure already exists and will not be affected by ending conscription. The volunteer force will have the same professional leadership as the present mixed force. Changes in the lower ranks will not alter the character of this leadership or the degree of civilian control.

A decision to use the all-volunteer force will be made according to the same criteria as the decision to use a mixed force of conscripts and volunteers because the size and readiness of the two forces will be quite similar. These military factors are key determinants in any decision to commit forces. Beyond initial commitment, the policy choice between expanding our forces by conscription or by voluntary enlistment is the same for both the all-volunteer force and a mixed force of conscripts and volunteers. The important difference between the two forces lies in the necessity for political debate before returning to conscription. With the all-volunteer force, the President can seek authorization to activate the standby draft, but Congress must give its consent. With the mixed system, draft calls can be increased by the President. The difference between the two alternatives is crucial. The former will generate public discussion of the use of the draft to fight a war; the latter can be done without such public discussion. If the need for conscription is not clear, such discussion will clarify the issue, and the draft will be used only if public support is widespread (chapter 12).

Other critics of an all-volunteer force argue that it will gradually erode the military's effectiveness. Some of their main concerns are taken up below.

*Objection 8:*   A voluntary force will be less effective because not enough highly qualified youths will be likely to enlist and pursue military careers. As the quality of servicemen declines, the prestige and dignity of the services will also decline and further intensify recruiting problems.

*Answer:*   The Commission has been impressed by the number and quality of the individuals who, despite conscription, now choose a career in the military. The fact that we must resort in part to coercion to man the armed services must be a serious deterrent to potential volunteers. A force made up of men freely choosing to serve should enhance the dignity and prestige of the military. Every man in uniform will be serving as a matter of choice rather than coercion.

The Commission recognizes the importance of recruiting and retaining qualified individuals. It has recommended improved basic compensation and conditions of service, proficiency pay, and accelerated promotions for the highly skilled to make military career opportunities more attractive. These improvements, combined with an intensive recruiting effort, should enable the military not only to maintain a high quality force but also to have one that is more experienced, better motivated, and has higher morale (chapters 4, 5, 7, and 12).

*Objection 9:*   The defense budget will not be increased to provide for an all-volunteer force, and the Department of Defense will have to cut back expenditures in other areas. Even if additional funds are provided initially, competing demands will, over the long term, force the Department of Defense to absorb the added budgetary expense of an all-volunteer force. The result could be a potentially serious deterioration of the nation's overall military posture.

*Answer:*   Ultimately, the size of the military budget and the strength of our armed forces depend upon public attitudes toward national defense. Since World War II, our peacetime armed forces have been consistently supported at high levels. The public has supported large forces because it has felt them essential to national security. The change from a mixed force of volunteers and conscripts to an all-volunteer force cannot significantly change that feeling.

The contention that an all-volunteer force is undesirable because it would result in smaller defense forces raises a serious issue regarding the conduct of government in a democracy. Conscription obscures a part of the cost of providing manpower for defense. When that cost is made explicit, taxpayers may decide they prefer a smaller defense force. If so, the issue has been resolved openly, in accord with the Constitution, and in the best tradition of the democratic process. Those who then argue that too little is being devoted to national defense are saying that they are unwilling to trust the open democratic process; that, if necessary, a hidden tax should be imposed to support the forces they believe are necessary (chapters 3 and 12).

Source: Gates Commission, *Report on an All-Volunteer Armed Force*, Part I, Chapter 2, pp. 11–20.

# DOCUMENT 10

## Gates Commission, "Conscription Is a Tax," February 20, 1970

Any government has essentially two ways of accomplishing an objective whether it be building an interstate highway system or raising an army. It can expropriate the required tools and compel construction men and others to work until the job is finished or it can purchase the goods and manpower necessary to complete the job. Under the first alternative, only the persons who own the property seized or who render compulsory services are required to bear the expense of building the highway or housing project. They pay a tax to finance the project, albeit a tax-in-kind. Under the second alternative, the cost of the necessary goods and services is borne by the general public through taxes raised to finance the project.

Conscription is like the first alternative—a tax-in-kind. A mixed force of volunteers and conscripts contains first-term servicemen of three types—(1) draftees, (2) draft-induced volunteers, and (3) true volunteers. Draftees and draft-induced volunteers in such a force are coerced into serving at levels of compensation below what would be required to induce them to volunteer. They are, in short, underpaid. This underpayment is a form of taxation. Over 200 years ago, Benjamin Franklin, in commenting on a judicial opinion concerning the legality of impressment of American merchant seamen, recognized the heart of the issue, and even estimated the hidden tax. He wrote:

> "But if, as I suppose is often the case, the sailor who is pressed and obliged to serve for the defence of this trade at the rate of 25s. a month, could have £3.15s, in the merchant's service, you take from him 50s. a month; and if you have 100,000 in your service, you rob that honest part of society and their poor families of £250,000. per month, or three millions a year, and at the same time oblige them to hazard their lives in fighting for the defence of your trade; to the defence of which all ought indeed to contribute, (and sailors among the rest) in proportion to their profits by it; but this three

millions is more than their share, if they did not pay with their persons; and when you force that, methinks you should excuse the other.

But it may be said, to give the king's seamen merchant's wages would cost the nation too much, and call for more taxes. The question then will amount to this; whether it be just in a community, that the richer part should compel the poorer to fight for them and their properties for such wages as they think tit to allow, and punish them if they refuse? Our author tells us it is *legal*. I have not law enough to dispute his authority, but I cannot persuade myself it is *equitable*."

The levy of taxes-in-kind is not a modern innovation. Such taxes have existed throughout history. The impressment to which Benjamin Franklin objected is an example. Also, it was common practice in the Middle Ages to require specific service of citizens in farming, construction, defense, and other activities. Traditionally, however, in the United States, taxes-in-kind have been rejected for three reasons. First, they deprive individuals of their freedom to pursue their careers where and how they choose—in essence their right to liberty and the pursuit of happiness. Second, they are often accompanied by serious inequities; i.e., a few people are forced to bear the burden of accomplishing a task for the general good of the government and its citizens. Third, they tend to conceal taxes and government expenditures so that both the general public and public officials are misinformed as to the costs of government services.

Under conscription, each inductee and reluctant volunteer is compelled to render services to the government. He is required to pay a tax—a tax paid (and collected) in kind rather than cash—but the form of the payment does not alter the substance of the relationship. The amount of the tax is the difference between the pay that the inductee or reluctant volunteer actually receives as a first-term serviceman and the pay that would be required to induce him to enlist. Even true volunteers who serve in a mixed force are paid less than they would receive in a volunteer force. In that sense, they too are taxed by conscription.

Prevailing government accounting practices do not recognize taxes paid in kind. Therefore, the tax on first-term servicemen never gets recorded in the budget either as revenue or as expenditure. In an all-volunteer force, the additional military compensation will be paid in cash or other benefits, and the taxes to make those payments will be collected in cash. Recorded budget expenditures will have to be increased to reflect these payments. This is the source of the budget "increase" we have estimated for an all-volunteer force. If current government accounting practices fully reflected revenues and expenditures, whether in money or in kind, there would be *not* a budget increase, but a budget decrease.

The real significance of the larger recorded budget for an all-volunteer force is the adjustment of the burden of defense costs. What appears on the surface to be an increase in expenditures is actually a shift in the tax burden from first-term servicemen to taxpayers at large. If government accounts reflected taxes-in-kind, tax revenues from first-term servicemen would go down with the inauguration of an all-volunteer armed force, and (assuming a balanced budget) tax revenues from the general public would go up.

This shift in tax burden lies at the heart of resistance on "cost" grounds to an all-volunteer armed force. Indeed, this shift in tax burden explains how conscription gets enacted in the first place. In a political democracy conscription offers the general public an opportunity to impose a disproportionate share of defense costs on a minority of the population.

We have made estimates of the amount of the tax-in-kind imposed on draftees and draft-induced enlistees for the period immediately prior to Vietnam, adjusted to reflect changes in civilian and military compensation through 1969. The tax can be separated into two components: first, the financial loss suffered by draftees and draft-induced enlistees because their total military compensation (including veterans benefits) falls short of the income they would have earned in civilian life; and second, the additional burden measured by the excess of military over civilian compensation that would be required to induce these same individuals to become true volunteers. We estimate that the financial loss due to the first of these, the difference between military compensation and potential civilian earnings, was $1.5 billion for draftees or draft-induced volunteers in the pre-Vietnam force. To induce these same individuals to become true volunteers we estimate would have required an additional $500 million. Thus the total implicit tax on draftees and draft-induced volunteers was $2.0 billion.

This implies an average tax rate of 48 percent of the income that draftees and draft-induced enlistees would have earned in civilian life. Taking into account the personal income tax they paid, their total tax rate was 51 percent. In 1967, the average personal income tax paid by all persons whose gross earnings were equal to the amount that would have been earned by draftees and draft-induced enlistees as civilians, was less than 10 percent of that gross income. Since draftees and draft-induced enlistees have fewer than the average number of dependents, it is estimated that they would have paid perhaps as much as 15 percent of their gross income in personal income tax. Hence, draftees and draft-induced enlistees are bearing a tax burden over three times that of comparable civilians.

This concept of the tax does not include the income loss suffered by true volunteers whose military compensation is held below the level which would be required to maintain an all-volunteer force, nor does it include the amount by which all-volunteer pay rates would exceed the pay levels at which some of the current draftees and draft-induced enlistees would enter on a voluntary basis. The sum of these two amounts has been estimated at $1.25 billion annually, again for the period immediately prior to Vietnam.

As is pointed out in detail later in this chapter, the concept of the implicit tax considered above does not fully encompass the costs of conscription. Prospective inductees also incur costs in their efforts to escape conscription—costs which manifest themselves in a variety of ways such as additional college attendance, movement into occupations which carry deferments, emigration, etc. Indirect evidence suggests that these costs may be 1.5 times the implicit tax, or about $3.0 billion. They can be viewed as the cost of collecting the implicit tax. Thus for each $1.00 of tax-in-kind collected, an average of $2.50 is foregone by the public. Quite apart from considerations of equity and freedom, this feature of conscription is enough to call it into question.

The fact that conscription imposes a tax is not in itself immoral and undesirable. Taxes are required to enable government to exist. What is of questionable morality is the discriminatory form that this implicit tax takes; and even more, the abridgement of individual freedom that is involved in collecting it.

The tax is discriminatory because the first-term servicemen who pay it constitute a small proportion of the total population. During the next decade the number of males reaching age 19 each year will average 2.2 million. To maintain a stable mixed force of 2.5 million men at present relative military/civilian pay levels, draft calls will average about 100,000 per year. We estimate that draft-induced enlistments might be 75,000 per year. Therefore the draftees and draft-induced enlistees paying the tax-in-kind will represent only 8 percent of the male population reaching age 19 each year.

The extent of the discrimination resulting from conscription depends on the proportion of the population forced to serve, and on the level of compensation provided to those who serve. When a large fraction of the population is conscripted as it was, for example, in World War II, the tax is levied on a larger fraction of the population. Even then, however, the discrimination is by no means eliminated. Not everyone eligible to serve does so. Moreover, such wars do not occur every generation, hence some generations never pay though they benefit from the defense provided by others. Even in World War II, the 16.4 million men who served in the armed forces represented only 12 percent of the total population, 17 percent of the adult population, and 56 percent of the adult male population between 18 and 45.

Defenders of conscription often argue that every young person has the duty to serve his country. The above discussion makes it clear that the real question is not whether young people have such a duty, but whether that duty does not extend to the entire populace. Is it right and proper that a large tax be confined to a small fraction of our young able-bodied males in order to relieve taxpayers in general from having to pay higher taxes?

In addition to being discriminatory, conscription as a tax is also generally regressive, falling on individuals whose income is low. The amount of benefits in the form of defense that individuals receive as a consequence of the tax is not related to the amount of tax they pay. Finally, and most importantly, the tax requires payment in kind, rather than money, and the payment in kind takes the form of involuntary service.

It is unlikely that any Congressman would ever propose enactment of a general tax of the kind now imposed by the draft. If one ever were proposed, it would have little chance of being approved by Congress. If approved by Congress, it is hard to imagine that it would be held constitutional by the courts. This is a hidden tax which persists only because it is obscure. No tax is perfect, of course, but it is hard to imagine a means of imposing the cost of defense, or any other government activity for that matter, more in conflict with accepted standards of justice, equality and freedom in the United States.

## The Cost of an All-Volunteer Force

The larger budget required to sustain an all-volunteer armed force is frequently referred to as the "cost" of such a force. We have deliberately refrained from using that language. We have done so in order to stress the difference between "costs" on the one hand and "budget expenditures" on the other. Budget expenditures need not correctly reflect costs. Indeed, as we have indicated above, government accounting practices do not recognize the expenditure in kind implicit in conscription. To that extent the cost of a mixed voluntary/conscript force is consistently understated in the budget. But the cost of such a force is also understated in other ways.

When the hidden costs of conscription are fully recognized, the cost of an all-volunteer armed force is unquestionably less than the cost of a force of equal size and quality manned wholly or partly through conscription. The all-volunteer costs are lower for four reasons.

1.   Conscription leads to low re-enlistment rates among first-term servicemen, thereby increasing turnover rates. Most inductees and draft-induced volunteers are not seriously interested in careers in the military. First-term re-enlistment rates for inductees pre-Vietnam were about one-fourth as high as for enlistees. In an all-volunteer force, first-term re-enlistment rates will be higher than those currently experienced because those who enlist will be more likely to choose the military as a career. Moreover, the term of service for inductees is only two years while regular army enlistments are three years and Air Force and Navy enlistments are four years. With an all-volunteer force these longer terms of enlistment will also reduce turnover and the need for accessions.

Both factors will generate real cost savings. For a mixed voluntary/conscript force of 2.5 million men we estimate that annual first-term accessions in FY 1977 to 1979 would have to be 452,000. For an all-volunteer force with equal effectiveness, accessions would be only 342,000, or 110,000 less. Lower accessions will mean a smaller training establishment; that is, fewer trainers, trainees and support personnel and less training equipment and facilities. We estimate this will reduce the cost of a stable 2.5 million man peacetime force by $675 million per year.

In addition to the savings in training costs, there will also be savings in the number of personnel who are in a non-effective status because of transfers generated by high personnel turnover. An all-volunteer force will have fewer separations, hence fewer changes of status to accommodate separations. This also will result in cost savings. The number of servicemen in ineffective status will decline as will transportation and administrative costs. We estimate that these savings will be $68 million per year for a stable peacetime force of 2.5 million men.

In our study we have recognized these particular cost reductions by appropriately reducing the required size of the forces. Thus, a mixed voluntary/conscript force of 2.5 million men is equated to an all-volunteer force of 2.44 million. The latter represents the same effective force as the former taking account of the savings in training and transients which we estimate will accrue.

2. Conscription induces the military services to use manpower inefficiently. They make manpower decisions on the basis of the costs as they perceive them, namely, those that are reflected in their budget. Because budget expenses significantly understate the cost of first-term servicemen, the services are led to use more of them than they otherwise would. This is not because they are profligate or inept. By minimizing the costs as they see them of meeting specific security requirements, they are behaving as the nation would want them to behave. The problem arises because conscription greatly understates these costs.

When military compensation is raised to a level consistent with an all-volunteer armed force, the services will find it desirable to economize on manpower. In particular, they will discover ways to substitute non-human resources for manpower in a wide variety of activities. They will find it desirable to mechanize tasks now performed manually, and to emphasize, even more than at present, durability, reliability and ease of maintenance in the design of equipment and vehicles and in the construction of facilities. It would be a prodigious research effort to examine each activity for potential savings from such substitutions. Moreover, as a practical matter, there will be a long period of transition before the process of effecting such substitutions is completed. For these reasons we have not attempted to estimate the total savings that could result from labor-saving substitutions if the forces were all-volunteer.

We have, however, examined one area of potential substitutions; namely, that of using civilians instead of military personnel in particular positions. Conscription leads to the assignment of servicemen to some billets which could be filled by civilians at lower costs. If a civilian is hired, the Defense Department must pay the full cost thereof, but if a first-term serviceman is used the price is only his military compensation. An extensive study was conducted of specific billets where potential savings from such substitutions exist. These savings accrue because military training costs are reduced or because a civilian can be hired at a salary below the real cost of a serviceman performing the same task, that is, below the salary required to fill the position with a volunteer. We estimate that for a force of 2.5 million men, 117,000 civilians could be substituted for servicemen at a savings of perhaps $100 million per year.

3. Conscription, whether by lottery or by Selective Service, is relatively insensitive to the alternative value of the draftee in the civilian economy and to his tastes for military employment. Thus, suppose a draftee or draft-induced volunteer is compelled to enter the service who would do so voluntarily only if he were offered $8,000 per year. If there exists a true volunteer who would be equally productive in the military, prepared to enlist for $6,000 per year, the difference of $2,000 is an additional real cost imposed by the draft. The $2,000 can reflect either a difference in the productivity of the two persons in the civilian economy, or differences in taste for military life. Whichever it is, the loss is a real cost (and a waste) in precisely the same sense as is any other cost.

4. Finally, there are many subtle costs imposed by conscription that are no less real for their subtlety. Their effects ramify throughout society, impinging on a variety of individual and institutional decisions.

The costs imposed on potential draftees are perhaps the most obvious. The draft erodes ideals of patriotism and service by alienating many of the young who bear the burden. American youths are raised in an atmosphere where freedom and justice are held dear. It is difficult for them to cope with a situation which falls far short of these ideals just as they enter adulthood. The draft undermines identification with society just at the age when young men begin to assume social responsibilities. It thwarts the natural desire of youths to commit themselves to society.

Many of the implicit costs of the draft arise out of the system of deferments and exemptions currently in effect, and out of the qualification requirements for military service. Young men distort their career and personal plans to take advantage of opportunities to postpone or avoid being drafted. They enter college when they otherwise would not. They stay in school longer than they otherwise would. They accept employment in positions they otherwise would not take. They marry and have families before they otherwise would. There is no doubt that the costs of these distorted choices are real and often cruelly high. Popular support for making 19 the year of primary draft eligibility stems largely from the desire to reduce uncertainty and improve opportunity for personal planning. "Channeling" young men into colleges, occupations, marriage or fatherhood is not in their best interests nor those of society as a whole.

The procedures of the selective service system also impose hidden costs. In many ways the young registrant is denied due process of law. He is confronted with an intricate legal maze and denied the right of counsel and judicial review during its normal operation. To get his case before the courts, the potential draftee must risk jail sentences of up to five years. The operation of the draft abridges constitutional rights in many other ways. For example, a registrant must get permission to travel outside the country. In addition to the loss of rights, there is the problem of determining who is entitled to exemption as a conscientious objector. These, decisions are inherently difficult to make, and are harmful both to the group deciding and the persons requesting conscientious objector status.

The process weakens the political fabric of our society and threatens the delicate web of shared values that alone enables a free society to exist. These problems are completely avoided by an all-volunteer force.

Each problem faced by the individual registrant has a counterpart in the institutions with which he must deal. In addition to draft-induced volunteers for the military, selective service results in draft-induced college students, draft-induced ministerial students, draft-induced husbands and fathers, and draft-induced employees in exempt occupations.

The draft creates unnecessary problems for the military. Selection by lottery compels some to serve who have neither a talent nor a taste for military life, resulting in misfits and maladjustments to military service. Draftees who cannot adjust must nevertheless serve out a two-year tour. These men present morale and disciplinary problems which otherwise would not arise. Some spend much of their military service in confinement, because it is so difficult for them to adjust to military service. Dissent within the military presents particularly ticklish problems for the armed forces of a free nation. The problems raised by the forced military service of those who are unwilling or unable to adjust to military life will be largely overcome by voluntary recruiting.

Because of the influence of the draft, our schools and colleges must choose among more applicants than would normally apply. Inevitably they admit some young men more interested in exemptions than education. The presence of these individuals adds to the forces of disruption on the campus, imposing costs on all members of a university community.

Employers, too, must sort out true volunteers from draft-induced applicants for jobs which provide exemptions. For example, when school teachers are deferred, some young men will become teachers for a short time, even though they would rather follow another profession. They will stay in teaching only as long as they require an occupational deferment. This results in higher turnover and less experienced and less dedicated teachers for the young of the country.

It is difficult to add up these costs and measure their overall impact on society. Yet it is easy to cite examples of serious problems created by the draft, which voluntary recruiting would eliminate.

Source: Gates Commission, *Report on an All-Volunteer Armed Force*, Part II, Chapter 3, pp. 23–33.

# DOCUMENT 11

## Melvin Laird, "Future of the Draft," March 11, 1970

THE SECRETARY OF DEFENSE
WASHINGTON, D. C. 20301

*11 MAR 1970*

MEMORANDUM FOR THE PRESIDENT
SUBJECT: Future of the Draft

This memorandum presents DoD comments and recommendations on matters concerning the future of the draft, including the Report of the President's Commission on an All-Volunteer Armed Force.

The Department of Defense endorses the basic conclusion of the Report of the President's Commission on an All-Volunteer Armed Force that the draft should be phased out. This should occur when assured of the capability to attract and retain an Armed Force of the required size and quality through voluntary means.

It is our view that as we proceed toward this goal, the main emphasis should be on reducing draft calls to zero rather than achieving the All-Volunteer Force, even though the objective of each is identical. There are many Americans, including some in Congress, who reject the idea of an All-Volunteer Armed Force but support reduced reliance on the draft. It will be easier to reach your objective by focusing public attention on eliminating the draft rather than stirring those who object to the concept of an All-Volunteer Force.

My recommendations on draft reform, which we previously discussed, went to the National Security Council on January 10, 1970. For the purposes of this memorandum, it is sufficient to recommend the following actions on draft reform to be taken coincident with your forthcoming message to Congress:

1. You should proceed with an Executive Order that would phase out occupational and paternity deferments, and with proposed legislation that would phase out undergraduate student deferments.
2. You should advocate legislation to place the draft on a national call in order of sequence numbers. A method which uses sequence numbers for calls of pre-induction examinations was introduced by the Selective Service System just a week ago, and it shows early promise of accomplishing a result which is more consistent with the draft lottery. Even so, a change in the law is the only way of assuring that local Draft Boards will use sequence numbers uniformly.
3. You should request a two-year extension of the Induction Authority beyond June 30, 1971, with the provision that you will end the draft by proclamation if it becomes clear during the two-year period that the draft can be shifted to Standby Status without jeopardizing national security. An alternative would be to request an extension with a ceiling on the number that could be inducted in each of the extension years. The final result from Congress might be a one-year extension, or a ceiling, but I believe the initial request should be for two years without a ceiling.

Department of Defense studies confirm that, as currently-planned force level reductions occur, it will become increasingly feasible and less expensive to meet military manpower needs without reliance on the draft. Even if current relationships between military and civilian pay were to be maintained (and assuming that Vietnamization and other factors proceed favorably), it is reasonable to estimate that monthly draft calls will fall to the level of 5000–6000 by the beginning of FY 1973. With special pay increases and other actions to improve upon the attractiveness and satisfactions of military service, it may be possible to further reduce these draft call levels.

In a memorandum I sent to you on December 18, 1969, and in my statement before the Joint Session of the Senate Armed Services and Appropriations Committees regarding the FY 1971 Defense Program and Budget, I recommended a 20% pay increase to be effective early in 1971 for enlisted personnel with less than two years of service. This was to be in addition to the civilian-military general increase. Provision has been made in the FY 1971 Budget for both of these increases effective January 1, 1971.

We would like to be able to advance the effective date of this special increase to July 1, 1970, and to change the increase amount from 20% to 25%. To do so would demonstrate to the nation and to Congress the high priority you assign to getting on with eliminating the draft, and relieving the draftee and enlistee of a portion of the tax burden he carries in the form of inadequately low pay. Further, it would accelerate the timetable for reducing draft calls to zero, and thus increase the possibility that this objective might be achieved by the end of FY 1972.

The problem, however, is one of cost. The earlier effective date and the higher increase would involve an additional budget cost of $375 million over the $250 million already earmarked for FY 1971. Also, this action would invite nearly-certain action by Congress to make the civilian-military general increase effective July 1, 1970 instead of January 1, 1971, with a further additional cost to the Department of Defense of $800 million. It is simply not possible for this Department to absorb additional costs by cuts elsewhere in its FY 1971 budget. Reluctantly, therefore, we must decline to recommend either the earlier effective date or the higher amount. This leaves us with the civilian-military general increase and the 20% pay increase for enlisted personnel with less than two years of service, both to be effective January 1, 1971.

In the course of considering the special 20% increase for enlisted personnel with less than two years of service, consideration was given to skewing the pay line by assigning the recruit a difference percent than the second year man. The rationale of the President's Commission would assign the higher percent to the recruit, on the grounds that his pay is lowest compared with his civilian counterpart. Others argue, however, for giving the lower percent of increase to the recruit and holding back the higher amount, possibly to be paid as a lump sum bonus when he completes an honorable enlistment. While its power to attract new recruits may be questioned, this latter approach could encourage thrift when most military recruits, even though low paid, are able to assign a portion of their disposable income to savings. Further, by keeping entry pay at a low level, it would at least reduce the initial tax burden that would occur in the event of later mobilization.

Notwithstanding these considerations, we believe the 20% increase is the minimum that should be given to any enlisted personnel with less than two years of service. Equity demands no less, and a lower percent of increase would provide no basis for measuring the impact of a pay increase upon voluntary enlistments.

Three comments on the Report of the President's Commission are appropriate for this memorandum. The first is that the Department of Defense has considerably less confidence than is reflected in the President's Commission Report that draft calls could be reduced to zero by July 1, 1971. This is because of factors of uncertainty beyond our current reach or control and they include the following:

- The changing attitude of young people toward military service, and its effect upon enlistments and reenlistments. Many of the manpower supply estimates for an All-Volunteer Force rely on pre-Vietnam data, and upon after-the-fact surveys of what induced "voluntary" enlistments. It is not known how youngsters of high school age have been affected by widespread anti-war propaganda, nor is it known how those already engaged in ground combat in Vietnam will respond to reenlistment.
- The uncertainty of the effect of increased pay. It is assumed that more pay will buy additional enlistments, but there simply is no way to know at this time the extent of its drawing power.
- The availability of jobs in the labor market. Our ability to attract young men to the Armed Forces will be influenced by the range of occupations and number of jobs they have to choose from, in addition to the military option.

My second comment is to point out that the Commission Report is in serious error in suggesting that little or no problem exists with respect to compensation of career military personnel. The report compares pay of military personnel with "average" civilian earnings on the basis of the number of years out of high school or college. This basis of comparison fails to take into account the degree of knowledge and responsibility required at various position levels and other factors which should be considered in determining pay relationships and levels of pay within the military services. It would be wrong to assume that military pay can be equated with civilian pay on the simple basis of age and basic education. Such standards are not used as the sole basis for testing the adequacy of pay levels in either private or public civilian jobs, and neither can they be so used to measure the adequacy of military pay.

My third and final comment about the Commission Report relates to the Guard/Reserve Forces. The report relies primarily upon pay raises and increases in lower ranks as the means of assuring Reserve strength and readiness. Other factors besides these are vital as we increase reliance upon Guard/Reserve components. It is essential, for example, to retain more experienced officer and enlisted personnel to compensate for the losses of World War II and Korean veterans through retirement. This means attention to a broad range of Guard/Reserve interests, including the combat readiness of equipment on which they train, and the arrangements to compensate for the disruption of family and vocational pursuits while in training. The attitude of the civilian soldier toward military life, including his opinion of its performance quality, is a key factor in our national security.

In moving toward the goal of zero draft calls, the Department of Defense intends to take positive steps through leadership provided by this office, the Service Secretaries and Chiefs, and its Project Volunteer Committee. In addition to what may be done with respect to pay, we plan the following initiatives to implement this essential goal:

1. Expand the recruiting effort by each of the Services for Active and Guard/ Reserve Forces.
2. Restore the sense of "duty-honor-country" which should symbolize the uniform and the man in it. The spending of money for pay will not by itself restore this precious sense to our national life. In today's climate, with the military widely blamed for an unpopular war, and with the severe cutbacks in Department of Defense budgets, it is increasingly difficult to maintain morale. One of our major human goals is to enable the military serviceman to feel the highest pride in himself, his uniform and the military profession. This is paramount to the realization of a high-quality military organization, and it will receive our continuing attention.
3. Improve on-base military housing and increase housing allowances, particularly in high-cost metropolitan areas. The FY 1971 Budget already provides for substantial increases in military housing, and the recommendations to

Congress in support of increased housing allowances and further increases in military housing will be made later this year.

4.  Improve conditions of service and increase military career satisfaction through such actions as expansion of in-service educational opportunities, expansion of ROTC scholarships, extension of family moving expenses to short-service enlisted personnel, reduction of KP and other extra duty assignments, and a broader program to assist those leaving military service in their adjustment to civilian life.

I believe action on the foregoing recommendations will take us firmly and safely on our course of reducing draft calls to zero while at the same time supporting your determination to end inflation, preserve our defense strength, and keep the Administration in a strong and flexible position. The Administration cannot be placed in the position of having to reduce forces below National Security Council recommendations because it has acted too soon in taking irreversible steps to eliminate the draft.

Melvin R. Laird

Source: Melvin Laird, "Memorandum for the President, Subject: Future of the Draft," March 11, 1970, pp. 1–6, box 37, White House Central Files, Staff Member Office Files, Martin Anderson, RMNL, https://www.nixonfoundation. org/wp-content/uploads/2012/01/Memo-The-Future-of-the-Draft.pdf (accessed September 7, 2021).

# DOCUMENT 12

## Richard Nixon, "To End the Draft," April 23, 1970

FOR RELEASE AT 12:00 NOON, EST                          APRIL 23, 1970

Office of the White House Press Secretary

### The White House

### *To The Congress of the United States:*

The draft has been with us now for many years. It was started as a temporary, emergency measure just before World War II. We have lived with the draft so long, and relied on it through such serious crises, that too many of us now accept it as a normal part of American life.

It is now time to embrace a new approach to meeting our military manpower requirements. I have two basic proposals.

- The first deals with the fundamental way this nation should raise the armed force necessary to defend the lives and the rights of its people, and to fulfill its existing commitments abroad.
- The second deals with reforming the present recruitment system—part volunteer, part drafted—which, in the immediate future, will be needed to maintain our armed strength.

### *To End the Draft*

On February 21, I received the report of the Commission on an All-Volunteer Armed Force, headed by former Defense Secretary Thomas S. Gates. The Commission members concluded unanimously that the interests of the nation will be better served by an all-volunteer force than by a mixed force of volunteers and draftees, and that steps should be taken in this direction.

I have carefully reviewed the report of the Commission and have discussed the subject with many others knowledgeable in this field. The preeminent consideration in any decision I make involving the American Armed Forces must be the security of the United States. I have had to weigh carefully how our responsibilities in Vietnam and our overall foreign policy would be affected by ending the draft. I also had to consider the budgetary impact, and the possible effect on our economy.

On the other hand, we have all seen the effect of the draft on our young people, whose lives have been disrupted first by years of uncertainty, and then by the draft itself. We all know the unfairness of the present system, no matter how just we try to make it.

After careful consideration of the factors involved, I support the basic conclusion of the Commission. I agree that we should move now toward ending the draft.

From now on, the objective of this Administration is to reduce draft calls to zero, subject to the overriding considerations of national security.

In proposing that we move toward ending the draft, I must enter three cautions: First, the draft cannot be ended all at once. It must be phased out, so that we can be certain of maintaining our defense strength at every step. Second, existing induction authority expires on July 1, 1971, and I expect that it will be necessary for the next Congress to extend this authority. And third, as we move away from reliance on the draft, we must make provisions to establish a standby draft system that can be used in case of emergency.

To move toward reducing draft calls to zero, we are proceeding with a wide array of actions and proposals:

- This administration proposed, and the Congress has approved, a six percent across-the-board pay increase for Federal employees, retroactive to the first of this year. This raises the pay of members of the Armed Forces by $1.2 billion a year.
- I shall propose an additional 20 percent pay increase for enlisted men with less than two years of service, to be effective January 1, 1971. This action, if approved by the Congress, will raise the annual pay of enlisted men with less than two years of service by $500 million a year, and is a first step in removing the present inequity in pay of men serving their first two years in the Armed Forces. The cost for Fiscal Year 1971 will be $250 million.
- In January 1971 I shall recommend to the Congress, in the Fiscal Year 1972 budget, an additional $2.0 billion for added pay and other benefits—especially for those serving their first two years—to help attract and retain the personnel we need for our Armed Forces.
- I have today directed the Secretary of Defense to give high priority to the expansion of programs designed to increase enlistments and retentions in the services. Further, I have directed that he give me a report every quarter on the progress of this program. Other agencies have been directed to assist in the effort.

- I am also directing the Secretary of Defense to review the policies and practices of the military services to give new emphasis to recognition of the individual needs, aspirations and capabilities of all military personnel.

No one can predict with precision whether or not, or precisely when, we can end conscription. It depends, in part, on the necessity of maintaining required military force levels to meet our commitments in Vietnam and elsewhere. It also depends on the degree to which the combination of military pay increases and enhanced benefits will attract and hold enough volunteers to maintain the forces we need, the attitude of young people toward military service, and the availability of jobs in the labor market.

However, I am confident that, barring any unforeseen developments, this proposed program will achieve our objective.

The starting pay of an enlisted man in our Armed Forces is—taking the latest raise into account—less than $1,500 a year. This is less than half of the minimum wage in the private sector. Of course, we should add to this the value of the food, uniforms and housing that is provided free. But it is hardly comparable to what most young men can earn as civilians. Even with special allowances, some married enlisted men have been forced to go on welfare to support their families.

The low pay illustrates another inequity of the draft. These men, in effect, pay a large hidden tax—the difference between their military pay and what they could earn as civilians. Therefore, on the grounds of equity alone, there is a good reason to substantially increase pay.

While we focus on removing inequities in the pay of men serving their first few years in the military, we must not neglect the career servicemen. They are the indispensable core of our Armed Forces. The increasing technological complexity of modern defense, and the constantly changing international situation, make their assignments ever more difficult—and critical. We shall continue to make every effort to ensure that they are fairly treated and justly compensated.

There is another essential element—beyond pay and benefits, beyond the best in training and equipment—that is vital to the high morale of any armed force in a free society. It is the backing, support and confidence of the people and society the military serves. While government can provide the economic justice our men in arms deserve—moral support and backing can come only from the American people. At few times in our history has it been more needed than today.

The consideration of national security contains no arguments against these historic actions; the considerations of freedom and justice argue eloquently in their behalf.

## To Reform the Draft

As we move toward our goal of ending the draft in the United States, we must deal with the draft as it now exists. This nation has a right to expect that the responsibility for national defense will be shared equitably and consistently by all segments of our society. Given this basic principle, I believe that there are important reforms that we must make in our present draft system.

It is my judgment, and that of the National Security Council, that future occupational, agricultural and student deferments are no longer dictated by the national interest. I am issuing today an Executive Order to direct that no future deferments shall be granted on the basis of employment. Very few young men at age 19 are in such critical positions that they cannot be replaced. All those who held occupational deferments before today, as well as any who may be granted such deferments from pending applications filed before today, will be deferred as they were previously.

This same Executive Order will also eliminate all future paternity deferments—except in those cases where a local draft board determines that extreme hardship would result. All those who held paternity deferments before today, as well as any who may be granted deferments from pending applications filed before today, will be deferred as long as they are living with and supporting child dependents.

I am also asking the Congress today to make some changes in the Military Selective Service Act of 1967.

The first would restore to the President discretionary authority on the deferment of students seeking baccalaureate degrees. If the Congress restores this authority, I shall promptly issue a second Executive Order that would bar all undergraduate deferments, except for young men who are undergraduate students prior to today. These young men would continue to be eligible for deferment under present regulations during their undergraduate years. This Executive Order would also end deferments for young men in junior college, and in apprentice and technical training programs, except for those who entered before today. Men participating in such programs before today would continue to be deferred until they complete them.

Should Congress pass the legislation I have requested, those young men who start college or enter apprentice or other technical training today or hereafter, and subsequently receive a notice of induction, will have their entry into service postponed until the end of the academic semester, or for apprentices and trainees, until some appropriate breaking point in their program.

Even if college deferments are phased out, college men who through ROTC or other military programs have chosen to obligate themselves to enter military service at a later date would be permitted to postpone their active duty until completion of their study program.

In each instance, I have spoken of the phasing out—not the elimination—of existing deferments. The sudden elimination of existing deferments would disrupt plans made in good faith by individuals, companies, colleges and local school systems on the basis of those deferments.

My second legislative proposal would establish a direct national call, by lottery sequence numbers each month, to improve the operation of the random selection system. We need to ensure that men throughout the country with the same lottery number have equal liability to induction.

Under the present law, for example, a man with sequence number 185 may be called up by one draft board while a man with a lower number in a different draft board is not called. This can happen because present law does not permit a national call of young men by lottery sequence numbers.

Some local draft boards may not have enough low numbers to fill their assigned quota for the month. As a result, these local boards are forced to call young men with higher numbers. At the same time, other draft boards throughout the country will have more low numbers than necessary to fill their quotas.

I am recommending to the Congress an amendment to suspend this quota requirement while the random selection system is in effect. If the Congress adopts this amendment, I will authorize the Selective Service System to establish a plan under which the draft call each month will be on a national basis, with the same lottery sequence numbers called throughout the country. This will result in a still more equitable draft system.

As long as we need the draft, it is incumbent upon us to make it as fair and equitable as we can. I urge favorable Congressional action on these legislative proposals for draft reform.

## Conclusion

While I believe that these reforms in our existing draft system are essential, it should be remembered that they are improvements in a system to be used only as long as conscription continues to be necessary.

Ultimately, the preservation of a free society depends upon both the willingness of its beneficiaries to bear the burden of its defense—and the willingness of government to guarantee the freedom of the individual.

With an end to the draft, we will demonstrate to the world the responsiveness of republican government—and our continuing commitment to the maximum freedom for the individual, enshrined in our earliest traditions and founding documents. By upholding the cause of freedom without conscription we will have demonstrated in one more area the superiority of a society based upon belief in the dignity of man over a society based on the supremacy of the State.

RICHARD NIXON

THE WHITE HOUSE,
          April 23, 1970.

Source: Richard Nixon, "To End the Draft," April 23, 1970, pp. 1–5, box C1, folder All-Volunteer Force Documents 36–40, Melvin R. Laird Papers, GRFL.

# DOCUMENT 13

## Richard Nixon, "Special Message to the Congress About Draft Reform," January 28, 1971

To the Congress of the United States:

On April 23, 1970, in a message to the 91st Congress, I proposed that the nation embrace a new approach to meeting our military manpower requirements—an approach that recognized both the necessity for maintaining a strong national defense and the desirability of ending the draft.

In that message I put forth two sets of proposals.

The first set of proposals dealt with the fundamental question of how this nation should raise the armed force necessary to defend the lives and rights of its people and to fulfill its existing commitments abroad.

After carefully weighing both the requirements of national security and the desirability of reducing infringements on individual liberties, I urged that we should begin moving toward an end of the draft and its replacement with an all-volunteer armed force, with an eye to achieving this goal as soon as we can do so without endangering our national security.

The second set of proposals dealt with reforming the draft system itself, while this continues to be needed in the immediate future to maintain our armed strength as we move toward an all volunteer force.

Now, more than nine months later, I am even more strongly convinced of the rightness of these proposals. Now, as then, the objective of this administration is to reduce draft calls to zero, subject to the overriding considerations of national security—and as long as we need the draft, to make it as fair and equitable as we can.

Over the past nine months the Secretary of Defense and the Director of Selective Service have initiated a comprehensive series of steps designed to help us achieve that goal. Average draft calls are now substantially lower than they were when this administration assumed office, and we have significantly improved the consistency and fairness of the draft system. We shall continue these actions at an accelerated pace.

However, to continue the progress that now is possible toward both goals—toward ending the draft, and in the meantime making it more nearly fair—legislative as well as Executive action will be needed.

## Ending The Draft

Since my April 1970 message, a 7.9 percent across-the-board increase in the rate of basic pay has been enacted that will raise the pay of members of the Armed Forces by almost $1.2 billion a year.

Building on this base, I am submitting a number of legislative proposals (some of which were previously submitted to the 91st Congress) which, together with Executive actions I shall take, would move us substantially closer to the goal of an all volunteer force.

* I propose that we invest an additional $1.5 billion in making military service more attractive to present and potential members, with most of this to be used to provide a pay raise for enlisted men with less than two years of service, effective May 1, 1971. If approved by the Congress, this action would result in a total additional investment of $2.7 billion for military manpower, and would substantially reduce the present inequity in the pay of men and women serving in the Armed Forces. The proposed pay raise would increase rates of basic pay at the entry level by 50 percent over present levels. Also, I am proposing increases in the quarters allowance for personnel in the lower enlisted grades.
* I am proposing a test program of special pay incentives designed to attract more volunteers into training for Army combat skills.
* Existing law provides that as general adjustments are made in civilian pay, corresponding increases will be made in military pay. In addition, I am directing the Secretary of Defense to recommend for the 1973 fiscal year such further additions to military compensation as may be necessary to make the financial rewards of military life fully competitive with those in the civilian sector.
* The Department of Defense, through Project Volunteer, has been actively engaged in expanding programs designed to increase enlistments and retentions in the services. A fair level of pay, while necessary, is only one factor in increasing the relative attractiveness of a military career. I will propose that approximately one-fifth of the additional $1.5 billion be devoted to expanding our efforts in the areas of recruiting, medical scholarships, ROTC, improvement of housing, and other programs to enhance the quality of military life.
* During the past year, the Department of Defense has reviewed the policies and practices of the military services and has taken actions to emphasize recognition of the individual needs and capabilities of all military personnel. These efforts will be continued and strengthened.

## Extension of Induction Authority

No one knows precisely when we can end conscription. It depends on many things—including the level of military forces that will be required for our national security, the degree to which the combination of military pay increases and enhanced benefits will attract and hold enough volunteers to maintain the forces we need, and the attitude of young people toward military service.

Current induction authority expires on July 1, 1971. While I am confident that our plan will achieve its objective of reducing draft calls to zero, even the most optimistic observers agree that we would not be able to end the draft in the next year or so without seriously weakening our military forces and impairing our ability to forestall threats to the peace. Considerations of national security thus make it imperative that we continue induction authority at this time.

Normally, the Congress has extended induction authority for four year intervals. I propose that this Congress extend induction authority for two years, to July 1, 1973. We shall make every endeavor to reduce draft calls to zero by that time, carefully and continually reexamining our position as we proceed toward that goal.

## Reform of the Draft

As long as we must continue to rely on the draft to meet a portion of our military manpower requirements, we must make the draft as equitable as possible. To that end I am proposing legislation to modify the present draft law, including the resubmission of recommendations I sent to the Congress last year. This proposed legislation would:

- Permit the phasing out of undergraduate student deferments, and also exemptions for divinity students.
- Establish a uniform national call, by lottery sequence numbers each month, to ensure that men throughout the country with the same lottery numbers have relatively equal liability to induction by their local boards.

In addition, the legislation I am proposing includes a number of other amendments which will improve the administration of existing law.

For the immediate future we will need the draft and, moreover, even when the draft has been ended, we will have to maintain some form of a standby system that could be re-activated in case of emergency. Therefore, I urge favorable Congressional action on these proposals to reform the draft and make it as nearly fair as we can for the time it is needed.

While the reforms proposed in our existing draft system are essential, however, it must be remembered that they are improvements in a system that will be used only as long as the draft is necessary.

This Congress has both the power and the opportunity to take an historic action. As I stated in last year's message, with an end to the draft we will demonstrate to the world the responsiveness of our system of government—and we will also demonstrate our continuing commitment to the principle of ensuring for the individual the greatest possible measure of freedom.

I urge the 92nd Congress to seize this opportunity, and to make the bold decisions necessary to achieve this goal.

RICHARD NIXON
The White House
January 28, 1971

Source: Richard Nixon, "Special Message to the Congress About Draft Reform," January 28, 1971, American Presidency Project, https://www.presidency.ucsb.edu/documents/special-message-the-congress-about-draft-reform (accessed September 11, 2021).

# DOCUMENT 14

## Richard Nixon, "Extension of the Draft and Increases in Military Pay," September 28, 1971

TODAY I am signing into law H.R. 6531. This legislation achieves two objectives of major significance:

- It is a significant step toward an all volunteer armed force, as it remedies the long-standing inequities in military pay for the lower grades.
- It introduces important, additional reforms of the draft, making it as fair and equitable as possible as we progress toward the volunteer force.

I am most hopeful that this is the last time a President must sign an extension of draft induction authority. Although it will remain necessary to retain a standby draft system in the interest of national security, this Administration is committed to achieving the reforms in military life as well as the public support for our Armed Forces which will make possible an end to peacetime conscription. The more equitable pay scales provided by this act are essential to achieving this goal.

Much of the money authorized by this bill will be used to raise the pay of first term recruits, whose pay scales have been unconscionably low. A married man without children who has just completed basic training and lives off the military base now receives only $255 a month, including his allowances. Under this new law, he will receive $450 a month. A single man living on base who now receives $149 will receive $299 under this new law.

By law the pay increases provided in this act are subject to the 90-day wage price freeze. I should further point out that under a plan I have previously submitted to the Congress the annual comparability pay adjustment for the military, like the Federal civilian employees pay adjustment, will take effect July 1, 1972, rather than on January 1, 1971. However, these short deferrals will not materially impair our ability to achieve an all-volunteer force.

I thank the Congress for its cooperation in enacting this legislation. In particular, I want to express my own gratitude and that of the Nation for the fine leadership of Senators John Stennis and Margaret Chase Smith and Congressmen F. Edward Hébert and Leslie C. Arends, who conducted the most penetrating hearings on the draft since 1948, and skillfully guided this legislation to final passage.

Source: Richard Nixon, "Statement on Signing Bill Authorizing Extension of the Draft and Increases in Military Pay," September 28, 1971, American Presidency Project, https://www.presidency.ucsb.edu/documents/statement-signing-bill-authorizing-extension-the-draft-and-increases-military-pay (accessed September 11, 2021).

# DOCUMENT 15

## Melvin Laird, "Progress in Ending the Draft and Achieving the All-Volunteer Force," August 28, 1972

### Chapter I Background

On October 17, 1968, Richard M. Nixon told the American people his views on compulsory military service.

> "I say it's time we took a new look at the draft—at the question of permanent conscription in a free society. If we find we can reasonably meet our peacetime manpower needs by other means—then we should prepare for the day when the draft can be phased out of American life."

A variety of student and other deferments had undermined confidence in the fairness of the draft system. For seven long years, from age 19 to 26, young men endured the uncertainty of an inequitable draft system which selected a few among the many who were subject to it. This prolonged term of uncertainty made it extremely difficult for them to plan for their education, career, and family.

The chance of being drafted varied by state and local community, and by one's economic status. Many young men entered college solely to avoid the draft, and their interaction with the educational community was often unsatisfactory. Those who could not afford college were drafted and felt the sting of discrimination.

In the years preceding this Administration, draft calls were increased to supply manpower for the massive build-up of troops in Vietnam:

## Draft Calls

|      |   |         |
| ---- | - | ------- |
| 1964 | – | 108,000 |
| 1965 | – | 233,000 |
| 1966 | – | 365,000 |
| 1967 | – | 219,000 |
| 1968 | – | 299,000 |

In addition to those drafted, more than half of the young men enlisting in military service did so because of the draft, not because they were true volunteers. Thousands more enlisted in the Guard and Reserve because they perceived these organizations to be without a mission, undeployable, and a safe haven from the draft and the war in Vietnam.

These were the conditions when this Administration took office. The remainder of this report deals with progress that has been made in correcting these conditions and in reducing reliance on the draft, and the additional steps that must be taken to solve the remaining problems as we move to an All-Volunteer Force.

## Chapter II Draft Reform and Planning for the All-Volunteer Force

### Draft Reform

One of the early initiatives taken by this Administration was to make major improvements in the Selective Service draft by minimizing its disruptive and unsettling effect on individual lives.

On November 26, 1969, the President signed into law a bill which reduced the period of draft vulnerability from seven years to one year, the latter being the calendar year following a young man's 19th birthday. The bill further provided that draft selections would be made by the drawing of sequence numbers at random, rather than by birth date.

Thus young men were enabled to make career and other life plans while being subject to a more equitable draft system for one year only.

In April 1970, the President issued an Executive Order phasing out occupational and paternity deferments, thereby further reducing the inequities of the draft system.

The Draft Extension and Military Pay Bill, recommended by this Administration and enacted in September 1971, contained key additional draft reforms. Principally, these reforms eliminated undergraduate student deferments for those entering college in the Fall of 1971 and thereafter, and established a uniform national call to insure that men throughout the country with the same sequence numbers would be equally liable to induction.

Additional reforms enacted by Congress, coupled with administrative improvements made by the Director of Selective Service, helped to restore confidence in the fairness of the draft system and defuse the intense opposition of young people to its inequitable and divisive effects.

## Planning for the All-Volunteer Force

As long as the draft is needed, the improved Selective Service System developed under this Administration's leadership is the fairest possible. But is [sic] is still conscription, and prompt and effective action was taken by this Administration to determine whether an All-Volunteer Force was feasible, and, if so, the steps necessary to attain it.

In March 1969, the President appointed a distinguished commission on the All-Volunteer Force under the Chairmanship of the Honorable Thomas S. Gates, Jr., former Secretary of Defense. The Commission's charter was "to develop a comprehensive plan for eliminating conscription and moving toward an All-Volunteer Force."

As an independent public advisory body with its own staff, the Commission examined all aspects of the All-Volunteer Force issue from a fresh and unbiased perspective. Its comprehensive report was a significant contribution to the public's understanding of a complex issue and to the broad acceptance of the All-Volunteer concept.

The Commission concluded in February 1970, after a year of intensive study, that:

> "We unanimously believe that the nation's interest will be better served by an all-volunteer force, supported by an effective stand-by draft, than by a mixed force of volunteers and conscripts; that steps should be taken promptly to move in this direction; and, that the first indispensable step is to remove the present inequity in the pay of men serving their first term in the armed forces."

Providing a working dialogue with the Gates Commission, and serving as the link point for its data, was the Project Volunteer Committee convened in April 1969 at my direction. This Committee consisted of key manpower officials of the Defense Department under the Chairmanship of Assistant Secretary of Defense (Manpower and Reserve Affairs), Roger T. Kelley. It continues as the Department of Defense steering group responsible for directing overall plans for the All-Volunteer Force and for monitoring the effectiveness of action programs.

There was a consensus in the conclusions of the Gates Commission and our Project Volunteer Committee regarding the feasibility of the All-Volunteer Force and the principal steps needed to end reliance on the draft. Both recommended substantial pay increases for junior enlisted personnel, selective pay incentives for specialists, additional ROTC scholarship support, and a greatly expanded recruiting program. The Project Volunteer Committee placed additional stress upon the need to retain members of the career force and to preserve the strength of Guard and Reserve Components.

The main difference between Department of Defense conclusions and those of the Gates Commission was in timing the end of the draft. The Gates Commission, assuming quick implementation of its legislative and other recommendations, recommended termination of induction authority on June 30, 1971, while we recommended extension of induction authority to July 1, 1973.

President Nixon accepted the basic conclusions and recommendations of the Gates Commission, but cautioned that the draft could not be ended prematurely. In his January 1971 message to Congress he said:

> "While I am confident that our plan will achieve its objective of reducing draft calls to zero, even the most optimistic observers agree that we would not be able to end the draft in the next year or so without seriously weakening our military forces and impairing our ability to forestall threats to the peace … . I propose that this Congress extend induction authority for two years, to July 1, 1973. We shall make every endeavor to reduce draft calls to zero by that time, carefully and continually reexamining our position as we proceed toward that goal."

After extensive hearings by the House and Senate Armed Services Committees, and full floor debate, the 92nd Congress extended induction authority to July 1, 1973 as the President had recommended.

Our experience to date in reducing reliance on the draft confirms the wisdom of having extended the authority to July 1, 1973, thus allowing sufficient time to phase-out of draft reliance and test the effectiveness of a variety of programs for the All-Volunteer Force while maintaining the strength and quality of our military forces.

The draft extension granted by Congress has strengthened our resolve to end the draft on July 1, 1973. I am still convinced that the interests of the nation and the Armed Forces would be best served by achieving an All-Volunteer Force. This conviction rests on the following conclusions:

1. In a peacetime environment, the Armed Forces will function best in a free environment where they compete with others for people.
2. An organization composed of volunteers, having survived the test of free competition, tends to be more efficient than one that relies on forced entry.
3. The alleged pitfalls of the voluntary military organization—that it will be dominated by mercenaries, who will take over our nation, or be all black—are false and unfounded claims.

The draft is an infringement on the liberties of our young people. As President Nixon stated in his 1968 address, "A system of compulsory service that arbitrarily selects some and not others cannot be squared with our whole concept of liberty, justice and equality under the law. Its only justification is compelling necessity ... . Let's show our commitment to freedom by preparing to assure our young people theirs."

## Legislative Programs

The Administration recommended, and the Congress enacted, legislation needed to reduce reliance on the draft and move us toward an All-Volunteer Force.

The key element in this legislative program was a substantial and costly increase in pay and allowances for personnel in the lower enlisted grades—reflecting the fact that for 13 years, from 1952 through 1964, there were no pay increases for military first-term members.

The higher pay rates became effective November 14, 1971, and were followed by a cost-of-living increase in January 1972. A single man living on base, having just completed four months training, previously received $149 a month. His basic pay was more than doubled to $321. By correcting this inequity in pay, particularly as it affected junior enlisted personnel, the military services were enabled to compete for young people in the labor market.

Other legislative provisions expanded ROTC scholarships and subsistence support, and provided funds to improve recruiting activities, and upgrade the quality of life at military installations.

The transitional cost of ending the draft will be significant. Funds for Volunteer Force programs in FY 1972 were about $1.9 billion, will be about $2.7 billion in FY 1973, and may increase in succeeding years. It is proper that the American people should bear this transitional cost in order to remove the financial penalties earlier placed on first-term service personnel, to realize the benefits of ending compulsory military service, and to achieve a more effective military organization.

## Chapter III Signs of Progress

The enactment of the draft extension bill provided two short years to make the transition to an All-Volunteer Force. One year of induction authority remains. We are encouraged by signs of substantial progress, while focusing sharply on the remaining problems and actions needed to solve them.

## Draft Calls Have Declined

The most direct evidence of progress toward ending reliance on the draft is, of course, the sharp decline in draft calls which has occurred during the years of this Administration.

From the level of 299,000 in 1968, the year preceding this Administration, draft calls this calendar year will be no more than 50,000, and every effort will be made to minimize draft calls, if not avoid them entirely, between January and July 1973 when the current induction authority expires.

The dramatic decline in draft calls has been made possible by substantially reducing the size of the Active Force and by attracting more voluntary enlistees to military service.

The size of the Active Forces declined from a Vietnam war peak of 3.5 million to 2.3 million in FY 1972.

Active military strengths for FY 1973 will be:

- 1,200,000 less than in 1968 at the peak of the Vietnam build-up.
- 300,000 less than in 1964 before the Vietnam build-up.

This decrease in active force strength is due to major changes in defense policy initiated by this Administration.

- When this Administration took office, military strength in Vietnam was 549,500. By Vietnamizing the war in Southeast Asia, troop strengths in Vietnam have been reduced by more than half a million.
- The Nixon Doctrine places increased responsibility on our allies to provide military manpower and greater overall capability for their own defense.
- The Total Force Concept places increased responsibility on the National Guard and Reserve Forces as the initial and primary augmentation force for the Active Forces.

## The Role of the Guard and Reserve in the Total Force Concept

The credibility and overall effectiveness of the Guard and Reserve suffered badly during the build-up of the active forces in Vietnam prior to 1969.

- The Guard and Reserve had a questionable combat role, since their mission was ill-defined and their units were seldom called to duty.
- Their effectiveness was marginal to poor, due largely to the fact that their equipment was diverted to build up the Active Forces in Vietnam.
- Their units included many men who joined them not in the tradition of volunteer citizen-soldiers, but because they wanted to avoid the draft and the war in Vietnam.

These conditions are being corrected, and there is highly encouraging evidence of revitalization within the Guard and Reserve.

- Their units have a mission. Within the total force concept, the Guard and Reserve Components are relied upon as the initial and primary augmentation for the Active Forces.
- Equipment inventories of the Army Guard and Army Reserve, badly depleted to build up the Active Forces in Vietnam, are being replenished at an annual rate approaching $1 billion.

- Reserve Forces of the Navy and Marine Corps have been substantially modernized.
- The Air Guard and Air Force Reserve are being transitioned into more modern aircraft at the fastest rate in their history.
- Training has been intensified in all Guard and Reserve Components, and readiness is improving.
- The Guard and Reserve portion of the Defense budget has increased from $2.1 billion in FY 1969 to $4.1 billion in FY 1973. This latter will be the largest single investment in the Guard and Reserve in our nation's history.

A well-equipped and fully-manned National Guard and Reserve, deployable on short notice, is potentially the most economical part of our defense system. An effective Guard and Reserve is also the best guarantee against having to use a peacetime draft in future years.

The actions described have given renewed hope to Guard and Reserve commanders, have re-spirited their units, and have begun to restore their credibility in the public eye. Now massive efforts must be directed toward the challenge of solving Guard and Reserve manpower supply problems without draft pressure. To do this will require the early response by Congress to Administration proposals, along with an improved public understanding of the Guard and Reserve role and enlightened support by American employers on their behalf. The details of these matters will be discussed in the next chapter.

### Enlistment Trends

A further and significant sign of progress is the favorable enlistment experience of the Services in FY 1972 compared to the previous year. The number of true volunteers increased and the quality of those who enlisted improved overall.

### Increase In True Volunteers

Draft calls in FY 1972 were only 25,000 contrasted with 152,000 in FY 1971. Despite this sharp drop in draft calls in FY 1972, enlistment levels have been maintained and the proportion of true volunteers among those who enlisted increased from 59 percent to 75 percent. This is evidence of real progress toward the goal of replacing enlistments previously obtained by pressure of the draft with true volunteers in a no-draft environment.

Several factors contributed to this improvement. Certainly the increase in military entry pay provided by the Congress in Public Law 92-129, which became effective in November 1971, attracted additional true volunteers.

Improving the conditions of Service life, modernizing the training of personnel, and renewing the emphasis on professionalism in the Services—and communicating these changes to the public—also have attracted additional volunteers.

But the factor which may have contributed most to these volunteer increases is the improvement of the recruiting program. During the years of heavy draft pressure, military recruiting was often little more than "order taking." The draft induced many young men to enlist, and gaps in enlistments were made up by drafting more young men. The draft served as an ever-present crutch to support unaggressive recruiting.

A great and successful effort has been made to improve the quality of military recruiting and to expand the recruiting force. Highly qualified officers and NCOs are seeking and being assigned to recruiting billets. Increasingly the military recruiter is capable of describing the challenges and satisfactions of military service, and of competing effectively in the labor market with those who offer other job options. Thus, he reflects to the prospective enlistee the best of Service life.

Recruiting funds in FY 1972 were 80 percent higher than they were two years ago, and the number of people assigned to recruiting was increased by 50 percent. Further expansions are programmed for FY 1973. Public Law 92-129 provided much needed allowances to recruiters for expenses incurred in recruiting.

## Ground Combat Enlistments

The impact of aggressive and creating recruiting is illustrated by the Army's experience in enlisting men for the ground combat specialties—infantry, artillery, and armor. During July to December 1970, enlistments for these specialties average 227 a month compared with requirements averaging 5,000 a month. Most of the men assigned to ground combat jobs were either draftees or men who enlisted without selecting a military specialty. During July to December 1971, ground combat enlistments reached a one-month high of 3,900 and averaged 3,000 a month. It continued at this level in 1972. This spectacular rise was achieved by offering the choice of overseas locations and unit assignments to combat arms enlistees, by advertising these new options, and by aggressively recruiting candidates for them.

With Army combat arms enlistments stabilized at 3,000 a month for one year, we began a test on June 1st of the combat arms bonus authorized earlier by Congress. A bonus of $1,500 is being offered to Army and Marine Corps ground combat volunteers who enlist for four years. Before the bonus test there were some Marine Corps four year ground combat enlistments, but none in the Army.

The test results in June show that the bonus is effective in securing longer term enlistments. The Army enlisted 5,400 men for the combat arms, with approximately half enlisting for four years under the bonus program. The Marine Corps enlisted 1,500 in June with 87 percent accepting the bonus in return for an additional year of service.

The test will continue through October enabling us to determine whether the bonus will increase the total number of combat arms enlistments and its effect on Navy and Air Force enlistments.

The longer enlistment of four years associated with the bonus, rather than two or three years without it, is significant. It has the effect of substantially reducing the high cost of training and reducing personnel turnover in the future. It is also an indication that an enlistment bonus can be used effectively to attract people for longer enlistments in sophisticated skills that require long training, thus further reducing the cost of training.

## Quality of Enlistments

There have been some dire predictions that ending reliance on the draft would produce an organization of substandard volunteers. Our experience during the past two years does not support this claim. During a period in which draft calls were sharply reduced, the quality of enlistees has remained high.

The single exception to improved quality among enlistees is the Navy. In the final months of FY 1972, the Navy experienced a higher than normal enlistment rate among people of lower mental capacity. The recent trend will be observed closely and as Navy recruiting performance improves it is hoped that the enlistment quality will improve also.

One indication of improved quality is the overall increase in high school graduates enlisting in FY 1972 (with draft calls of 25,000) over the previous year (with draft calls of 152,000). High school graduates in FY 1972 accounted for 70 percent of enlistments compared with 67 percent the previous year. High school graduates have consistently performed better in their military jobs, and have had fewer disciplinary problems, than those who have not graduated. The enlistment of more high school graduates under conditions of greatly reduced draft pressure is a favorable quality sign.

The mental test scores of those who enlisted this past year provide another indication that the quality factor can be controlled without draft pressure. Standardized tests, which provide a measure of an individual's learning capacity, are administered to all incoming personnel. The test scores are summarized by broad mental groups. Mental Group I indicates the highest capacity and Mental Group IV is the lowest category accepted for military service. Persons who score in Groups I and II are good to excellent college material.

The primary market for enlisted volunteers is among non-college youth of military age. As shown in the next chart, the Services in FY 1972 enlisted a significantly higher proportion of young men in Groups I and II than is contained in the non-college youth population. They also enlisted a much lower percentage of Group IV men than is represented in this population. Group V men are not acceptable for military service.

The next chart shows that as the number of true volunteers increased in FY 1972, there was no decrease in quality. The additional true volunteers were primarily men with average and above average learning capacity.

It is clear from the previous charts that as draft calls declined last year, the quality of enlistments has been maintained. It is also clear that more enlistees could have been obtained if entrance standards had been eased to admit a blending of enlistees more nearly representative of the non-college population.

Our quality objectives are:

1. To enlist people whose learning capacities match the requirements of military jobs. An organization composed of bright people unchallenged by their jobs would be as much of a quality mismatch as an organization made up of people who lack the ability to perform their jobs. In this regard, tests have been useful in selecting people whose aptitudes match specific job requirements.
2. To enlist people who display self-discipline and control—with all capable of following and some capable of leading. Past accomplishments of the individual such as high school graduation and good citizenship record, have proven to be the best predictors of behavior.

The fine balance between the quality of the force, its mission requirements, and its costs must be monitored closely. The goal should be to obtain people who can perform the required job in a completely adequate fashion. It may be necessary to offer bonuses to attract people in sufficient numbers for more difficult jobs or reenlistment bonuses to selectively retain them. Authority for the payment of such bonuses is contained in the Uniformed Services Special Pay Act of 1972 which awaits action by Congress. These provisions will be discussed in the next chapter.

## Racial Composition

The concern has been expressed that a voluntary force will be composed primarily of blacks and low-income youth of all races. This concern appears to lean on the argument that the higher pay rates at the military entry level would appeal principally to the so-called "disadvantaged" among our young people.

Regarding the possibility of a black-dominated volunteer force, the Gates Commission concluded that,

> "The frequently heard claim that a volunteer force will be all black, or all this or all that, simply has no basis in fact. Our research indicates that the composition of the armed forces will not be fundamentally changed by ending conscription."

The facts support this conclusion. For the total Active Forces, officer and enlisted, the current rate of participation by blacks (11 percent) is lower than their percent of the military age population (13.5 percent). The service participation rate varies from a low of five percent in the Navy to a high of 15 percent in the Army. Among the career force, all of whom are volunteers, the black proportion is close to the percentage of blacks in the Nation's population.

The proportion of blacks and other racial minorities in the Armed Forces is expected to grow in the next decade, keeping pace with population trends, the improving education level of blacks and increased service attractiveness. For several years this proportion may exceed the percentage of minorities in the Nation's population, reflecting the apparent fact that minority members find better career opportunities and overall treatment in the military than in civilian life. For example, the current rate of black enlistments and reenlistments in the Army increased this year and is currently higher than the national percentage of black youth. Long range, however, we do not foresee any significant difference between the racial composition of the All-Volunteer Force and racial composition of the Nation.

The charge that a volunteer force will be dominated by low-income youth is not relevant. Young people applying for military service are considered on the basis of their physical, mental, and moral qualifications. To the extent that large numbers of low-income youth apply and qualify, so much the better for them, the Armed Forces, and the Nation.

We are determined that the All-Volunteer Force shall have broad appeal to young men and women of all racial, ethnic, and economic backgrounds. This objective was reinforced by the Human Goals program initiated by the Department of Defense in 1969, which emphasizes equality of opportunity for all uniformed members.

## Officer Requirements

The Military Services met their requirements for 43,000 new commissioned officers last year.

In meeting these requirements for new officers, the Services drew on the supply of ROTC graduates who had enrolled in the program in previous years when draft pressure was high. Recent legislation which increased the number of ROTC scholarships and subsistence payments is expected to abate any serious decline in ROTC enrollment.

Except for medical officers and a few other highly skilled and professional categories, we do not anticipate that the procurement of officers will present a major problem with the ending of the draft. Legislation has been proposed to Congress to assist in meeting the expected shortage of doctors and other specialized officers.

Currently blacks comprise only 2.3 percent of the officer corps. The Services are not satisfied with this low representation and are making special efforts to increase the percentage of blacks and other minorities in the various officer commissioning programs. The percentage of blacks enrolled in ROTC is now nine percent. The enrollment of blacks was improved by increasing the number of ROTC detachments at predominately black colleges from 16 in FY 1969 to 27 in FY 1972, and will be further increased to 35 detachments in the next school year. The number of blacks entering the Service Academies increased by 150 percent in the past three years, from 48 to 123. Black representation in the officer corps will rise as black participants in these officer programs graduate and enter service.

Source: Melvin Laird, "Report to the President and the Chairmen of Armed Services Committees of the Senate and of the House of Representatives (P.L. 92-129): Progress in Ending the Draft and Achieving the All-Volunteer Force," August 28, 1972, pp. 1–27, box A51, folder All-Volunteer Force, 1971–1972, Melvin R. Laird Papers, GRFL.

# DOCUMENT 16

## Richard Nixon, "Progress Toward Establishment of an All-Volunteer Force," August 28, 1972

Based on the report submitted to me this morning by Secretary Laird, and provided the Congress enacts pending legislation I have recommended, we will be able, as planned, to eliminate entirely by July 1973 any need for peacetime conscription into the armed forces.

Four years ago I pledged that if elected I would work toward ending the military draft and establishing in its place an all volunteer armed force—and that during such time, as the need for a draft continued, I would seek to make its working more equitable and less capricious in its effect on the lives of young Americans.

Immediately on taking office, my Administration began its fulfillment of that pledge—and I take deep and special satisfaction in the progress that has been made.

Within 18 months, the old, outmoded draftee selection process, with its inequitable system of deferments, was replaced by an even-handed lottery system based on random selection. The uncertainty created by the draft was further minimized by reducing the period of draft vulnerability from 7 years to one. As a result of these and other reforms, confidence in the fairness of the Selective Service System has been restored.

Meanwhile, we have also been working toward the all-volunteer force.

Secretary Laird today delivered to me an encouraging report detailing the substantial progress we have made in reducing dependence on the draft to meet military manpower needs. The experience of the past 3 years, as indicated in this report, seems to show that sufficient numbers of volunteers can be attracted to the armed forces to meet peacetime manpower needs, and that ending all dependence on the draft will be consistent with maintaining the force level and degree of readiness necessary to meet our vital long-term national security needs.

This remarkable record of progress in reducing our dependence on the draft is a direct result of the strong support given by Secretary Laird, by the Service

Secretaries, by the Service Chiefs, and by the entire Defense Department. They can all be justifiably proud of the record:

- Draft calls have been reduced from 299,000 in 1968 to 50,000 in 1972 one-sixth of the previous level.
- The proportion of enlistees who are "true volunteers"—that is, who enlist out of their own free will and not because of pressure from the draft—has increased from 59 percent to 75 percent in the last year alone.
- The quality of enlistees has remained high, even improving slightly, while the economic and racial profile of the enlistees has not been significantly changed.
- Our military readiness has not suffered.

Some problems, however, remain to be overcome, and doing so will require the full support of the Department of Defense, the Congress, and the public. These problems include:

- Avoiding potential manpower shortages which will occur unless legislation currently pending before the Congress is passed, so as to bolster vigorous Service efforts already underway to improve manpower utilization enlistments and retention;
- Providing sufficient numbers of doctors and other highly trained specialists in critical skills;
- Maintaining Guard and Reserve force manning, which will remain below congressionally mandated strength unless pending legislation is passed.

I am confident that these problems can and will be overcome—assuming prompt action by the Congress on the necessary pending legislation and assuming continued public and Service support. In particular:

- The benefit and worth of a military career must be more effectively communicated to the American people, while all four Services continue to improve their personnel management and manpower utilization procedures. Military careerists deserve the respect and the gratitude of the public they serve.
- The Congress must assist through timely passage of pending legislation—particularly the Uniformed Services Special Pay Act of 1972, which will provide needed bonus authority to help fill projected shortages in critical skills and other possible shortages in the number of enlistees available under a zero draft.

Given this kind of support, we will no longer need conscription to fill manpower requirements after July 1973. This means that it will not be necessary to require from the Congress an extension of induction authority of the Selective Service Act past July of 1973; further authority to conscript thereafter would rest with the Congress.

In reaching this goal, we will finally—28 years after the end of World War II—have done what I said in 1968 that we should do: that we should "show our commitment to freedom by preparing to assure our young people theirs."

Source: Richard Nixon, "Statement About Progress Toward Establishment of an All-Volunteer Force," August 28, 1972, American Presidency Project, https://www.presidency.ucsb.edu/documents/statement-about-progress-toward-establishment-all-volunteer-armed-force (accessed August 31, 2021).

## Notes

1 The Commission investigated the possibility of encouraging more enlistments through an active 2-year enlistment program and finally concluded that such a program would have little beneficial effect because the increased numbers of enlistees would be largely counterbalanced by a higher rate of turnover.
2 Charts 1 and 2 show the number of inductions which have been necessary to sustain various force levels since 1950. Chart 3 projects, from this experience, the numbers of inductees necessary to maintain different strength levels.
3 General Eisenhower outlined his views in a Readers Digest article in September 1966, and elaborated on them for the Commission in an interview with several Commission members the following month. The Commission chairman endeavored to obtain an interview with former President Truman but Mr. Truman advised the Commission that personal reasons prevented him from making such arrangements.
4 The largest board in the country is in North Hollywood, Calif; its registrants number 54,323. (See appendix tables 5.1 and 5.2.)
5 See appendix table 5.4.
6 A delinquent is any registrant who, in the opinion of a local board, has failed to meet the requirements of the Selective Service law. This has been construed to include men who neglect to report a change of address promptly, as well as those who refuse to report for induction. Regulations permit a local board to classify delinquents I-A and order them for induction ahead of all other eligibles.
7 Responses to a December 1966 telegraphic inquiry by the Selective Service System show 261 Negro members out of 17,123 local board members, or 1.5 percent.
8 Statistical information on the composition of local boards is shown in the tables in sec. 1 of the appendix.
9 See tables 7.5 and 7.6 of the appendix.
10 See sec. II of the appendix.
11 This is primarily because of written test failures; physical rejections among Negroes are actually lower than those for whites.
12 The estimates cited here are based upon overall disqualification rates, including experience of both volunteers and draftees. The disqualification rates for those called for induction alone have been consistently higher than these overall rates.
13 Statistics relating to the Negro serviceman are contained in the tables in sec. V of the appendix.
14 See table 5.7 in the appendix.
15 Reclassification statistics are contained in the tables in Sec. III of the appendix.
16 See Sec. VI of the appendix.
17 See Sec. IV of the appendix.
18 See table 4.1 in the appendix.
19 Local board and appeal board responses are presented in sec. IV, of the appendix.

# BIBLIOGRAPHY

## Primary Sources

*Archives, Manuscripts, and Collections*

National Archives and Records Administration, College Park, Maryland
RG 147 Records of the Selective Service System, 1940–
Harry S. Truman Presidential Library, Independence, Missouri
Harry S. Truman Papers
President's Secretary's Files
White House Central Files: Official File
J. Howard McGrath Papers
Dwight D. Eisenhower Presidential Library, Abilene, Kansas
Dwight D. Eisenhower Papers
Pre-Presidential Papers
Papers as President of the United States
White House Central Files, Official File
Lyndon B. Johnson Presidential Library, Austin, Texas
Lyndon B. Johnson papers
Administrative Histories
Richard M. Nixon Presidential Library, Yorba Linda, California
White House Central Files, Subject Files
FG 216 Selective Service System
FG 249 Commission on an All-Volunteer Armed Force
White House Central Files, Staff Member and Office Files
Martin Anderson Files
Gerald R. Ford Presidential Library, Ann Arbor, Michigan
Arthur F. Burns Papers
Gerald R. Ford Congressional Papers
Robert T. Hartmann Papers
Melvin R. Laird Papers

*Government Documents*

Aspin, Les. *All Volunteer: A Fair System; A Quality Force.* Washington, DC: U.S. Government Printing Office, 1991.

Burrelli, David F. "Women in Combat: Issues for Congress." *Congressional Research Service Report.* May 9, 2013.

Congressional Budget Office. *The All-Volunteer Military: Issues and Performance.* Washington, DC: Congressional Budget Office, 2007.

Dawson, David A. *The Impact of Project 100,000 on the Marine Corps.* Washington, DC: History and Museums Division, Headquarters U.S. Marine Corps, 1995.

Department of Defense. *Modernizing Military Pay: Report of the First Quadrennial Review of Military Compensation.* Vol. 1, *Active Duty Compensation.* Washington, DC: U.S. Government Printing Office, 1967.

Department of Defense. *Report of the Task Force on Women in the Military.* Washington, DC: U.S. Government Printing Office, 1988.

Griffith, Robert K., Jr. *The U.S. Army's Transition to the All-Volunteer Force, 1968–1974.* Washington, DC: Center of Military History, 1997.

Kamarck, Kristy N. "The Selective Service System and Draft Registration: Issues for Congress." *Congressional Research Service Report.* August 18, 2021.

Kamarck, Kristy N. "Women in Combat: Issues for Congress." *Congressional Research Service Report.* August 18, 2015.

Laurence, Janice. *The All-Volunteer Force: A Historical Perspective.* Washington, DC: Office of Under Secretary of Defense (Force Management Policy), 2004.

Military Manpower Task Force. *A Report to the President on the Status and Prospects of the All-Volunteer Force.* Washington, DC: U.S. Government Printing Office, 1982.

National Advisory Commission on Selective Service. *In Pursuit of Equity: Who Serves When Not All Serve?* Washington, DC: U.S. Government Printing Office, 1967.

National Commission on Military, National, and Public Service. *Inspired to Serve: The Final Report of the National Commission on Military, National, and Public Service.* Washington, DC: U.S. Government Printing Office, 2020.

National Commission on Military, National, and Public Service. *Interim Report: A Report to the American People, the Congress, and the President.* Washington, DC: U.S. Government Printing Office, 2019.

President's Commission on an All-Volunteer Armed Force. *The Report of the President's Commission on an All-Volunteer Armed Force.* Washington, DC: U.S. Government Printing Office, 1970.

Selective Service System. *Selective Service in Peacetime: First Report of the Director of Selective Service, 1940–1941.* Washington, DC: U.S. Government Printing Office, 1942.


*Magazines and Newspapers*

*Army Times*
*Boston Globe*
*Chicago Daily News*
*Christian Science Monitor*
*Detroit News*
*Look*
*Los Angeles Times*
*Newsday*
*Newsweek*

*New York Times*
*New York Times Magazine*
*Saturday Evening Post*
*Stars and Stripes*
*Time*
*U.S. News and World Report*
*Wall Street Journal*
*Washington Post, Times Herald*


*Reference Works*

Congressional Quarterly. *Congress and the Nation: A Review of Government and Politics.* Vol. 3, *1969–1972.* Washington, DC: Congressional Quarterly, 1973.


## Secondary Sources

*Books*

Adams, Gordon, and Shoon Murray, eds. *Mission Creep: The Militarization of US Foreign Policy?* Washington, DC: Georgetown University Press, 2014.
Avant, Deborah D. *The Market for Force: The Consequences of Privatizing Security.* Cambridge: Cambridge University Press, 2005.
Bacevich, Andrew J. *Breach of Trust: How Americans Failed Their Soldiers and Their Country.* New York: Henry Holt, 2013.
Bailey, Beth. *America's Army: Making the All-Volunteer Force.* Cambridge, MA: Belknap Press of Harvard University Press, 2009.
Biank, Tanya. *Undaunted: The Real Story of America's Servicewomen in Today's Military.* New York: NAL Caliber, 2014.
Bicksler, Barbara A., Curtis L. Gilroy, and John T. Warner, eds. *The All-Volunteer Force: Thirty Years of Service.* Washington, DC: Brassey's, 2004.
Bristol, Douglas W., Jr., and Heather Marie Stur, eds. *Integrating the US Military: Race, Gender, and Sexual Orientation since World War II.* Baltimore: Johns Hopkins University Press, 2017.
Caraley, Demetrios. *Politics of Military Unification: A Study of Conflict and the Policy Process.* New York: Columbia University Press, 1966.
Chambers, John W. *To Raise an Army: The Draft Comes to Modern America.* New York: Free Press, 1987.
Clifford, J. Garry. *The Citizen Soldiers: The Plattsburg Training Camp Movement, 1913–1920.* Lexington: University Press of Kentucky, 1972.
Clifford, J. Garry, and Samuel R. Spencer. *The First Peacetime Draft.* Lawrence: University Press of Kansas, 1986.
Cohen, Eliot A. *Citizens and Soldiers: The Dilemmas of Military Service.* Ithaca, NY: Cornell University Press, 1985.
Davies, Robert B. *Baldwin of the Times: Hanson W. Baldwin, A Military Journalist's Life, 1903–1991.* Annapolis, MD: Naval Institute, 2011.
Feaver, Peter D., and Richard H. Kohn, eds. *Soldiers and Civilians: The Civil-Military Gap and American National Security.* Cambridge, MA: MIT Press, 2001.

Fiss, Owen. *Pillars of Justice: Lawyers and the Liberal Tradition.* Cambridge, MA: Harvard University Press, 2017.

Flynn, George Q. *Lewis B. Hershey: Mr. Selective Service.* Chapel Hill: University of North Carolina Press, 1985.

Flynn, George Q. *The Draft, 1940–1973.* Lawrence: University Press of Kansas, 1993.

Friedman, Norman. *The Fifty-Year War: Conflict and Strategy in the Cold War.* Annapolis, MD: Naval Institute, 2000.

Frost, Jennifer. *"Let Us Vote!": Youth Voting Rights and the 26th Amendment.* New York: NYU Press, 2022.

Gerhardt, James M. *The Draft and Public Policy: Issues in Military Manpower Procurement, 1945–1970.* Columbus: Ohio State University Press, 1971.

Hanson, Thomas E. *Combat Ready? The Eighth U.S. Army on the Eve of the Korean War.* College Station: Texas A&M University Press, 2010.

Hewlett, Richard G., and Francis Duncan. *A History of the United States Atomic Energy Commission.* Vol. 2, *Atomic Shield, 1947–1952.* University Park: Pennsylvania University Press, 1969.

Hewlett, Richard G., and Oscar E. Anderson Jr. *A History of the United States Atomic Energy Commission.* Vol. 1, *The New World, 1936–1946.* University Park: Pennsylvania State University Press, 1962.

Holley, I. B. *General John M. Palmer, Citizen Soldiers, and the Army of a Democracy.* Westport, CT: Greenwood, 1982.

Jensen, Geoffrey W., and Matthew M. Stith, eds. *Beyond the Quagmire: New Interpretations of the Vietnam War.* Denton: University of North Texas Press, 2019.

Kennedy, David M., ed. *The Modern American Military.* Oxford: Oxford University Press, 2013.

Kindsvatter, Peter S. *American Soldiers: Ground Combat in the World Wars, Korea, and Vietnam.* Lawrence: University Press of Kansas, 2003.

Kofsky, Frank. *Harry S. Truman and the War Scare of 1948: A Successful Campaign to Deceive the Nation.* New York: St. Martin's, 1995.

Krehbiel, Nicholas A. *General Lewis B. Hershey and Conscientious Objection during World War II.* Columbia: University of Missouri Press, 2011.

Kriner, Douglas L., and Francis X. Shen. *The Casualty Gap: The Causes and Consequences of American Wartime Inequalities.* Oxford: Oxford University Press, 2010.

Laich, Dennis. *Skin in the Game: Poor Kids and Patriots.* Bloomington, IN: iUniverse, 2013.

Marble, Sanders, ed. *Scraping the Barrel: The Military Use of Substandard Manpower, 1860–1960.* Bronx, NY: Fordham University Press, 2012.

Miller, James C., III, ed. *Why the Draft? The Case for a Volunteer Army.* Baltimore: Penguin, 1968.

Millett, Allan R. *The War for Korea, 1950–1951: They Came from the North.* Lawrence: University Press of Kansas, 2010.

Millett, Allan R. *The War for Korea, 1945–1950: A House Burning.* Lawrence: University Press of Kansas, 2005.

Mittelstadt, Jennifer. *The Rise of the Military Welfare State.* Cambridge, MA: Harvard University Press, 2015.

Moskos, Charles C. *A Call to Civic Service: National Service for Country and Community.* New York: Free Press, 1988.

Nixon, Richard. *The Real War.* New York: Simon & Schuster, 1980.

Reeves, Richard. *President Nixon: Alone in the White House.* New York: Simon & Schuster, 2001.

Rostker, Bernard. *I Want You! The Evolution of the All-Volunteer Force*. Santa Monica, CA: RAND, 2006.

Roth, Tanya L. *Her Cold War: Women in the U.S. Military, 1945–1980*. Chapel Hill: University of North Carolina Press, 2021.

Roth-Douquet, Kathy, and Frank Schaeffer. *AWOL: The Unexcused Absence of America's Upper Classes from Military Service—and How It Hurts Our Country*. New York: HarperCollins, 2006.

Rutenberg, Amy J. *Rough Draft: Cold War Military Manpower Policy and the Origins of Vietnam-Era Draft Resistance*. Ithaca, NY: Cornell University Press, 2019.

Segal, David R. *Recruiting for Uncle Sam: Citizenship and Military Manpower Policy*. Lawrence: University Press of Kansas, 1989.

Stoler, Mark A. *George C. Marshall: Soldier-Statesman of the American Century*. Boston: Twayne, 1989.

Stur, Heather M. *Beyond Combat: Women and Gender in the Vietnam War Era*. Cambridge: Cambridge University Press, 2011.

Tax, Sol, ed. *The Draft: A Handbook of Facts and Alternatives*. Chicago: University of Chicago Press, 1967.

Taylor, William A. *Every Citizen a Soldier: The Campaign for Universal Military Training after World War II*. College Station: Texas A&M University Press, 2014.

Taylor, William A. *Military Service and American Democracy: From World War II to the Iraq and Afghanistan Wars*. Lawrence: University Press of Kansas, 2016.

Unger, Debi and Irwin, with Stanley Hirshson. *George Marshall: A Biography*. New York: HarperCollins, 2014.

VanDeMark, Brian. *Road to Disaster: A New History of America's Descent into Vietnam*. New York: Custom House, 2018.

Vuic, Kara D. *Officer, Nurse, Woman: The Army Nurse Corps in the Vietnam War*. Baltimore: Johns Hopkins University Press, 2011.

Zarefsky, David. *President Johnson's War on Poverty: Rhetoric and History*. Tuscaloosa: University of Alabama Press, 1986.

*Articles*

Butler, Jack. "The All-Volunteer Armed Force: Its Feasibility and Implications." *Parameters* 2, no. 1 (Summer 1972): 17–29.

Eikenberry, Karl W. "Reassessing the All-Volunteer Force." *Washington Quarterly* 36, no. 1 (Winter 2013): 7–24.

Friedman, Milton. "Why Not a Volunteer Army?" *New Individualist Review* 4, no. 4 (Spring 1967): 3–9.

Gates, Robert M. "The Overmilitarization of American Foreign Policy." *Foreign Affairs* 99, no. 4 (July/August 2020): 121–132.

Janowitz, Morris. "Volunteer Armed Forces and Military Purpose." *Foreign Affairs* 50, no. 3 (April 1972): 427–443.

Janowitz, Morris, and Charles C. Moskos Jr. "Five Years of the All-Volunteer Force: 1973–1978." *Armed Forces and Society* 5, no. 2 (Winter 1979): 171–218.

MacKenzie, Megan H. "Let Women Fight: Ending the U.S. Military's Female Combat Ban." *Foreign Affairs* 91, no. 6 (November/December 2012): 32–42.

Moos, Felix. "History and Culture: Some Thoughts on the United States All-Volunteer Force." *Naval War College Review* 26, no. 1 (July 1973): 16–27.

Perri, Timothy J. "The Evolution of Military Conscription in the United States." *Independent Review* 17, no. 3 (Winter 2013): 429–439.

Runey, Michael, and Charles Allen. "An All-Volunteer Force for Long-Term Success." *Military Review* 95, no. 6 (November/December 2015): 92–100.

Segal, David R., Thomas J. Burns, William W. Falk, Michael P. Silver, and Bam Dev Sharda. "The All-Volunteer Force in the 1970s." *Social Science Quarterly* 79, no. 2 (June 1998): 390–411.

Taylor, William A. "From WACs to Rangers: Women in the U.S. Military since World War II." *Marine Corps University Journal*, Special Issue: Gender Integration (2018): 78–101.

Taylor, William A. "The Cavalcade of Universal Military Training: Training and Education within the Experimental Demonstration Unit." *Marine Corps University Journal* 9, no. 1 (Spring 2018): 97–119.

## Sources for Main Primary Documents

*Document 1*

Marshall Commission, "Introduction and Summary of Conclusions," February 1967:
Marshall Commission, *In Pursuit of Equity*, Chapter I, pp. 3–10.

*Document 2*

Marshall Commission, "The Need for the Draft," February 1967:
Marshall Commission, *In Pursuit of Equity*, Chapter II, pp. 11–16. This document does not include three charts from the original report.

*Document 3*

Marshall Commission, "Profile of the Present System," February 1967:
Marshall Commission, *In Pursuit of Equity*, Chapter III, pp. 17–29. This document does not include four charts from the original report.

*Document 4*

Anderson, Martin, to Richard Nixon, "An Outline of the Factors Involved in Establishing an All-Volunteer Force," July 4, 1967:
Anderson, Martin, "Memorandum to Richard Nixon, Re: An Outline of the Factors Involved in Establishing an All-Volunteer Armed Force," July 4, 1967, pp. 1–7, box 2, Martin Anderson Donated Collection, RMNL, https://www.nixonfoundation.org/wp-content/uploads/2012/01/An-Outline-of-the-Factors-Involved-in-Establishing-an-All-Volunteer-Armed-Force-by-Martin-Anderson.pdf (accessed August 31, 2021).

*Document 5*

Nixon, Richard, Presidential Candidate, "The All-Volunteer Armed Force," October 17, 1968:

Nixon, Richard, "The All-Volunteer Armed Force," October 17, 1968, pp. 2–10, box 3, Martin Anderson Donated Collection, RMNL, https://www.nixonfoundation.org/wp-content/uploads/2012/01/Candidate-Nixon-Statement-on-an-All-Volunteer-Force.pdf (accessed August 25, 2021).

*Document 6*

Laird, Melvin, "The First Five Months: Problems and Progress," June 27, 1969:
Laird, Melvin, "The First Five Months: Problems and Progress," Armed Forces Staff College, Norfolk, VA, June 27, 1969, pp. 7–10, box A76, folder Laird – First Five Months, 1969, Melvin R. Laird Papers, GRFL.

*Document 7*

Brehm, William, "Ongoing, Planned and Other Actions to Reduce Reliance on the Draft," July 12, 1969:
Brehm, William, "Memorandum for the Assistant Secretary of Defense (Manpower and Reserve Affairs), Subject: Ongoing, Planned and Other Actions to Reduce Reliance on the Draft," July 12, 1969, pp. 1–4, enclosure pp. 1–6, box C1, folder All-Volunteer Documents 10–15, Melvin R. Laird Papers, GRFL.

*Document 8*

Gates Commission, "Protecting the Free Society," February 20, 1970:
Gates Commission, *Report on an All-Volunteer Armed Force*, Part I, Chapter 1, pp. 5–10.

*Document 9*

Gates Commission, "The Debate," February 20, 1970:
Gates Commission, *Report on an All-Volunteer Armed Force*, Part I, Chapter 2, pp. 11–20.

*Document 10*

Gates Commission, "Conscription Is a Tax," February 20, 1970:
Gates Commission, *Report on an All-Volunteer Armed Force*, Part II, Chapter 3, pp. 23–33.

*Document 11*

Laird, Melvin, "Future of the Draft," March 11, 1970:
Laird, Melvin, "Memorandum for the President, Subject: Future of the Draft," March 11, 1970, pp. 1–6, box 37, White House Central Files, Staff Member Office Files, Martin Anderson, RMNL, https://www.nixonfoundation.org/wp-content/uploads/2012/01/Memo-The-Future-of-the-Draft.pdf (accessed September 7, 2021).

*Document 12*

Nixon, Richard, "To End the Draft," April 23, 1970:

Nixon, Richard, "To End the Draft," April 23, 1970, pp. 1–5, box C1, folder All-Volunteer Force Documents 36–40, Melvin R. Laird Papers, GRFL.


*Document 13*

Nixon, Richard, "Special Message to the Congress About Draft Reform," January 28, 1971:
Nixon, Richard, "Special Message to the Congress About Draft Reform," January 28, 1971, American Presidency Project, https://www.presidency.ucsb.edu/documents/special-message-the-congress-about-draft-reform (accessed September 11, 2021).


*Document 14*

Nixon, Richard, "Extension of the Draft and Increases in Military Pay," September 28, 1971:
Nixon, Richard, "Statement on Signing Bill Authorizing Extension of the Draft and Increases in Military Pay," September 28, 1971, American Presidency Project, https://www.presidency.ucsb.edu/documents/statement-signing-bill-authorizing-extension-the-draft-and-increases-military-pay (accessed September 11, 2021).


*Document 15*

Laird, Melvin, "Progress in Ending the Draft and Achieving the All-Volunteer Force," August 28, 1972:
Laird, Melvin, "Report to the President and the Chairmen of Armed Services Committees of the Senate and of the House of Representatives (P.L. 92-129): Progress in Ending the Draft and Achieving the All-Volunteer Force," August 28, 1972, pp. 1–27, box A51, folder All-Volunteer Force, 1971–1972, Melvin R. Laird Papers, GRFL.


*Document 16*

Nixon, Richard, "Progress Toward Establishment of an All-Volunteer Force," August 28, 1972:
Nixon, Richard, "Statement About Progress Toward Establishment of an All-Volunteer Force," August 28, 1972, American Presidency Project, https://www.presidency.ucsb.edu/documents/statement-about-progress-toward-establishment-all-volunteer-armed-force (accessed August 31, 2021).

# ABOUT THE AUTHOR

 **William A. Taylor** is the holder of the Lee Drain Endowed University Professorship, previous department chair, and award-winning professor of global security studies in the Kay Bailey Hutchison Center for Security Studies at Angelo State University in San Angelo, Texas. Taylor is the book series editor for both Studies in Civil-Military Relations, with the University Press of Kansas, and Studies in Marine Corps History and Amphibious Warfare, with the Naval Institute Press. He is the author or editor of four other books, including *George C. Marshall and the Early Cold War: Policy, Politics, and Society* (Norman: University of Oklahoma Press, 2020); *Contemporary Security Issues in Africa* (Santa Barbara, CA: Praeger, 2019); *Military Service and American Democracy: From World War II to the Iraq and Afghanistan Wars* (Lawrence: University Press of Kansas, 2016); and *Every Citizen a Soldier: The Campaign for Universal Military Training after World War II* (College Station: Texas A&M University Press, 2014), which won the Crader Family Book Prize Honorable Mention in 2015.

# INDEX

Acosta, Joie 93n56
active-duty requirements 131
Active Forces 16n15; augmentation for 82, 83; decrease in 179; quality 183; size 179; total 183; volunteers 8
African American military service 61–62
Agnew, Spiro T. 66
all-black army 61
Allen, Charles 88, 94n74
all-out non-nuclear war 126
All-Volunteer Force (AVF) 2–5, 129; advantages of 120–121; American democracy 2; arguments during 1960s 38–42; Armed Forces by 177; challenges 90; characteristics 2; civil-military relations 59–60; contemporary critiques 87–88; contemporary relevance 89; cost 154–157; current status 86–87; early impacts 82–84; economic analysis 42, 120–121; fifty years of service, reflections after 89–90; legacy 84–85; major turning point 1968 45–47; nascent campaign for 36–38; Nixon administration 66–68, 70–71; objections to 121–123, 158; officer requirements 184–185; planning for 176–178; pre-Vietnam data 160; progress toward establishment, 1972 186–188; proper role 2; racial composition 183–184; Report of the President's Commission on 158; resistance against 14–15; significance 45, 172
Altman, Stuart 53
Anderson, Annelise Graebner 45, 50n29, 66

Anderson, Martin 44–45, 50n22, 50n24, 66, 69n34, 70, 90n1, 91n24
Arends, Leslie C. 173
arguments: against all-volunteer force 144–149; draft center 125; against exclusively volunteer force 103; Ford's 39; mercenary 128; military 39–40; during 1960s 38–42; threat of universal military influence 128
Armed Forces 6, 81, 102; basic pay of members 169; blacks and racial minorities proportion 183–184; public support for 172; size of 129; student deferments 114
Armed Forces Medical Academy 138
Armed Forces Qualification Test 22
Armed Services Committee 10
Army Reserve and National Guard 98
Association for Volunteer Army 40
Avant, Deborah D. 15n5
AVF. see All-Volunteer Force (AVF)

Bacevich, Andrew J. 88, 94n70
Bailey, Beth 63, 69n25
Baldwin, Hanson W. 20, 26, 27, 33n7, 34n28
Berryman, Clifford K. 11
black army 128
Boston Globe 75
Brehm, William 131–138
Brewster Jr., Kingman 25, 47
Bristol Jr., Douglas W. 15n6
Buchanan, Patrick J. 49, 51n42

budget expenditures 154
Burke, Vincent 51n43
Burns, Arthur 50n20

Califano, Joseph C. 20–21, 23, 34n19,
  34n30, 34n37
Callard, David J. 53
Cancian, Mark F. 86–87, 93n59, 93n60
Carter, Ashton B. 85
Center for Strategic and International
  Studies (CSIS) 87
Chinman, Matthew 93n56
civilian community housing 137
Civilian Health and Medical Program of the
  Uniformed Services (CHAMPUS)
  134–135
Civil Rights Division 25
Civil War 112
Claiborne, William 84, 92n40
Clark, Mark W. 28
Clark Panel's report 28
Cold War 9, 13–15, 29, 36, 58, 62, 83
Cold War draft 64
Congress in Public Law 92-129 180
Congress of the United States: draft reform
  169–170; end to draft 163–165;
  extension of induction authority
  177, 187
conscription: in America 2–15; hidden cost
  of 154; tax-in-kind 57, 150–154
cost, all-volunteer armed force 152,
  154–157
Curtis, Thomas B. 37, 42, 49n3, 52

Democratic National Convention 36
Dent, Frederick 52
Department of Defense (DOD) 19, 81;
  Armed Forces payment 169; challenges
  75–77; draft study 4, 23–25; vs. Gates
  Commission 177; nonwhite men, unfit
  for service 115; women volunteer for
  military duty 107
DiBona, Charles J. 48–49
division force equivalent (DFE) 131
DOD. see Department of Defense (DOD)
"Don't Tread on Me" flag 40
Doyle, Lee 91n24
draft: abolition 39; end to 163–167, 169;
  extension 172–173, 177; future of
  158–162; implicit costs of 156;
  infringement 177–178; Johnson
  administration 28–30; ongoing or
  planned actions to reduce reliance on
  133–138; process of 7; during 1940s 5–8;

during 1950s 12–14; signs of substantial
  progress 178; unpopularity of 30–33; and
  Vietnam 76
The Draft: A Handbook of Facts and
  Alternatives (Tax, Sol) 41
draft calls: declined 178–179; Fiscal Year
  1972; in 180; increased 174–175;
  reduced 187
draft during 1960s: arguments 38–42;
  demographic changes 20–21; increased
  use of draft 19–20
draftees 156; payment to 145; taxation 152;
  tax-in-kind 153; term of service 76
Draft Extension and Military Pay Bill
  (1971) 175
draft-induced volunteers 146, 150, 154,
  156, 157; payment to 145; taxation 152
'The Draft is Dead'—'Draft
  Finished'—'Congress Repeals Draft
  Law' 38
draft-motivated volunteers 7
draft reform 72–75, 169–171, 175–176; bill
  79; to end draft 165–167; endeavor 75;
  recommendations on 158–159
Dunwoody, Ann 86

Eaker, Ira C. 39, 49n12
Ehrlichman, John 47
Eikenberry, Karl W. 15n4, 88, 94n71
Eisenhower, Dwight D. 52, 108, 109, 188n3
enlistees: proportion of 187; quality of 187
enlistment: ground combat 181–182;
  quality of 182–183; rates 115; true
  volunteers, increase in 180–181
Esch, Marvin L. 66–67, 69n36, 78–79,
  91n27
European Recovery Act 10
Executive Order 159, 166, 175
Executive Order 11289 25, 34n23
Executive Order 11497 73, 91n10

Finney, John 92n42
First Quadrennial Review of Military
  Compensation 39
Fiscal Year 2017 National Defense
  Authorization Act (Public Law
  114–328) 89
Flanigan, Peter M. 47, 50n36, 71, 91n5
Flynn, George Q. 8, 15n5, 16n16, 24, 25,
  34n20, 34n25
Ford, Gerald R. 38–39, 49n6, 49n10, 65,
  66, 67, 69n35, 83, 92n38
Fort Knox Experiment 11
Franklin, Ben A. 84–85, 92n41

Franklin, Benjamin 150–151
Friedman, Milton 41, 42, 49n15, 50n19, 52, 54, 57
Friedman, Norman 20, 33n4

Gates Commission 2, 5, 52–58, 66, 76, 89, 129–130; appointment of 129; arguments against all-volunteer force 144–149; defense of society 139–143; vs. Department of Defense 177; feasibility of All-Volunteer Force 176; major critiques of AVF 58–63; outcome of 63–66; pay and benefits of first-term enlisted servicemembers 55; political costs, criticism of 57; political issue 55–56; standby draft 56; tax, conscription as 150–157
Gates Jr., Thomas S. 2, 25, 52, 57, 64, 65, 68n6, 69n30, 129, 163, 176
Gerald R. Ford Library 33n9
Gerhardt, James M. 10, 12, 17n29, 17n37
Gilman, Harry J. 53, 62
Goldwater, Barry 66, 67, 68
Greenewalt, Crawford 52
Greenspan, Alan 52, 54
Griest, Kristen 85
Griffith Jr., Robert K. 76, 91n19
Griffith, Paul H. 8–9, 17n20
Gruenther, Alfred 52
Gurney, Chan 9

Haldeman, H. R. 47, 50n35
Harris, Louis 91n16
Hatfield, Mark O. 40, 49n13, 67, 68
Haver, Shaye 85
Hébert, F. Edward 173
Heck, Joseph J. 89
Hershey, Lewis B. 6–8, 13, 16n13, 35n38, 37, 45–49, 50n30, 72, 110, 111, 112
Hershey Task Force 38
Hesburgh, Theodore 53
Hess, Stephen 50n37
hidden tax 44, 127, 150–151, 153–154
Hinton, Harold B. 14, 18n48
Hoffman, Anna Rosenberg 25
Holland, Jerome 53, 55
Hoover, J. Edgar 48
Hoppy, Oveta Culp 25
Horton, Frank 37, 75
House of Representatives 46, 73, 78
House Rules Committee 10–11
*How to End the Draft: The Case for an All-Volunteer Army* 37, 67
Hubbell, Lester E. 38–39

Hubbell Pay Plan 130
Hubbell Pay Study 135
Hubbell Report 39
Hull, Hadlai A. 77
Humphrey, Hubert 42, 45

implicit tax 152–153
induction authority: Congress extension 177, 187; expiry 83, 84, 164; extension 30, 70, 159, 170, 172; recommended termination of 177
Iraq and Afghanistan Wars 89

Jennings, Paul J. 25
Jensen, Geoffrey W. 33n10
Johnson, Lyndon B. 16n11, 19–25, 27–32, 33n8, 34n19, 34n21, 34n23, 37, 38, 39, 43, 45, 46, 48, 49n3, 53, 55, 82, 122

Kamarck, Kristy 94n75
Kassing, David 53
Kelley, Roger T. 76, 129
Kemper, John 53
Kerwin Jr., Walter T. 77
Kindsvatter, Peter S. 7, 16n13
Korean War 3, 12–15, 20, 21, 32, 61, 64
Kriner, Douglas L. 93n60, 93n62

Laich, Dennis 16n7, 88, 94n67
Laird, Melvin 67, 73, 76, 79–83, 90n1, 91n20, 91n21, 92n31, 92n34, 92n35, 92n36, 129–130, 158–162, 174–184, 186
large-scale conventional war 126
legislative programs 178
Linehan, Adam 93n54
List, William R. 13
*Look* magazine (Wolff, Anthony) 30

manpower: requirement 187; utilization procedures 187
Mansfield Amendment 78–79
Mansfield, Mike 38, 79
Marin, Allan 51n39
Markovitz, Deborah 49n14
Marshall, Burke 26, 30, 34n27
Marshall Commission 4, 25–28, 30, 37–38, 41–42, 89; aliens in United States 102–103; Clark Panel's report 28; conscientious objectors position 104–105; defense establishment by volunteers 106–108; draft 26–28; draft-eligible men 100–101; enlistment procedures of Reserve and National Guard programs 102; final report 27;

introduction 97–98; issues 112–118;
Johnson administration 28; leaders from
American society 25; local board
members 111–112; national and state
headquarters 111; problem of men
rejection 103; registrant and the general
public 100; Selective Service System
99–100, 110–118; student or
occupational deferments 101; summary
of conclusions 97–98; universal military
training 103, 108–109; volunteer for
military service, opportunities for
101–102; volunteer national service
103–104
Marshall, George C. 8, 13, 18n47
Marshall Plan 10, 11
McCartney, James 92n33
McCormack, John 38
McCrocklin, James H. 25
McGrath, J. Howard 8, 17n20
McNamara, Robert S. 22–24
Meckling, William H. 53, 56–58
medical service 138
mental test scores 182
mercenary argument 128
military commitments 107
military compensation 155
military duty attractiveness 132–133
military pay 172–173
military recruitment policy 106
Military Selective Service Act (1967) 30,
84, 166
military service 22, 23, 25–29, 43–45, 54,
57, 60, 61, 76, 88, 97–98, 102–104, 107,
108, 114, 120, 143, 144, 146, 147, 156,
161, 162, 165, 166, 175, 178, 179, 181,
182, 184; African American 61–62; age
group 115; altered conception of 39;
American 89; American youth 32, 125;
attractiveness and satisfactions 159;
"available and qualified" for 74; basic pay
for 142–143; benefit and worth of 71,
187; black army 128; compulsory 32, 52,
124, 174, 178; conscription 155;
eligibility for 100; exemption from
102–103; Gates Commission 58, 63–65;
investment 169; manpower 126; men
rejection for 103; misfits and
maladjustments 157; policies and
practices 169; prevalence of 59; Project
100,000 21; race and gender within 3;
reconceptualization 90; recruitments 10;
requirements 184; rewards 39; during
1960s and 1970s 2; Selective Service

System and 22; sexual harassment in 86;
size 12; United States 102–103;
volunteers 140; widespread poverty and,
connection between 21; women in 77,
85–87; young people attitude toward
160, 165, 170
military, U.S. 40; demographic changes
20–21; draftees 13; obligation 103; in
Vietnam War 4, 19
Miller III, James C. 41, 49n15
minimum wage 126
Mittelstadt, Jennifer 15n4
Moskos, Charles C. 15n5

nascent campaign, AVF 36–38
National Advisory Commission on
Selective Service 20, 25, 37
National Association for the Advancement
of Colored People (NAACP) 53
National Guard and Reserve 180
national security requirements 107
National Selective Service Appeals
Board 72
*Newsday* 46
*New York Times* 14, 20, 32, 45, 77, 84
Nixon, Pat 72
Nixon, Richard M. 2–6, 42–45, 47–49,
50n21, 51n39, 52–56, 64–68, 68n2, 70,
72–76, 78–80, 84, 85, 91n10, 91n11,
92n44, 129, 144, 177–178, 186–188;
administration 42, 47–49, 55, 65–67,
70–72, 75, 78–82, 129; all-volunteer
armed force establishment 119–123;
compulsory military service 174;
Congress of the United States 168–171;
crusade against Hershey 47–49; doctrine
179; draft extension and increased
military pay 172–173; end to draft
163–167; presidential campaign 43–46;
presidential candidate 124–128;
Vietnamization plan 66, 73
Noble, Jeanne L. 25
Norris, John 34n18
nuclear war 126

Ogrysko, Nicole 94n78
O'Hanlon, Michael 86, 93n55, 93n62
Oi, Walter Y. 53, 54

Palmer, John M. 8
Patterson, Bradley 20, 33n8, 35n45
Pentagon 19–20, 22–25, 48, 61, 65, 75–77,
80, 82, 85, 86
Pepitone, Byron 83–84, 92n38

Petersen, Howard 16n18
Philipps, Dave 93n50
political support 121
Project 100,000 Program 4, 21–23, 29, 134
Project Volunteer Committee 131, 161, 176–177
Project Volunteer in Defense of the Nation (PROVIDE) 76, 129, 169; women, as civilian employees 77

reform: draft 165–167, 169–171, 175–176; military pay 130
Renshaw, Edward F. 41, 42, 50n16, 50n20
Report of the President's Commission 158, 160–161
Republican National Committee (RNC) 80
Republican National Convention 36
reserve components 137–138
Reserve Forces of the Navy and Marine Corps 180
Rico, Puerto 111, 112
Rivers, L. Mendel 23
Robinson, Lori 86, 93n55
Rose, Jonathan 48, 51n40
Rosenberg, Matthew 93n50
Rostker, Bernard 39, 49n9, 62, 69n22, 85, 92n43
ROTC scholarships 162, 178, 184
Rumsfeld, Donald 37, 49n3
Runey, Michael 88, 94n74
Rutenberg, Amy J. 14, 15n5, 18n49

Schafer, Amy 93n64
Schmidt, Dana Adams 91n23
Schweiker, Richard S. 37
Selective Service Act (1948) 11, 12
Selective Service Act (1973) 28, 77, 187
Selective Service System 4, 6–9, 11–14, 20–22, 24, 25, 28, 37, 38, 41, 46–49, 56–57, 59–62, 64, 65, 79, 83–85, 89, 98–100, 110–118, 129, 130, 156, 159, 167, 176, 186
Selective Training and Service Act (1940) 8, 112
Semple Jr., Robert B. 45
Senate Republican Conference 49
Servicemen's Group Life Insurance (SGLI) 136, 137
sexual harassment, in military service 86
Shearer, Amy 93n56
Sheehan, Neil 35n43, 35n47
Shen, Francis X. 93n60, 93n62
Shoup, David Monroe 25

Shriver, Garner E. 37
Sisk, Richard 93n53
Smith, Margaret Chase 49, 173
socio-economic factors 114, 116
Soviet ground attack 126
Soviet Union 9, 11, 15
Stafford, Robert T. 37, 49n4, 49n5
Stanwood, Henry C. 13
state headquarters 116–117
Stennis, John 173
student deferment issue 116
Stur, Heather Marie 15n6

Tarr, Curtis W. 49, 79
tax-in-kind 150–154
Tax, Sol 41
Taylor, William A. 15n5, 17n34, 92n45, 93n49
Thimmesch, Nick 46, 50n33
Total Force Concept 5, 66, 82–83; Guard and Reserve role in 179–180
Towe, Harry L. 9
true volunteers 187; increase in 180–181; raising and maintaining of armed forces 140
Truman, Harry S. 8–14, 17n23, 18n47

Ulrich, Marybeth P. 88, 94n73
Uniformed Services Special Pay Act (1972) 183, 187
United Service Organizations (USO) 86
United States Youth Council 47
universal military training (UMT) 3, 5, 8–12, 14, 103, 108
Universal Military Training and Service Act (1951) 8
U.S. Army Recruiting Command 134–136
U.S. civil-military relations 59–60
U.S. Commission on Civil Rights 1963 115
U.S. Military Assistance Command, Vietnam (MACV) 73
*U.S. News and World Report* 10

Veterans of Foreign Wars (VFW) 9
Vietnam 19–20, 22, 29, 32, 42, 52, 58, 70–72, 76, 79, 80, 83, 104, 106, 115, 122, 124, 125, 126, 129, 152, 160, 164, 165, 174, 175, 179
Vietnam Conflict Servicemen and Veterans Act 1967 29
Vietnam rotation policy 80
Vietnam War 4, 19, 21, 23, 28, 32, 33, 36, 42, 43, 45, 46, 55, 56, 58, 61–64, 68, 70, 76, 79, 82, 88, 97, 122, 124

volunteer army 41, 128
volunteer national service 103–104
volunteers 106; term of service 76;
  women 107

Wallis, W. Allen 53
*Wall Street Journal* 23
*Washington Post* 75
Westmoreland, William C. 31, 73, 76
Whalen Jr., Charles W. 37
White House 10, 23–26, 31, 36, 43, 47, 48,
  49, 53, 67, 70, 73, 80, 146, 163–167
Wilkins, Roy 53, 65, 69n31
Wofford, Harris 34n30
Wolff, Anthony 35n44

women: in military service 77, 85–87;
  volunteers 107
Women's Army Corps (WAC) 136
World War I Act 6
World War II 8, 10, 13–14, 20, 28, 58, 75,
  80, 107, 108, 110, 114, 124, 161, 188;
  conscription 142; tax during 153; U.S.
  Army Research Branch 7; U.S. military
  from 61
written test failure 188n11

'youngest-first' draft system 48
youngest-first lottery selection system 72

zero draft calls 158–161